D1265391

MINISTERING ANGELS

A Study of Nineteenth-century Evangelical Writing for Children

MINISTERING ANGELS

A Study of
Nineteenth-century Evangelical Writing
for Children

by

MARGARET NANCY CUTT

1979
FIVE OWLS PRESS

Published by
Five Owls Press Ltd.
67 High Road, Wormley
Herts., England

ISBN 0903838 02 8

Printed in England by
The Blackmore Press,
Shaftesbury, Dorset

To
W.T.C.
my husband, whose unfailing support and encouragement has made this book possible
and
H.M.P.
my mother, who showed by example what Victorian Evangelicalism could be at its best

CONTENTS

ILLUSTRATIONS

SECTION 1 between pp. 98 and 99

SECTION 2 between pp. 114 and 115

Acknowledgements

The author wishes to express her gratitude to the following for permission to reproduce illustrations: *Toronto Public Libraries Osborne Collection of Early Children's Books* for Figs. 2, 5, 7, 9, 10, 11, 12, 13, 17, 18, 22, 23 and 25; *Wandsworth Public Libraries* for Figs. 3, 4 and 14; *The British Library Reference Division* for Fig. 19 and *Jeanette White* for Fig. 26.

The author also wishes to thank: Ernest Benn Ltd., for permission to quote from S. Bamford's *Passage in the Life of a Radical*, J. M. Dent & Sons Ltd., for permission to quote from the *Memoirs of J. M. Dent*; Longman Group Ltd., for permission to quote from *Studies in Social History*, edited by J. H. Plumb; Lutterworth Press for permission to quote from Mrs Walton's *A Peep Behind the Scenes*; John Murray for permission to quote from Henrietta Keddie's *Three Generations*; Oxford University Press for permission to quote from *Victorian Essays* edited by W. D. Hancock; Penguin Books for permission to quote from J. H. Plumb's *England in the Eighteenth Century*; S.P.C.K. for permission to quote from *The Victorian Crisis of Faith* edited by A. Symondson; The University of London Library for permission to quote from a letter from Hesba Stretton to Mr Pattison (A.L.225) and Shropshire County Library for permission to quote from Sarah Smith's (Hesba Stretton) *Log Books* and R. S. Webb's *Notes.*

She also wishes to thank Brian and Valerie Alderson for their advice and help in preparing the manuscript for publication.

PREFACE

ALTHOUGH nineteenth-century prose writing and fiction have both been for some years the subject of intensive research and analysis, no similar study has been made of a vast body of tract fiction which followed the Cheap Repository Tracts of 1795–98. In this writing directed chiefly to the theologically illiterate—i.e. children and newly-literate adults—much of nineteenth-century children's literature seems to be rooted. These tract tales, read by children and adults alike, made up in sheer bulk and number a sizable proportion of the printed matter of the century. Few other Victorian authors could rival the records set by the circulation of works like Hesba Stretton's *Jessica's First Prayer* or Silas Hocking's *Her Benny*.

Thanks to the Evangelical success in establishing by about 1840 strict Sunday observance and, in literate homes, the habit of specialised Sunday reading, the cheap and copious output of Tract Societies and other religious publishing houses was widely circulated. It formed until after 1900 a large proportion of children's literature in the Dominions. While most Victorian children of educated families had access to excellent books from extensive family libraries, they also read *Jessica's First Prayer*, *The Wide Wide World*, *Christie's Old Organ*, and the works of A.L.O.E. (See for instance the reminiscences in E. V. Lucas: *Reading, Writing and Remembering*; M. V. Hughes: *A London Child of the Seventies*; and Edith Tyrrell: *I was There*.) At the same time, these tales, others like them, and related printings of the tract societies supplied most of the official school and Sunday School reading matter for children of workmen, farm labourers, lesser tradesmen, artisans and villagers, and for those slum children who could read. According to his biographer, Margaret Lane, Edgar Wallace, a child of the slums in the 1880's, read *Christie's Old Organ* and *The Wide Wide World* in Sunday School, and discussed them with an adult—a woman who kept a sweet-shop and knew and enjoyed the books. This double readership had existed from the end of the eighteenth century, when Hannah More's enthusiastic upper-class supporters bought bound volumes of the Cheap Repository Tracts for their own libraries and the use of their children. Mrs. Trimmer's suggestion in 1802 that the "seasonable and edifying lesson" of *The History of Susan Gray* might be "applied with great propriety to the higher classes" worked to the same effect.

Most tract tale writers were far from democratically inclined (except where the lessons of religion were concerned). But as the century drew to a close, their subject matter inevitably gave increasing importance to the working classes. Supplied with cheap books by the tract societies, lower-class readers found edifying tales about their own sort of people, written sometimes in excellent English, often with cloying sentimentality. Not until the 1860's were stories with a working-class viewpoint generally available.

Until after 1870 the fiction produced by the tract societies was ostensibly Christian. The limited background knowledge of so much of its readership meant that the religious lesson had to be simple and concrete. Much of it was uncompromisingly Protestant as well, and its writers attempted to communicate both knowledge and belief. But the same Evangelical teaching which assumed education to be the prelude to conversion was equally efficacious in making it the prelude to increased respectability and independence. The tract tales suggest that the widespread Victorian concern with respectability was a by-product of mass education and a concomitant of that literacy fostered from 1840 onward. They show, too, some ground-level links between tract society printings and the utilitarian economic theory of the mid-century.

The tract tales have not been examined in this book only as cheap literature infinitely inferior to *Alice in Wonderland*, *The Princess and the Goblin*, or *The Jungle Books*. Of course they are inferior as literature. But they were read by many more children than were their literary superiors; and when they were written, the high standards of the last years of the century had not always been set. They have been approached as far as possible from the viewpoint of their own day with an eye to their significance to the first two or three generations of their readers. They were a logical if not inevitable follow-up to the ideas of Berquin, Rousseau, John Wesley, the Edgeworths, Mrs. Trimmer and Mrs. Sherwood: they represented in effect, a *laminated* theory of education intended to supply mental nourishment and improve the spiritual health of the deprived masses.

In the vast flat prairie of tract literature surveyed there are several interesting landmarks, which, like Mrs. Sherwood's *History of Little Henry and his Bearer* (1814), or Mrs. Walton's *Peep Behind the Scenes* (1877), have been constantly in print since they first appeared. These books and their writers helped to shape and perpetuate habits of thought and belief; in some instances, their influence has lasted down to our own time. Who would have thought that Maria Charlesworth's pious tale of village life, *Ministering Children* (1854), could have influenced North American theories of prisoner rehabilitation and parole?

The writers selected for close study here were conspicuous among the tract tale writers of the century. Their backgrounds and beliefs have been outlined, and the close relation of their best-known works to the events and the thinking of their times demonstrated, as well as the influence of these works upon children's books and the thinking of later generations.

CHAPTER I

THE BACKGROUND TO THE EVANGELICAL TALE FOR CHILDREN:

The Moral Tale for Children 1760–1820

APPROVED reading matter for children up to about 1815 was still dominated by the extensive eighteenth-century literature of morality and instruction. In addition to those enduring classics, *Goody Two-Shoes, Sandford and Merton, The Parent's Assistant*, and *Evenings at Home*, it included translations of works by Berquin, Mme. d'Épinay and Mme. de Genlis, and numerous conversations and dialogues modelled upon them. Volumes of letters were plentiful, written ostensibly to absent children by anxious parents such as Lord Chesterfield, Mrs. Chapone, Mrs. Taylor, or Mrs. Rundell. The *Fables* of Aesop and of Gay were there, and lengthy narratives in "fabulous" form which were the animal stories of the day: *The Life and Perambulation of a Mouse, The Memoirs of Dick, the Little Poney, The History of the Robins*, etc. "Moral fairy tales", all very much alike, were as fraudulent as those of which Dickens complained fifty years later,[1] their elegantly-named characters, reminiscent of seventeenth-century novels—Mirtillo, Florimond, Glorinda, Paridel—existing only to advocate "the pursuit of those graces and beauties which are proof against time and sickness", or to point out the value of a "*tranquil mind*, exempt alike from the illusions of vanity, and the agitation of the passions."[2] Instructive accounts of travel further swelled the publishers' lists, along with books of natural history: *The Children's Cabinet*, perhaps; *The History of Frugal, the Wild Bee*; or *A Natural History of British Quadrupeds*, with its delightful Bewick illustrations.

This highly didactic literature served two important purposes apart from entertainment. It provided for immediate instruction of several kinds, and it attempted to give a moral and ethical training directed towards the improvement of society. Thus a young reader was constantly bombarded with useful facts of history, geography, or (as in *Evenings at Home*) science, ranging from the Linnaean classification of plants to the manufacture of paper. The Rev. Isaac Taylor's *Scenes of Commerce, by Land and Sea* (1830) and *Scenes of British Wealth* (1823) show that the Victorians were not the first to hold up the progress of national trade or industry to admiring approval. Mrs. Hofland's *Young Northern Traveller* (1813) under a thin guise of fiction is one of many extended geography lessons; the books of Thomas Day, the Edgeworths, Maria Hack, and many others are solid with practical information. Undoubtedly the insatiable Victorian appetite for facts and figures is rooted here.

Since these writers were intent upon moulding the raw material of childhood into the socially-acceptable adult and guiding him into his allotted station in life, their works often included lessons on deportment and conduct, or stressed the duty and the advantages of contentment. Harry Sandford, after sampling the Merton hospitality, returns thankfully to his father's farmhouse; Miss Sandham's *Alithea Woodley* (c. 1810) is a variation on the same theme; and an accommodating little Jemima Placid at the age of six is displayed as

> . . . always contented and good-humoured, even when she was not in a state agreeable to her wishes, and by learning to submit to what she did not like, when it could not be altered, she obtained the love of everybody who knew her, and passed through life with less trouble than people usually experience; for by making it a rule to comply with her situation, she always enjoyed the comforts it afforded, and suffered as little as possible from its inconveniences.[3]

Another large section of this immediately instructive literature, the much-derided cautionary tales and rhymes, warned its readers of dangers lurking everywhere in the child's world of the time. It is true that the cautionary tale could easily be carried to the point of absurdity: Mrs. Trimmer's tale of Miss Julia Sandford who *would* swallow ends of sewing cotton is not one of her best.

> . . . think-ing to her-self, a lit-tle thread is not poi-son, it will do me no harm, but she was mis-tak-en, it prov-ed to be a dread-ful poi-son, for when it came in-to her sto-mach, it un-rol-led, and got a-bout her bow-els, and ti-ed them to-ge-ther in pla-ces, which gave her such ex-cess-ive pain as you can-not i-ma-gine. . . .[4]

And the incongruously cheerful job-trot rhymes of Adelaide O'Keeffe and Elizabeth Turner, celebrating the dismal fates of children who ". . . thought it clever to deceive", or "played at lighting straws" have lent themselves to parody ever since. Nevertheless, in an age without fireproof fabrics, a regular police force, or knowledge of the germ theory, these awful warnings had strong practical value.

Works for younger children, often enlivened by woodcuts and rhyme on the model of Newbery's printings, attempted to follow John Locke's suggestion that instruction be sweetened by amusement. Childhood was short, however, and little readers were soon forced to come to grips with serious matters. The age of ten was generally recognised as a dividing line between childhood and impending maturity.

> EMILY: . . . Tomorrow will be an important day. When I rise, I shall no longer be a child; the first ten years of my life will be past.
>
> MAMA: And past never to return! If you have passed them well, so much the more agreeable will be your reflections; but if otherwise, the misfortune is without remedy.
>
> EMILY: That is exactly what I said to myself as I came in. I dare not hope that I have employed them so well as I might have done, yet I flatter myself that I have not wasted them entirely. . . . . . . I think I shall have no taste for dancing to-morrow; there is something too serious in a birth-day.
>
> MAMA: It is a day for reflection. You will think of the past, however you have been employed. The veil which covers futurity is raised a little, and makes us look forward with a degree of anxiety. . . .[5]

This "degree of anxiety" mentioned by Mme d'Épinay anticipates the long-range purpose of moral education: the all-important improvement of society. The theory was a part of eighteenth-century preoccupation with the untrammelled use of human reason. Mary Wollstonecraft's observation in the preface to *Original Stories* (1788) that she had "accommodated [her tales] to the present state of society; which obliges the author to cure those faults by reason, which ought never to have taken root in the infant mind" takes account of it, as does the more optimistic Dr. Aikin's Epilogue to *Evenings at Home*.

Hope of the world, *the rising race*,
May Heaven with fostering love embrace,
And turning to a whiter page,
Commence with them *a better age!*
An age of light and joy, which we,
Alas! in promise only see.

To hasten the coming of this better age, children's writers sought to inculcate the social virtues in order to strengthen morality. There was some disagreement about the definition of *virtue* and the identity of the highest duties. According to Erasmus Darwin in 1797,

> the criterion of moral duties has been variously delivered by different writers: Expediency, by which is meant whatever increases the sum of public happiness, is by some called the criterion of virtue; and whatever diminishes that sum is term'd vice. By others, the happiness or misery of the individual, if rightly understood, is said to be the bond of moral obligation. And lastly, by others the will of God is said to constitute the sole criterion of virtue and vice.

Darwin divided morals into five departments "for the greater conveniency of instruction", listing them thus:

1. A sympathy with the pains and pleasures of others, or compassion.
2. A strict regard to veracity.
3. Prudence, justice, chastity.
4. Fortitude.
5. Temperance.[6]

Pinnock's Catechism of Morality (c. 1827) is probably a fairly complete distillation of the principles underlying the theory of moral education in the previous half-century. Its definitions clarify the aims of the moralists and indicate the extent of the foundations upon which the Evangelicals and the Victorians erected their own systems of education and morality.

Morality, according to Pinnock, is "that science which teaches those rules of human conduct, the observance of which will best promote the happiness of mankind". *Duty* is subdivided: *Personal duties* "promote our *own* permanent security and happiness"; *relative duties*, "the permanent security and happiness *of society in general*". The first group consists of Cleanliness, Economy,

Industry, Temperance, Contentment, Prudence, Self-Examination, Self-Improvement, and Self-Government. The relative duties are Obedience, Gratitude, Civility, Benevolence, Charity, Veracity, Honesty, Candour, and Justice.[7]

Tales for the very young naturally stressed obedience, honesty, cleanliness and industry, other duties and qualities being brought in by degrees in the hope that all would become habitual. Moral tales for older children (e.g. those of Maria Edgeworth's *The Parent's Assistant*) were devised to illustrate the application of personal and relative duties to more complicated situations at home or at school, and thus to lead by degrees into the responsibilities of adult life. Some introduced serious social issues, among them the perennially-deteriorating relation of landlord and tenant which had been the background to *Goody Two-Shoes* in 1765. Mrs. Hofland concludes *The Blind Farmer and his Children* (c. 1815) with moral reminders that the ideal tenant should be honest and industrious, that landlords must exercise discretion and knowledge, wisdom and benevolence, and that young readers should consider that "next to honesty and industry, piety and duty, unassuming modesty and propriety of manners, insure the success of the Blind Farmer and his Children".

Many moral writers between 1780 and 1830 supported the spectacular anti-slavery campaign. William Darton, the Quaker publisher, a true eighteenth-century moralist, produced in 1787 a rational but uninspired dialogue on the subject in *Little Truths for the Instruction of Children*:

> . . . I am sorry to say that the lawmakers still countenance the slave-trade, though they have spoken against it and condemned the cruelty occasioned by the traffic.
> *Then what is the cause of its being continued?*
> From an evil desire of gain, that kind of love of money "which is the root of all evil". To hear the groans of dying men—the cries of many widows and fatherless children,—the bitter lamentations of a husband when torn from the arms of his beloved wife,—and the mournful cries of a mother and her children when violently separated,—one would think that these things would so affect the human mind, as to cause such practices to cease.[8]

Darton, sincerely concerned with justice, benevolence, and charity, appeals to "the human mind", and deals with the social group—

lawmakers, slaves, owners. By 1830, the same issue had been treated in emotional verse by Mrs. Opie (*The Black Man's Lament . . .*, 1826), and evangelically with skilful use of sentiment and suspense by Mrs. Sherwood (*Babes in the Wood of the New World*, c. 1830). Both ladies, taking full advantage of romantic freedom in literary form, emphasized individual suffering and individual responsibility.

Following the lead given by Mrs. Trimmer in *Fabulous Histories* (1786), the same writers and others protested against cruelty to animals; and a growing humanitarianism appeared in tales stressing the duty of the rich and the comfortable toward the less fortunate. In 1765, Little Goody Two-Shoes (metamorphosed into Lady Jones) began to set a good example to young readers of the next hundred years. Mary Wollstonecraft's Mrs. Mason, from 1788, encouraged them to economise in order to have money for charity. In 1804, Jane Taylor's Greedy Richard "Felt inconceivably asham'd" because he had spent his money on pastry before meeting the beggar who

> . . . held his hat to beg;
> And while he told his mournful case,
> Look'd at him with imploring face.

Indeed the matter of charity came to occupy a progressively larger space in books for children as the new century got under way, and moralists and Evangelicals alike, troubled by the hardships of the times, sought to persuade the reader of his duty to the poor. At the end of Mrs. Hofland's *Ellen the Teacher* (1814), Ellen in her new prosperity wishes that she may be able to

> . . . select from the neighbouring poor such children as have been hitherto neglected in their education, and form them into a school, which I will superintend myself. I wish my little seminary to open on the day when peace is proclaimed . . . and I particularly wish that the spirit of the Prince of Peace should be instilled into their young hearts; so that quietness, good-humour, obedience and every other social virtue, may spring from them, and spread through the circle to which each may belong; and I am persuaded no little good may arise from so small a beginning.

A generation later an equally dedicated Ellen would have worked in a Ragged School, or like Maria Charlesworth's heroines, visited the cottages. But at the later date, instead of stressing the "social virtues", she would have sought to convert her individual pupils as well as forward their training in useful employment. She would, in fact, have been a Ministering Child and fervent Evangelical.

For, in spite of its seriousness of purpose and gravity of tone, the moral literature of the late eighteenth and early nineteenth centuries lacked a sense of urgency. It presupposed the stable society and the traditional parish organisation. Its rational approach and dependence upon logical argument in the overworked form of dialogue precluded activity and humour. Child characters, with a few happy exceptions like Maria Edgeworth's Rosamond, were not childlike; present, like the young reader, to be instructed, they had the sameness of creatures of fable, obviously contrived to show the progression from ignorance to knowledge. The point of view in all this literature was that of the parent or mentor. Reason was exalted, and emotion either discouraged or directed into approved channels.

> "O dear! I cannot look at blood. Besides I cannot bear to see you hurt, mama!"

cries little Eliza, bidden to remain in the room while her mother is bled.

> "O, if I can bear to feel it, surely you may to see it,"

responds her brisk, practical mother. "It will do you good to be accustomed to such sights."

> "Why, mamma?"
>
> "Because instances are every day happening in which it is our duty to assist fellow-creatures in circumstances of pain and distress; and, if we were to indulge a reluctance to come near to them on those occasions, we should never acquire either the knowledge or the presence of mind necessary for the purpose."

Driving her point home by a series of anecdotes displaying the value of presence of mind, she concludes with a long dissertation on courage and reason:

> "[Courage is] . . . of two kinds; one the gift of nature, the other of reason and habit. Men have naturally more courage than women; that is, they are less affected by danger; it . . . does not flutter their spirits so much. This is owing to the difference of their bodily constitutions. . . . But the other kind of courage may, in some measure, be acquired by every one. Reason teaches us to face smaller dangers in order to avoid greater. . . . Habit makes us less affected by particular dangers which have often come in our way. . . ."

"I think I should not be afraid again to see anybody bled," says little Eliza doubtfully. "But would that make me like to be bled myself?

> "Not to *like* it, but to lose all foolish fears about it, and submit calmly to it when good for you. . . ."

replies her mother, and on this note the story ends.[9]

Not all moral works were as directly didactic. A fair amount of amusement crept into Sarah Fielding's *The Governess* (1749), as into *The History of Little Goody Two-Shoes* (1765). Mrs. Teachum's nine pupils, all differentiated from each other and learning to live in harmony with their neighbours, exist in a different world from the two little girls in Mary Wollstonecraft's humourless *Original Stories* (1788), who, barely distinguishable as individuals, undergo a chillingly rational training under the eye of the omniscient Mrs. Mason. It *was*, in fact, a different world, divided during those forty years by that revolutionary doctrine that Mary Wollstonecraft found liberating and her contemporary, Hannah More, discovered to be the work of Satan. The varied and substantial work of the Aikins was rooted in it, as were those of the Edgeworths and Thomas Day. The tales of this group were good-humoured in tone and reasonably entertaining; all were informative. Contemporary with them is the miscellany of books by lesser moralists, among them the Quaker writers and the talented Taylors of Ongar.[10]

But it was a world on the brink of shattering social and industrial change, and soon after 1800 children's books began to reflect the growing tensions of the time. During the forty years between the publication of *The Governess* and that of *Original Stories*, the educational theories of Locke and Fénelon had been overlaid in England by those of Rousseau, Mme. d'Épinay and Mme. de Genlis (particularly in upper-class homes), and in many serious-minded circles, by those of John Wesley and Mrs. Trimmer. The whole question of education was coloured by feelings of anxiety stemming from fear of revolutionary doctrine and the distresses of war.

During these years, writers for the young separated into two opposing camps divided by one major issue: the place of religion in education. Rational moralists, many of them deists, were far more excited by science than by religion. (Erasmus Darwin, for instance, invariably left comment on religion until the end of his chapter or section, dismissing it briefly like a postscript.) Their theory, a modified and anglicized form of Rousseauism, was displayed in Thomas Day's *Sandford and Merton* (1783–1789) and in the Edgeworths' *Harry and Lucy* (1801), these and similar works being intended to guide both parent and child. Little was written for children of the lower classes, whose instruction, if any, came from Bible and Catechism, but all writers, rational or religious, kept the rising middle class in mind, particularly the wealthy East Indian merchants or West Indian planters, who, retiring with large fortunes, were buying their way into the old, privileged landowning levels of English society.[11]

The opponents of the rational moralists were the Sunday School and Evangelical writers who collected around Mrs. Trimmer and Hannah More, and built upon the groundwork raised by these industrious educators between 1780 and 1800. This group had more in common with the earlier moralists than they cared to admit later: having grown up in the same world, they shared the greater part of the field of immediate instruction; most of the books of factual information and the cautionary tales; as well as anti-slavery works and others advocating a greater degree of humanitarianism. But they disagreed sharply upon the long-range purpose of education for the young; and in the name of religion, the disciples of Mrs. Trimmer and Hannah More carried an elementary education to the children of the poor, arguing that all, regardless of station, were entitled to be able to read the word of God. Their basic tenet was that education must subserve religion and be directed to preparation for the after-life. They claimed emphatically that the degree of human happiness was in direct proportion to the degree of submission to the divine Will. Thus they repudiated the moralists' view that learning should exalt reason and work to the temporal happiness of the individual, which was governed by the best interests of society.

Mrs. Trimmer, the most famous of the group in the eighteenth century, was convinced, like Dr. Watts and the Puritans, that religious training should be stressed in infancy, the earlier the better. Thus the child, rich or poor, would be

> . . . prepared for longer days,
> Or fit for early death.

". . . [For] persons of all ranks and degrees," she wrote in *The Good Schoolmistress*,

> RELIGION is the principal concern, and . . . it is of the utmost importance to sow the seeds of piety in the minds of children, and give them as early as possible, strong impressions respecting the being of a GOD, the immortality of the soul, the certainty of a future state.[12]

The rationalist moralist, on the other hand, treated religion casually, giving it no preference over any other aspect of education, and because of its associations with "enthusiasm",* often evading all mention of it. Sarah Fielding, for instance, cautions in *The Governess* (xiv) ". . . not to be partial to any of your Companions, only because they are agreeable without first considering whether they are good enough to deserve your Love. . . ." If one deduced from this that Prudence was one of the higher duties, the assumption would be borne out by Mrs. Chapone's *Letter on the Regulations of the Heart and Affections* (1773). Erasmus Darwin was speaking for most of the rational moralists when, in *A Plan for the Conduct of Female Education* (XIX), he urged delaying the religious training of the young until ". . . their minds are capable of perceiving [its] force to co-operate with the effects of the laws of society and of the opinions of the wise and virtuous". In other words, man is the measure and man the judge. "The virtuous" had been touched on earlier by Mme. d'Épinay in Conversation II of *The Conversations of Emily*. Six year old Emily having enquired about "becoming reasonable", her Mamma explains.

> MAMMA: In time your mind will expand, and you will become, by degrees, a reasonable being. . . .
> EMILY: Yes; because I shall endeavour to correct my faults.
> MAMMA: And to acquire a government over yourself, which is called *virtue*; and without it neither happiness, esteem, nor success can be obtained.

Similarly, Mrs. Chapone asserted in "Letter on the First Principles of Religion" that "the great laws of morality are . . . written in our hearts, and may be discovered by reason," following this by a hope that the reader "will examine . . . the evidence of the Christian religion, and be convinced on rational grounds, of its divine authority."

* Throughout the century the word was used in Dr. Johnson's sense of irrational or ill-governed emotion. An *enthusiast* was, in the popular mind, a "crackpot". By the end of the century the term was being applied to Methodists and Evangelicals.

That any sort of virtue and Christian religion could be acquired through self-control and reason was directly contrary to Evangelical belief. Peculiarly offensive was the lukewarm and nominal Christianity inculcated by such teachings as Dr. Darwin's:

> . . . [T]he precepts . . . are best taught by requiring the young pupils regularly to attend such places of divine worship as their parents direct; and by reading on Sundays select parts of the holy scriptures, and some approved book of sermons; . . . and by inculcating the reasonableness of daily thanksgiving, and the duty of daily prayer. . . . (*Plan* . . ., XXI.)

Quickening the religious sensibilities and thus making religion *vital* was one of the chief aims of the Evangelical writer, and no one was more skilful in this line than Mrs. Sherwood. Writing for parents and children of the Bengal Army barracks about 1810, she represents two of the few conscientious mothers talking.

> "Teaching children to repeat catechisms, and verses from the Bible, will not do much," said Mrs. Browne, "unless we press upon them the necessity of practicing what they learn."
>
> "And," said Mrs. Francis, "we should be careful to let them know that they have not in themselves the power to do one good thing, or to think one good thought; but that for these purposes they are, by diligent prayer, to seek power from God, who, through his blessed Son, will help them to do all good things. . . ."[13]

This is the authentic tone of that wave of urgent religious teaching which, between 1810 and 1830, largely displaced the older moral tale. The latter, so practical, prudent and secular, was too thoroughly engrained to disappear, but for nearly half the century it went into eclipse. The purely informative books such as those about geography or natural history were, of course, retained and sometimes brought up to date; but those directed to moral training were either taken over and "evangelized" by the writers of tracts and tract fiction, or superseded. (As Mrs. Trimmer did with *The Ladder to Learning*, and Mrs. Sherwood with Sarah Fielding's *The Governess*. The process was usually described as "correction".) With the publication (1795–98) of the Cheap Repository Tracts, the great age of the tract began. For seventy years or more, tract printing was to be one of the most prolific and profitable forms of publishing, a very large proportion of its output being aimed at the young and written by women.

CHAPTER II

EVANGELICAL BEGINNINGS IN CHILDREN'S BOOKS:
Tract to Tract Fiction 1795–1820

CHEAPLY produced, widely distributed, energetically and often vituperatively expressed, the tract had been for two centuries an offensive weapon in the war of words. Seventeenth-century Puritans justified their religious and political policies in tracts; eighteenth-century Whigs and Tories carried on bitter political debates. It was only natural for Methodists, and later the Evangelicals to adapt the well-established pattern of the tract to their own particular battle against infidelity, immorality and ignorance.[1]

Around 1740, the Methodists began using tracts to foster literacy among lower-class converts. Recognizing the need for cheap, available printed matter for new readers, Wesley called for a religious literature in which ideas should be "simply and nakedly expressed in the most clear, easy and intelligible language".[2] This requirement, adopted by the Religious Tract Society founded in 1797 soon after Wesley's death, was still in force a century later; Hesba Stretton and Mrs. Walton wrote in accordance with it.

Wesleyan tracts included homilies, explication of Bible passages and religious doctrine, obituaries of the godly, advice to the newly-converted, and extracts from the lives and writing of famous figures (Richard Baxter and Bunyan being prime favourites). At all times, the tract and its extension, the religious periodical, exhorted the reader to renew his spiritual life by Bible study and prayer. These publications, some especially for juveniles, were distributed from the Methodist Book Room in London, and carefully supervised by Wesley himself during his lifetime. Schools were set up by Wesley, Rowland Hill and others to demonstrate their carefully thought-out system of religious education.[3]

The distressing fact remained that a number who were trained in Sunday Schools upon the Catechism, the Bible and the tract, became backsliding adults. Samuel Bamford, for instance, testifies that, having learned to read by the time he was eight, he studied with attention

> . . . the wondrous accounts in the Revelation. . . . After I had gone through the Revelation, I began with the Gospel of Saint Matthew, and was deeply interested in the miracles, sufferings and death of our Lord. The New Testament was now my story book. . . .[4]

Discovering shortly afterwards a bookshop which "exhibited numerous songs, ballads, tales and other publications, with horrid and awful-looking woodcuts at the head", he became equally absorbed in "Jack the Giant Killer", "Saint George and the Dragon", "Tom Hickathrift", "The Witches of the Woodlands" and the like (Fig. 6). Nothing in this array of chapbooks seems to have been positively harmful; his tolerant father, who described it all as trash, did not forbid it. A few years later, however, Bamford was back to solid reading—Wesley's *Journals*; *The Arminian Magazine*—but he thought the latter's accounts of travels were inferior to *Robinson Crusoe*. An intelligent and superior reader, Samuel Bamford was obviously seeking at this stage *narrative*, the Tale, and not finding it in the pious output of the Methodist Book Room.

The adult backslider had no trouble finding a gaudy assortment of ballads, tales and romances in chapbooks (many extremely crude); lurid crimesheets; and, most sinister of all in the 1780's and 1790's, radical political pamphlets. All could be grouped together as "infidel publications"; against them, government and Evangelicals alike waged a lively battle.

The dismal economic conditions of the decade had rendered workmen and labourers extremely restive, a situation coinciding with the excesses of the French Revolution and the growing strength of the Evangelical Movement. The influence of Evangelicalism steadily widened for over twenty years. Its success was the result of a particular combination of circumstances. War losses and war weariness during the long struggle with Napoleon were sapping the national optimism.

> Another year! another deadly blow!
> Another mighty empire overthrown!
> And we are left, or shall be left, alone;
> The last that dares to struggle with the foe.

wrote Wordsworth in 1806, reflecting the mood of many. The better world that was to have grown out of the Enlightenment had disintegrated into war and revolution. A prolonged economic depression followed upon the breakdown of world trade; it gave rise in turn to the spread of radical agitation among poverty-stricken rural labourers and destitute factory workers. Paine's *Rights of Man* (1791–92) and the diatribes of William Cobbett, Richard Carlile and others against an inept government and an indifferent church circulated freely in these years in defiance of official attempts at suppression.[5]

The end of the Napoleonic Wars brought little relaxation of the general anxiety. "In 1815", writes J. H. Plumb,

> ... Great Britain seemed on the edge of bankruptcy and social revolution. Starvation was driving the poor to wreck the machinery which seemed to them to be the cause of the misery, and the government ... repressed brutally what in its turn it could not comprehend. To thinking men the horizon was dark and foreboding. ... In 1815, at the end of long endurance, there was fear, and envy, and greed, but little hope.[6]

The fact that no revolution occurred can be credited in some measure to the sobering influence of Evangelicalism. An outgrowth of the latent strain of Puritanism which had survived eighteenth-century humanism, the Movement had been two generations in the making and by 1800 had behind it half a century of effort. The quality of its leadership was the greatest factor in its success; the organisation of its campaign was masterly. It appealed to every section of the population. Before 1760, the Wesleys and George Whitefield had established it among the working classes; Hannah More wrote persuasively of it for the literate, and around 1790 turned her talents to the establishment of Sunday School work in an absolutely illiterate country area. William Wilberforce carried the Movement into the circles of the wealthy and powerful; he argued and won its causes in the House of Commons. Henry Venn and Charles Simeon made devout Evangelicals of two generations of theological students at Cambridge. Simeon established a trust fund to buy up vacant livings for Evangelical graduates in theology, a practice followed by other wealthy members of the Movement such as the Thorntons.

By 1810, the steady pressure exerted by the Evangelicals at all influential levels of English society was showing results. In a little over twenty years they brought about their quiet domestic revolution—in taste, in standards of conduct, in intensity of religious feeling, and in the outward manifestation of religion. They had re-educated a high proportion of their contemporaries, and brought respectability into fashion.[7]

In working with the illiterate, the poor and the young, Evangelicals, like the Methodists earlier, made extensive use of tracts. Beginning in 1795, three years after the publication of *The Rights of Man*, a group of churchmen and prominent laymen sponsored a mass printing of anti-Jacobin and morally-improving tracts, enlisting the aid of Hannah More. She organised the series of Cheap Repository Tracts which ran until 1798, writing about fifty herself. Varied in style and content, illustrated with good-quality woodcuts, many were cunningly devised to resemble popular ballads or political discussions. Some took the form of well-written, entertaining "histories", either of admirable, industrious, pious lower-class worthies such as *The Shepherd of Salisbury Plain*, or of awful warnings—*Tawny Rachel, the Fortune Teller*, or *Black Giles the Poacher*—who came to a well-deserved bad end. These particular tracts read like fiction, with brisk dialogue, vivid description and genuine suspense; one could make a good case for their being the first true tract tales.

The series also contained conventional dialogues arguing against radical or infidel belief; sermons; and discourses on the Bible. Some were in verse. By 1796 a total of two million Cheap Repository Tracts were said to be in circulation, and the printing kept several publishers hard at work. They were also said to have driven out a large proportion of the vicious chapbooks of the time, and to have effectually discredited (for the moment at least) the current radical and revolutionary propaganda.[8] Judging however by the vehemence and wide distribution of the unstamped press publications from 1820 onward, these claims should perhaps be qualified.

From Cheap Repository Tract to Evangelical tract tale for the young was but a short step. Many of the former were, indeed, printed for children's reading. *Betty Brown, or The St. Giles Orange Girl* is still of interest as a picture of an eighteenth-century working child; *The History of Hester Wilmot* was the prototype of most Victorian tract tales for young village girls and servants.

Most of the early nineteenth-century Evangelical writers

recalled the terrors of the French Revolution which had overshadowed their youth. Mrs. Sherwood and her sister, Mrs. Cameron, for instance, knew a number of well-born French emigrés; Captain Sherwood as a boy of fifteen caught in France with his family had narrowly escaped with his life, spending months half-starved in detention at Abbeville.[9] "Charlotte Elizabeth" remembered vividly the childish determination of her brother and herself

> . . . to stand by our mother to the last, and try if we could not by some means ourselves kill Bonaparte . . . this man seemed to embody in himself all that was terrifying in the idea of invasion. . . . God made him a scourge, and rendered his name very terrible among men.[10]

These memories, the depressing effect of the long war, and the disillusionment of those who had hoped for better things from two generations of moral education, affected the tone and content of children's books for years to come. French-inspired educational theories on which so many moral tales were based were repudiated, partly on the grounds that they had led to deism, infidelity and revolution, partly (according to "Charlotte Elizabeth"), "checked by the tone of national defiance universally breathed against France".

The result was that the principal supporters of instruction dominated by religion were brought for a time into working agreement, their intent being that of Hannah More: "to persuade children of the absolute claims of religion". The prevailing note in children's books became one of home-grown religious strictness.

Mrs. Trimmer's thirty years of insistence upon revealed religion, and her stubborn determination to subordinate all aspects of education to religious training were now of inestimable value to the Evangelicals. She was a pillar of the Established Church, a firm believer in class distinctions. About her teaching clung none of the lower-class connotations of Methodism; on the contrary she was *persona grata* in the highest circles. Her daughter, Selina, was governess at Devonshire House; Queen Charlotte asked Mrs. Trimmer's advice upon Sunday Schools and charities. Moreover Mrs. Trimmer was herself something of a moralist, so there was no sharp break with the desirable aspects of moral education. Unlike Wesley, she had never been labelled "enthusiast"; unlike Hannah More, she was never involved in violent controversy about her schools.[11] Evangelical educators like Mrs. Sherwood and Mrs. Cameron who followed closely in Mrs. Trimmer's footsteps were assured of a cordial reception: indeed, *The History of Susan Gray* (1802) and *The History of Margaret Whyte* (1799) had been warmly recommended in Mrs. Trimmer's *The Guardian of Education*.[12]

Mrs. Trimmer likewise supplied the Evangelicals with a second convenient precedent: objecting to the "leaven of false philosophy" that had found its way into school books, she had written her own. Her *Essay upon Christian Education* explained her essential principles in doing so.

> Even Geography, Writing and Arithmetic may be made, in some measure, subservient to religious instruction, by proper observations on the form and division of the earth among the different nations which inhabit it; by a judicious use of copies; and by quotations relative to Scripture History, etc. (*Guardian of Education*, II (1803), p. 403.)

Within fifteen years Mrs. Sherwood was writing textbooks on this pattern, all geared to the strictest Evangelical doctrine, or, after 1825, to Millinarianism.[13]

The books condemned by Mrs. Trimmer undoubtedly included those of Joseph Priestley and of that most improper clergyman, the Rev. John Horne Tooke, which Dr. Erasmus Darwin had listed and recommended in his *Plan for the Conduct of Female Education* (1797). He also included Mrs. Trimmer's *Histories*; unappeased by this compliment, she dismissed *Zoonomia*, and *The Botanic Garden* as "ingenious and amusing [but] by no means proper to put into the hands of young Readers".[14]

Concurring fully with her judgments and convinced that the deification of reason and the dependence upon French educational theory were largely responsible for the troubles of the times, the Evangelicals proceeded to replace the Rule of Reason in children's books by the Rule of Religion. Like Mrs. Trimmer, they asserted that ". . . one of the worst passions that can infect the mind is *the pride of Human Reason*. Religion alone can rule them ALL [i.e., the passions], and bring the Reason itself into subjection to the revealed will of God." (*Guardian of Education*, I (1802), p. 287.) They objected also to the deistic avoidance in works for children of testimony to Christian belief and revealed religion. For most of the eighteenth century, discussion of these points (and of the essential tract themes of conviction of sin and the consequent religious conversion) had been held to be marks of "enthusiasm", undignified and Methodistical. Thus Thomas Day's Mr. Barlow, a clergyman, is never seen at church and rarely mentions religion and the soul. He instructs his little pupils with tales from the classics or from contemporary accounts of travel; Harry Sandford's account of Christ and the apostles denies the divinity of Christ.

> . . . and all the world was very bad, very bad indeed; and then there came a very good man indeed, whose name was Christ; and he went about doing good to every body and curing people of all sorts of diseases, and taught them what they ought to do—and he chose out twelve apostles; and those apostles went about the world, doing as he did, and teaching people as he taught them . . . and so they made the world a great deal better. . . .[15]

In marked contrast to this tone of religious indifference was that of Mrs. Cameron's first tale, *The History of Margaret Whyte* (1799). She too pictures a child explaining her understanding of religion:

> . . . (M)y kind parents have instructed me in many good habits which every Christian should strive to acquire: they have taught me that I should be obedient to them, and above all that I ought to serve my God and Saviour to the best of my power, and never fail to be thankful to the goodness of my God towards me. . . . (I)f you desire to make God love you, and to gain the good-will of your fellow-creatures, endeavour to acquire a meek and peacable temper; and in all your dealings, whether with the rich or poor, remember that our blessed Saviour has commanded us to return good for evil.[16]

The usual eighteenth-century moral teaching of personal and relative duties has been replaced here by emphasis upon the Catechism and the Commandments; the tale is a direct outgrowth of the Sunday School instruction of Mrs. Trimmer and Hannah More. But in its blend of sentiment and religion, its fully developed background, and the long account of the child's life that precedes the usual obituary tract description of her pious death, *The History of Margaret Whyte* looks ahead to Victorian fiction for children. With this story and Mrs. Sherwood's *History of Little Henry and his Bearer* (1814) the narrative tract came to life. Fictional children, who, before their early deaths, led interesting realistic lives, began to replace the faceless children of the doleful obituary tracts, who were dead before a young reader ever heard of them.[17]

Sentiment thus enters children's books before 1820 in the form of *pathos*; and tales for the young begin to show concern for the individual rather than with society, and with soul rather than reason. The romantic impulse in adult literature was filtering down into books for children through these tract tales: once religious feeling became important in the child's reading, other types of emotion quickly followed.

By 1810 new writers for children were mostly Evangelicals or Evangelical sympathizers, their work being a calculated part of the Evangelical determination to reform and convert the nation and eventually the world. The principal moralists of 1800 occupied a much smallar proportion of the expanded publishers' lists, some of them (Maria Hack, for instance, and Mary Belson Elliott) moving into the fringes of the religious camp and taking up a half-way position between Evangelicalism and eighteenth-century morality.

In *Harry Beaufoy*, or The Pupil of Nature (1821), Maria Hack simplifies for children some of the arguments of Paley's *Natural Theology* (1802). Wilberforce had remarked in 1803 that Paley did no more than bring his readers up to "the threshold of Christianity",[18] but Maria Hack was convinced that

> . . . the idea of God will become connected with every other idea; and the influence of this constant and lively sense of the divine presence and power, attending to, disposing, and governing all things, must have a favourable effect upon our characters. . . . Confidence in the goodness of the Almighty must naturally produce resignation to his will; and when once these dispositions are firmly settled in our minds, we shall have discovered the true secret of happiness.[19]

The passage begins in the spirit of deism, but the allusions to resignation and "the true secret of happiness" show a drift towards the new order of religious thought.

A stronger display of controlled piety crept into novels by Mrs. Hofland and Elizabeth Sandham, which by 1810 indicated clearly that eighteenth-century moral purpose was being re-directed into the channels of Evangelicalism. Here is the wealthy East Indian merchant, Mr. Stanley who has squandered his wealth in luxury and gaming, and is now sick and old and dependent upon the daughter he has long neglected.

> Here, too, Mr. Stanley saw an uniform respect paid to the Sabbath—that day which, if properly spent, adds grace and happiness to all the rest; and by the example of those about him, he was led to attend the church, and, like them also, he found comfort in so doing—He had all his life been seeking after happiness; but now, when nearly driven to despair, he came desponding, and not expecting, or scarcely wishing, to discover it in the country, he found in a quiet peaceful life, dedicated to religion and the good of others, the truest enjoyment: leaving far behind him the world, and all its visionary plans, he became acquainted with a higher source of pleasure, and was imperceptibly led to admit the claims of reason in its favour. . . .[20]

Evangelical emphasis on Sunday observance (a strong plank in their platform of moral reform) and on the life to come has made headway in 1810. Against the gloomy background of the time the rational life was coming to be equated with religious life, and the moralists' earlier conception of human happiness being reshaped. Since the light of reason had failed to illuminate the darkness of the age, and there was little evidence of that general improvement of society so confidently anticipated a generation before, educators were turning to the promise of a spiritually-regenerated society held out by the Evangelicals.

CHAPTER III

EVANGELICAL EFFORT BEFORE 1850: MISSION AND OMISSION

As the fundamental beliefs of the Enlightenment—its assumption of the progress and ultimate perfectibility of society, its implicit trust in human reason—dwindled under the pressures of war and revolution, those of Evangelicalism were enhanced. The Movement clarified for many the confusion of the times, assuring them that insoluble contemporary problems mattered less than the welfare of the individual soul. For those who could accept its tenets it charted a clear spiritual path through the intellectual wreckage of the past. By 1820, its older adherents had already exemplified the comforting stability of absolute religious conviction in a period of shifting values. Without losing the respect of their social equals or superiors, the noted Evangelicals had accomplished work of lasting value, gathering about them a host of devoted followers, who in thirty years had taken to heart Hannah More's *Thoughts on the Importance of the Manners of the Great to General Society* (1788), and Wilberforce's *Practical View of the Prevailing Religious System of Professed Christians* (1797).

Like romanticism, with which it had much in common, Evangelicalism asserted the worth of the individual. It encouraged too the expression of individual impulse, so long suppressed by the moralists; and the release of emotion, so long disciplined into social conformity. The fact that this release of feeling is shown in books for children as part of a religious lesson does not alter the fact that it *was* a release, and that the expression of emotion by the young was coming into favour. Grace Kennedy's *Anna Ross* (1823), for instance, makes much of emotion.

> Anna sat down by Marianne, and assisted her so much, that her little cousin two or three times forgot, and threw her arms around her "dear Cousin Anna's" neck to thank her; but every time she moved from the posture in which she had been placed, Miss Palmer added to her task, so that poor Marianne at last remembered

> Miss Palmer's instructions, to express what she felt by words. "You have a silly childish way, Miss Marianne," continued her governess, "of always putting your arms round one, crumpling one's ruff, and almost strangling those you love. You know your Mamma has often forbid your doing so."
>
> Poor little Marianne seemed to think that she had been guilty of a serious fault . . ., while Anna felt bewildered on hearing blame attached to those proofs of affection which her own Mamma had always received from her, and returned with the most tender kindness.[1]

Anna is exhorted to be prudent, reasonable, self-controlled only by the materialistic, cold-hearted aunt, the selfish cousins, or the indifferent governess. Those who are genuinely concerned about her give vent to emotion: kindly Uncle Ross, angry that she will not remain in his household; her jubilant country cousins; her tearful, affectionate Aunt Murray.

Emotion flows strongly in most books of the next fifty years. Tears are the order of the day in Mrs. Cameron's *Emma and her Nurse* (c. 1820) and others; Mrs. Sherwood was as adept in arousing fear (cf. the well-known passages in *The Fairchild Family*, or *The Little Woodman*) as she was in communicating pleasure, jealousy and affection.

Thus the range of emotion in children's books widened in the early nineteenth century, but, like a good deal of feeling loose in the adult world at the time, it was chiefly directed to religious ends.

Not since the time of the Reformation, perhaps, had there been such a widespread change in the public attitude to religion and morality. In 1777, Parson Woodforde, a genuinely charitable and conscientious clergyman, bought his tea, brandy and gin from the local smuggler without qualms of conscience or criticism from his parish.* Before his death in 1803, the situation was changing. A new generation of clergymen, often trained at Cambridge under Charles Simeon, was carrying Evangelical principles all over the kingdom. The leisurely routine of the Established Church, says Geoffrey Best, was disturbed by

> . . . a new model of an active parish clergyman—multiplying Sunday Services, introducing week-day services and religious meetings in the evenings, founding societies for spiritual and

* James Woodforde: *The Diary of a Country Parson* 1758–1802 (OUP, 1949) Entries for Jan. 16 and Mar. 29, 1777; Oct. 29, 1781.

> religious purposes, encouraging the laity to fill their non-working time with religious reading and activity, to do more and venture more for their beliefs. . . .[2]

Never before had the ordinary churchgoers of the upper or middle class been so involved in various good causes. Evangelicalism demanded individual effort; every true Evangelical was a missionary to the unconverted. Energies earlier directed to the general improvement of society were channelled into the work of universal conversion and the spiritual betterment of others. The number of societies formed after 1790 on behalf of missions, charities, education and rescue is evidence of the importance attached to this work.[3]

Of the many causes springing from Evangelical determination to reform and convert, that of the abolition of slavery was the most obviously successful, coming to a reasonably satisfactory conclusion before the death of its most famous advocate, William Wilberforce. In children's books, it was one of the themes taken over from eighteenth-century moral tales for the young. Early works had treated mostly of the humanitarian aspects of slavery. In Miss Edgeworth's "The Grateful Negro" (*Popular Tales*, 1812) and Mrs. Hurry's "Tyranny" (*Moral Tales for Young People*, 1807), the brutal masters and overseers are slaughtered in a slave rebellion, but just and kindly individuals are saved by grateful slaves. Mrs. Sherwood uses the same theme in *Babes in the Wood of the New World* (c. 1830), but the tale is also shot through with Evangelical concern for the conversion of slaves and masters alike.

In putting an end to the legal transportation of slaves to and from British colonies, the Abolition Act of 1807 had shown that total abolition was only a matter of time. Stories of the next two decades, displaying the current Evangelical preoccupation with the conversion and education of West Indian and African slaves are quite in tune with the hopes and fears of the times. M. G. ("Monk") Lewis, writing to Wilberforce in 1817 asks his advice as to the disposal of his hundreds of slaves on his Jamaican property.

> . . . [W]ere you in my situation, what would you do with those negroes at your disposal. . . . How can I secure them from being ill treated when I am dead? . . . Shall I leave them all their liberty? Then they must have a provision made for them; . . . But if I set them free, how can I be certain that the consequences may not be dangerous to the island and to its white inhabitants? There are so many difficulties on both sides. . . .[4]

He goes on to add that his enlightened treatment of his slaves has caused him to be blamed by other owners for the slave rebellion of 1816.

Nine years later, "Charlotte Elizabeth" took up the question of negroes about to receive their freedom. Her solution—found in *Perseverance*, or Walter and his Little School (1826)—is precisely that of Hannah More confronted by the abysmal ignorance of the population of Cheddar forty years earlier.[5]

> "In England," continued Mr. Shirley, "the places of worship are numerous . . . no man is excluded from hearing, if he cannot read, what God requires him to know; but we are aware that such privileges are not attainable by our slaves; and doubtless it is the duty of every proprietor to make good the deficiencies as far as lies in his power. . . ."

The school on the estate is conducted by the planter's son, a young man of eighteen.

> ". . . [W]e must be careful that you do not go beyond what is necessary and fitting for the negroes to learn. What do you principally teach in your school?"
>
> "Reading, Papa; a little writing to the most apt among them; and a general knowledge of Christianity, as set forth in the Catechism of our Church, and in Dr. Watts' Catechism; with selections from the New Testament, which they commit to memory and repeat to me." (*Perseverance*, p. 108–9.)

At the beginning of a moral tale of 1827, *The West Indian*, or The Happy Effects of Diligence and Self-Control, we are shown a rational rather than Evangelical Christianity at work on the plantation. A former slave, Caesar, had belonged to owners who had

> established schools for the education of the children of the slaves, and were so actively benevolent, that the slaves themselves became so attached to them, that they performed their work from a desire to shew their affection and gratitude to their good master. . . .

Converted by his master, Caesar made it his study "to practise the meekness, humility and forbearance, which ought to adorn the Christian character" and is so successful that he is entrusted with the care of their child after his owners' death. Taking the boy to a guardian in England, Caesar continues to exert a good influence upon him while he grows up. Coming to be regarded as "a friend rather than a servant", the former slave is rewarded by a house, an annuity, and an opportunity to return to Jamaica to find a wife. Like his young master, he is the happy result of a Christian education well subordinated to the moral duties.

The Evangelical mission drive was the second result of years of careful planning by Wilberforce and his associates. By calling year after year for action by Parliament, issuing effective propaganda on all fronts (including books for children), and finally by circulating petitions which gained nearly a million signatures in favour, the Evangelicals in 1813 forced the East India Company to open its Indian territories to missionaries. The ensuing enthusiasm for mission work lasted for a century, and is attested in hundreds of tract tales and missionary magazines for adults and children alike.

> "Go preach my gospel," Jesus said;
> "To every creature bear
> The stream of life, the living bread,
> And I will bless you there!"
>
> Lord, let us go, or let us send,
> This word of truth abroad;
> Gladly our little help we'll lend,
> That men may know the Lord.
>
> (*Hymns for Infant Minds*, XXXVIII)

Completely convinced of the rightness of missionary work, the Evangelicals passed on their urgent convictions to their Victorian descendants of all religious persuasions. Although a certain amount of opposition to mission work surfaced in the 1850's and 1860's,[6] missionary societies flourished in the English-speaking world, and active mission stations were scattered all over the globe. Sunday Schools devoted much of their effort to support of missions; tract fiction writers—Maria Charlesworth and A.L.O.E. (who became a missionary in her later years) being the most notable—wrote on their behalf, and so did Charlotte Yonge. Children's missionary magazines were produced by all sects; there was a missionary ship, "The John Williams".[7] And has anybody ever counted the missionary hymns?

No later writer, however, attained the perfect blend of romantic sensibility and Evangelical fervour that gave the first missionary story, Mrs. Sherwood's *History of Little Henry and his Bearer*

(1814), its lasting appeal. With the romantic attractions of colourful authentic details of Indian life, the book is one of the best early examples of the use of devices of the sentimental novel in the children's tract tale. It was particularly effective with pathos (Fig. 8).

> "You were kind to me when my own father and mother were dead,"

says the dying Little Henry to his faithful servant, Boosy,

> "The first thing I can remember is being carried by you. . . . Nobody loved me then but you; and could I depart in peace, and leave you behind me in the way to hell? I could not bear to think of it! . . . I know you will die a Christian. God has begun a good work in you, and I am certain that he will finish it. . . ."

But the early nineteenth-century Evangelical effort did not stop with the anti-slavery movement and the popular missionary drive. Its third and widest field was already charted by Mrs. Trimmer, Hannah More and Mrs. Sherwood: the education and conversion (or education *for* conversion) of the illiterate and the indifferent, the ungodly and the ignorant, the rich and the poor. And always, the young. In short, as Wilberforce expressed it, *the moral reform of the nation*. To this ambitious cause, the Tract Societies turned their energies, and tract fiction evolved out of the tract in response to the demand for narrative literature that should be sufficiently entertaining to hold the reader without distracting him from its moral and religious lesson. The tract was an essential tool of education.

Between 1820 and 1870, the cry for education was never silenced. "Groping their way in the labyrinth of social evils by which they were surrounded," noted Charles Knight in his recollections of the year 1818,

> . . . most benevolent persons had come to the conclusion that the Adults of their generation must take their chance of growing happier and better under our existing systems, but that improvements, to be real and genuine, must begin with the Young. The half-whispered cry was for Education.[8]

Individuals, groups and churches pursued their own policies of education. Textbooks and literature for schools came from the Tract Societies, the only publishers of the time equipped to deal in vast quantities of printed material of impeccable moral content. The Church of England favoured the Society for the Propagation of Christian Knowledge (founded 1698); the Dissenters, the Religious Tract Society (1799) which had followed fast upon the success of the Cheap Repository Tracts. The R.T.S. was principally a joint publishing scheme. The S.P.C.K. took an active part in erecting charity schools and aiding missions at home and abroad, as well as in publishing and distributing Bibles and tracts. It was not, said Charles Knight, very active around 1820, although by 1840 it was doing a great deal.[9]

There was also a Methodist Tract Society, direct descendant of John Wesley's London Book Room. A number of other publishers and printers: Rivington's, Hatchard's, Houlston of Wellington, Hazard (later Binns and Robinson) of Bath, Holdsworth, Seeley and Burnside, and others, brought out tracts, theological works, textbooks, and instructive tales for children. They favoured the Evangelical approach. Darton and Harvey, originally a Quaker firm, specialized more in moral works, as did the firm of Harris. Both were highly commended in 1831 by *The Quarterly Journal of Education* (I, II), published by Charles Knight for the Society for the Diffusion of Useful Knowledge.

Between 1810 and 1840, in spite of the efforts of government, Tract Societies and churches, the radical and revolutionary press attracted a vast number of readers among artisans and workmen, and promoted Chartism. In the instruction of children, however, the religious groups and the Tract Societies moved rapidly ahead. The moralists, who tended to group together under the wing of the S.D.U.K., made a significant contribution to a revived secularism. In spite of the general concern, progress was slow in the training of the illiterate masses. Nothing kept pace with the growth of the urban population; whatever was accomplished in the training of teachers or the building of schools was inadequate almost before it was completed. A second difficulty was the lack of machinery with which to institute the necessary improvement: no precedent existed for setting up or administering a national system of education, even if those most concerned had wished it done upon a national scale.

Schools of many kinds existed and others were being built. All functioned more or less independently: day schools and night schools; dame schools and town schools; workhouse, Ragged, Army, and Sunday Schools; charitable trusts and private academies.

They were supported by societies, by churches, by charitable bequests and donations, and by individuals (including factory owners). Anglicans had founded the National Society about 1811 to educate the poor; in the 1830's it was said to be educating around a million.[10] The Nonconformists set up the British and Foreign School Society in 1812; in the mid-thirties, its figure was seventy thousand. Each had its own system, Bell and Lancaster respectively; and the Education Act of 1870 found in their workings the only available machinery by which to set up the national system.

In 1820 that Act lay far in the future. Meanwhile the ever-increasing pauper population of swelling industrial cities demanded attention. Volunteer societies took a hand. Ragged Schools were set up, cheap, privately-supported, in the lowest slums. Their supporters gave generously of time and money, acting as teachers as well as sponsors. Lessons were given, a hot meal provided, and a little learning began to seep into grim back alleys and foetid courts—very little, but something.

Early nineteenth-century schools and their teachers have been unflatteringly pictured in mid-Victorian fiction. Dickens contributed Dotheboys Hall; the Castle of Mrs. Pipchin, the "ogress and child-queller" (a fraud, surely, rather than an ogress?); Mr. Bradley Headstone's Preparatory Establishment; and Mr. Gradgrind's model school in Coketown. Two or three inadequate schools appear in *Vanity Fair*; no reader can forget Jane Eyre's life at Mr. Brocklehurst's Lowood. She gave no details about the school after it was reformed. Books written for children between 1820 and 1870 also touched upon school life. As one might expect, the picture is generally a happier one, although the standard of education seems low. Mr. and Mrs. Fairchild support a village school in which their children instruct Sunday pupils, a point which must have appealed to young readers. Mrs. Sherwood's other tales display a range of girls' schools and at least two for boys. Later came *The Crofton Boys*, *Tom Brown's Schooldays*, and the pedagogical passages of *The Water-Babies* (Kingsley's comment upon current theories of education). Periodicals over these fifty years give as varied a view of schools and education.

Several interesting points arise from this mass of contemporary material. Whatever sort of a fictional picture of schools, scholars or teachers may have been drawn, it certainly had somewhere a counterpart in real life. Discernible too is the sharp anxiety of the age about getting its children educated, and the difficulty of doing so. The whole problem is further complicated on one hand by the serious desire to make education of moral and spiritual value, and on the other by the rapidly-hardening determination to make it materially useful.

Throughout the century the Tract Societies attempted to fill all needs by ensuring a constant supply of cheap printed matter. Until around 1840, the bulk of it was religious. Twenty-eight years after its founding, the R.T.S. claimed that "upwards of 300,000 Juvenile Readers are every year added by these institutions (i.e. Sunday and other schools), to the vast number already eager for books to read, and at a price suited to their ability to purchase". Their publications included the Series of Short Stories for children under ten, actually tracts for young children intended to oust "the vile trash . . . of *halfpenny books* for children". The circulation of the two juvenile magazines, *The Child's Companion* and *The Tract Magazine*, was at this date, twenty thousand and thirty thousand issues a month respectively.[11]

After the middle of the century, the Tract Societies catered more and more to secular interests. By 1851, the S.P.C.K. catalogue listed an ancient classical atlas; much biography; and material on Canada and Australia that testifies to the current interest in colonization and emigration. There were accounts of a summer spent in the Antarctic; of travels in Africa, Russia, North and South America. There was even an history of Mohammedanism. The many children dependent for reading matter upon the Tract Societies naturally benefited from this broadening of the subject matter. In 1828, the R.T.S. Committee dealing with publications for the young had said with pride that, as a matter of public duty, they had excluded "those publications which, although well meant, are calculated to injure rather than benefit the youthful mind, from the romantic and fanciful manner in which they are written". By 1860, they were offering the vigorous if stereotyped adventure stories of Kingston and Ballantyne, and accounts of the excavations of Thebes, Nineveh and Tyre. They probably had little more intention of admitting "the romantic and fanciful" than they had in 1828, but romance and fancy can hardly be excluded from tales of travel, adventure and exploration. Without the printings of the Tract Societies, children's libraries in the poorer homes of the last century would have been scanty indeed, and the self-education of the newly-literate adult would have often stopped short for lack of cheap books.

* * *

In spite of the acute Evangelical concern for slaves and Hindus, and the stress upon converting the godless and teaching the ignorant and the young, there was, until the 1860's, little or nothing in children's tract tales about the English working child: chimney-sweep, mine or factory worker, farm drudge. These children had been the subject of investigation even before 1800; there were Factory Acts in 1802 and 1819; Robert Owen had taken up the matter of factory children and gained the support of Sir Robert Peel. But working children as objects of sympathy were generally excluded from early tract tales, literature for the young being more concerned with little sinners

> Who curse and swear, but never pray;
> Who call ill names, and fight

or with little idlers

> Weary and wretched, in spite of their mirth
> For want of some pleasing employ.*

One reason for this omission may have been that so few of their influential fellow-citizens knew what went on in the industrial centres. In 1800, and for over thirty years afterwards, there was no train travel, cheap and speedy. Then too the shocking findings of Parliamentary Committees on mine and factory abuses were not regularly made public until the late 1830's. Tract writers were as ignorant as other literate persons of the real state of manufacturing cities. The visitors who were permitted, even encouraged, to view the workings of the mills, were not (as Mrs. Trollope says) allowed to interrogate the children.

> . . . (L)ed by a skilful official through the various floors of a factory, (they) retire . . . without having any feelings of sympathy excited by . . . the silent little unobtrusive beings, one moment of whose unchanging existence they have been permitted to witness. . . . Strangers do not visit factories to look at *them*! It is the triumphant

* Isaac Watts: "Against Evil Company" (*Divine Songs* XXI).
Jane Taylor: "Idleness" (*Original Poems*, Vol. II).

perfection of British mechanism which they come to see, it is of that they speak, and of that they think, of that they boast when they leave the life-consuming process behind them.[12]

The fact that the great age of railway building in Britain coincided with energetic investigation into working conditions in mills and mines helped to expose the worst of the industrial evils. The findings of Parliamentary Committees and Commissions between 1830 and 1850 were widely publicized, and concerned people were able to see the manufacturing cities (as Dickens visited "Coketown", and enquired at another time into Yorkshire schools). Many years passed, however, before the wider significance of the shocking statistics was really grasped. Most Victorians before 1870 equated the vast expansion of national prosperity with *progress*, a word of which they were inordinately proud. They were as fascinated by machinery and progress as we are today. Ironically, the same people who deplored the wretched state of factory workers took pride in the fact that goods made in Manchester, Preston, Birmingham, were exported to the ends of the earth. The concluding lines of Isaac Taylor's *Scenes of Commerce by Land and Sea* (1830) could have been echoed for decades afterwards:

May the commerce of the British realms long flourish! Especially as it is becoming, by the favour of Divine Providence, the means of conveying the Bible, with the temporal, spiritual, and eternal blessings of the Gospel to all nations under Heaven!

Few before 1840 realised the magnitude of the shift in population, or the potential dangers in the slow continuous drift since 1790 of faceless thousands of country people towards the cities, driven from farms and villages by depression and hunger. Steam and water power had undermined the eighteenth-century cottage industries which made villagers self-supporting, self-respecting. The Corn Laws kept up the price of food. Those who had earlier entered the cities of "the dark Satanic mills" did not return to tell their tale; nor was it easy to find influential listeners willing to help.

Tract tale writers in general were silent on these matters. Only one Evangelical children's writer of the first half of the century produced a detailed account of the abuse of child labour. This was the determined "Charlotte Elizabeth", an Evangelical of the old school, who let nothing silence her protests against Roman Catholicism (a favourite theme in her children's tales), against the

Tractarians, the theatres, and the exploitation of children in factories. Her circumstantially-detailed tract novel, *Helen Fleetwood* (1841), was still being read in 1877 and later. It was certainly not a book for the young.*

Its depressing picture of the factory town is corroborated by the evidence of William Cobbett, Peter Gaskell, Robert Owen and many others to Commissioners working on the various Reports between 1814 and 1842. Incidents paralleling events in *Helen Fleetwood*—the mutilation of the unhappy Sarah by the machinery, the beatings undergone by Helen and Mary—were brought before the House of Commons in 1832 by Michael Sadler:

> ... [D]rowsy and exhausted, the poor creatures fall too often among the machinery, which is not in many instances sufficiently sheathed; when their muscles are lacerated, their bones broken, or the limbs torn off ... [C]hildren are beaten with thongs prepared for the purpose. Yes, the females of this country, no matter whether children or grown up ... are beaten in your "free market of labour" as you term it, like slaves! (Speech of March 16, 1832.)[13]

The deformity of child workers; the illness or death from inhalation of dust and fluff from the textiles; the exhaustion following twelve or fourteen hours of labour with insufficient nourishment; the early recourse to gin-drinking—all part of the pathos of *Helen Fleetwood*—are fully authenticated by the Parliamentary Papers of the time.

There is more to this novel than the recital of the misfortunes of a healthy, happy country family, separated by the regulations of the New Poor Law, humiliated and degraded in the crowded city, and finally broken by death. "Charlotte Elizabeth" recognised those sinister long-range effects of the pressure of the industrial city upon the human personality that are called today "the alienation of the individual" from his kind. Young factory workers at the machines were, she said, "a community of automata" lacking all animation, their faces showing "cold listlessness", "vacancy, selfishness and gloom" instead of the lively interest and gaiety befitting their youth.[14] She noted too the depressing subservience of the human

* Mrs. Cameron who had spent many years in the Shropshire industrial area, read it with approval, noting "I hope she will not fail in her excellent object". (*Life of Mrs. Cameron*, 1862, p. 404.)

being to the machine, almost as if he were chained to it, obeying its movements without pause for rest or thought.

Like so much tract fiction, *Helen Fleetwood* is not of outstanding literary value. It is not, however, immoderately sentimental, and its compassion and indignation are fully justified. Nor does its element of other-worldliness exclude the demand for improvement of the conditions it describes. Moreover its date (1841) is two years earlier than *Past and Present*, and three years before *The Cry of the Children* and Engels' *Condition of the Working Class in England in 1844*. Earlier too than *Sybil*, and *Mary Barton*, it pointed out the fact of the two nations and the significance of the situation in terms of human lives.

"Charlotte Elizabeth", Mrs. Tonna, in this work as in *The Wrongs of Women* (1843–44), was not only well abreast of the times, but in some respects far ahead of them. But wisely she did not try to put the material into books for children.

Nothing in Mrs. Sherwood's writing bears upon the working children in industrial cities. A tract with the suggestive name of *The China Manufactory* (c. 1821–22) turns out to be an allegory of the Divine Potter shaping unpromising human clay. A vivid description of the industrial area around Wolverhampton, "this region of smoke and machinery, of pits and cinder banks" merits a better tale than *Dudley Castle* (1831) turns out to be. During the 1820's, Mrs. Sherwood held readings for the local gloveresses, an unruly crowd, and visited the local penitentiary; but after her attack on political reform in *Emancipation* (1831), she was requested to discontinue these activities and did so.

Only one of the Cheap Repository Tracts had approached the matter of very young working children. *The Lancashire Collier Girl* (ascribed to Hannah More) dealt with a child of nine, who, with a brother of seven, was taken down the pit by her father, to become a "drawer" (i.e. to haul the carts of coal along the low, narrow underground passages). Later, at twelve, after her father's death in a mine accident, she took on "task work" to support the family, thus ruining her health. The tract leaves an unpleasant impression: it flatters the parish officials "who give maintenance to those who apply to them"; flatters the miners among whom "Mary's virtue was safe"; flatters the pit-master who recommends the girl to a new employer; and the new employer himself. As for Mary, the Collier Girl, she is a pious object lesson

> . . . to teach the poor that they can seldom be in a condition of life so low as to prevent their rising to some degree of independence if they choose to exert themselves; and that there can be no situation whatever so mean, as to forbid the practice of many noble virtues . . . and to do their duty in that state of life unto which it hath pleased God to call them.

The situation taken for granted in this tract had not improved much by the time of the Factory Commission of 1833, or the Children's Employment Commission of 1842, although the public attitude had changed. The high moral rating given in the tract to all concerned was quite absent from the later reports, which asserted on irrefutable evidence the moral and physical degradation of women and children in the pits. They were accompanied by the well-known illustrations which aroused a national outcry, and at last matters began to improve. In 1847, Thomas Burt went into the pits at the age of ten. He was well treated, and, writing of his experiences many years later, records no ill effects and no resentment.[15] Not all were so lucky, even then.

Young Harriet Martineau's brief excursion into "tract" writing for Houlston of Wellington produced four moral tales of Unitarian leanings and two touching on industrial disputes. The latter seem to be for young adults and are very dull. Entitled *The Turn-Out* (1829) and *The Rioters* (1827), they sum up the consequences of industrial agitation, linking material and moral evils brought about by strikes.

> . . . the produce of ingenuity and industry destroyed; I have seen the wealthy brought down to poverty, and the poor to starvation; I have seen alarm and distrust spread over the face of a populous and once happy country; the minds of the young perverted and corrupted, the hearts of the old wrung with sorrow.[16]

The middle-aged Harriet Martineau, the populariser of Political Economy, would rather have forgotten these tales. She was extremely annoyed when the Houlston of the 1840's altered and re-issued *The Rioters* as an anti-Chartist pamphlet.

One working child, however, was impossible to miss: the Sweep, always in plain sight, who came like the swallow with the seasons (Fig. 11). Incredible as it seems, few who employed him in the early nineteenth century recognized his miseries or tried to help him. Attempts made by the eccentric reformer, Jonas Hanway, around

1780, to stiffen the regulations governing this dreadful occupation failed. Not for a century was it finally prohibited, following years of effort by Lord Shaftesbury and others. It was a blind spot in the acute but narrow Evangelical vision that was shared by many. Even the soft-hearted Charles Lamb who sympathised with the sweeps and treated them to an annual dinner, could write of them humorously as

> . . . young Africans of our own growth—these almost clergy imps, who sport their cloth without assumption; and from their little pulpits (the tops of chimneys) in the nipping air of a December morning, preach a lesson of patience . . . (In Praise of Chimney Sweeps).

Most readers of 1794 probably overlooked Blake's ironic juxtaposition of sweep and churchgoer:

> A little black thing among the snow,
> Crying "weep! weep!" in notes of woe!
> "Where are thy father and mother? Say!"
> "They are both gone up to the church to pray."
> (The Chimney Sweep)

Moral tales for children continued either to treat the sweep humorously, as in Adelaide O'Keeffe's "George and the Chimney-Sweeper" or to cite him as an Awful Warning. The Master Sweep had become the urban counterpart of the chapbook Ogre, lurking to pounce on a lost child, who must thereafter, like "pretty Jack" of Elizabeth Turner's verse,

> . . . creep
> Up chimneys, crying Sweep! Sweep! Sweep!
> (*The Daisy*, XXVII)

There were other reasons why early Evangelicals, enmeshed in their own teachings, found it difficult to protest these home-grown evils. Intensely concentrated (like Wilberforce) upon one or two favourite good causes, they were limited by a form of spiritual tunnel-vision which could exclude other pressing matters, particularly those involving bodily hardship, for which they advocated Christian resignation. Thus the very nature of early Evangelical belief sometimes cancelled its reforming energies: it was directed, not to the making of a better world to live in, but to the making of better people who lived in this world only in preparation for eternity. At no time, therefore, did the welfare of the body come before that of the soul. Since chimney-sweeper, factory or mine worker, lacemaker, crossing-sweeper and all lived in Christian England, where, as Dr. Watts had said,

> . . . Streams of Heavenly Mercy flow,
> And Words of sweet Salvation sound,
>
> (*Divine Songs*, V)

the highest duty of the Evangelicals was to see that all these children were instructed in religion. Despite their horrid working conditions (a factor of only temporal importance) they were in better case than

> A heathen, untaught and forlorn,
> And worshipping idols of stone!
>
> (*Hymns for Infant Minds*, XXXVII)

Similarly the Evangelical emphasis upon individualism and industry worked to the advantage of mine or factory owner, who, in many instances, had reached his position by the exertion of these same qualities, and who, moreover, was employing so many people so usefully. When it came to the sanctity of work, Evangelicals and Utilitarians found common ground.

Many tract tale writers of 1810–1830 (and a few later ones such as Maria Charlesworth) failed to realise that earlier tales for the working classes—the Cheap Repository Tracts among them—with rural backgrounds and simple religious lesson carried no message for the labourer in Manchester, Leeds or Birmingham, living under the harsh economic realities of the time. The radical writers—William Cobbett, Richard Carlile, William Hone, and others—were, however, thoroughly aware of the fact. They knew that for every poor shepherd on Salisbury Plain or elsewhere who received charity and employment from the affluent, there were probably ten thousand unaided hand-loom weavers in desperate poverty. Unable to retrieve any measure of independence, these men and others like them eagerly received political instruction from Chartists and trade unionists who did not talk down to them. Similarly, children's tract tales of an earlier generation, *The History of Margaret Whyte*, *The Young Cottager*, etc. written for village Sunday Schools, meant little to the collier child of the

1830's, "trapping" or "drawing" in the black pit tunnels, or to the little scavenger collecting fluff and scraps under the web on the power loom. Even if factory schools for children working twelve hours a day were not the merest farce; even if these children did learn to read, the world of existing tract literature was beyond their impoverished experience. Two or three generations removed from country life, they had probably started in mill or mine at five or six; as Mrs. Browning pointed out, religion and the beauty of nature had no place in these contracted lives.

> . . . [A]ll day, the iron wheels go onward,
>   Grinding life down from its mark;
> And the children's souls, which God is calling sunward,
>   Spin on blindly in the dark.
>
> (*The Cry of the Children*, 1843)

Like their elders, the factory children turned to the gin palace for companionship, and (if they could read) to the lurid broadside and chapbook for amusement. Family ties often disintegrated rapidly under such conditions.

This was a further embarrassment to Evangelical tract writers, who stressed implicit obedience to parents. As Mrs. Sherwood made so clear in all her work, the parent-child relationship was the *type* or symbol of God's relationship with man, Divine law proclaimed by the Fifth Commandment. No children's writer went against it, though few went as far as Dr. Watts in support of it.

> Have we not heard that dreadful Plagues
>   Are threatened by the Lord
> To him that breaks his Father's Law,
>   Or mocks his Mother's Word?
>
> (*Divine Songs*, XXIII)

Moreover there was the law of the land, giving the father complete control over his child and the husband over the wife.

Was the tract writer, then, to contravene the laws of God and man and contradict all his own previous teaching by suggesting that *any* parent be denied control over his own child? Although the parish workhouse or the big orphanage "apprenticed" orphans and pauper children to the Master Sweep, to the overseer of the rural labour gang, or to the factory owner, it was the sad fact that *most* children were placed in mines and factories by their own parents, and under legal contracts.

Doubtless it was so with Mary the Collier Girl, whose father, "finding that he had but little employment for her above ground, took her to work with him in the coal-pit". Hannah More is careful to add that this father "had an eye [to his children] . . . there is no particular reason to suppose that . . ., they were ever much overworked".

Fathers pocketed the earnings of children and wives as a matter of course, the Collier Girl and her brother earning "no less than seven shillings a week for their parents". They were certainly luckier than most of their contemporaries in having a mother who cared for her children and her home. Dr. Percival of Manchester in 1796 had protested against the employment of young children in cotton mills, partly on the grounds of ". . . idleness, extravagance and profligacy in the parents, who, contrary to the law of nature, subsist by the oppression of their children"; Dr. Gaskell found no improvement in the 1830's.[17] Josiah Wedgwood, a conscientious employer although an opponent of the legislation to curtail child employment, admitted in 1816 that a child's wages were always paid to his parents, who all too often spent them on liquor. Even good parents, if impoverished, were forced to sacrifice children to factory employment; they got no parish relief unless they did so when there was a factory at hand. The callous parent was still in evidence in "Charlotte Elizabeth's" time:

> . . . thousands of delicate little girls . . . habitually oppressed, overworked, starved, beaten and that of men, frequently by their own fathers, to swell the gains of their labour . . . under the hardening influence of covetousness, or the cravings of wretched want, more barbarous usage awaits the girl at the hand of a father or brother than that of a stranger. . . .[18]

Like the real picture of the Chimney-sweep's fate, none of this made pleasant reading and none of it appeared in children's books.

Nevertheless, at this distance of time, it is impossible to be sure about the facts of family life in industrial cities. Mrs. Gaskell, whose clear, dependable voice must be listened to, discovered affectionate parents and dutiful children in Manchester slums, but she did not write about them for children. Those who did, Charles Kingsley, for instance, and Hesba Stretton, used approved novel conventions, selected and isolated their one oppressed child, setting him at the centre of the tale. Their carefully-chosen details were guaranteed to touch the heart without turning the stomach or offending the enlarged Victorian sense of delicacy, but they got down to the basic evils. The climate of opinion had changed, but as Dr. Barnardo and others were to discover in the 1870's and 1880's, the law moved very slowly.

Another factor keeping the unfortunates of mill and factory out of children's books was that dropsical sense of delicacy typified by Thomas Bowdler's editing of Shakespeare. It was a continuation of the earlier reaction against the grossness of the Regency, and for several generations it had a profound effect upon writing for children. Episodes in *Helen Fleetwood* and *Michael Armstrong* show how it hampered the rescue efforts of would-be helpers. Why is it, asks the young heroine of the latter, that ". . . this, their painful labour should subject them to such habits of inevitable ignorance and degradation, that all decent and respectable people must be taught to shun them?"

The wickedness of industrial cities was a by-word, and the corruption of their children extremely well-attested. It is notable that the hero of the tract tale throughout the century is always exceptional: *someone* has taught him morals, or brought him up better than the average before he appears in the pages of *Christie's Old Organ*, *Alone in London*, or *Mother's Last Words*.* Usually the average street child is the Awful Warning.

More potent than the general reluctance to criticize the conduct of the parent (save when he was a drunkard), or the fear of contaminating the innocence of the young, may have been the economic reason for ignoring the working child. Had the Evangelicals made a genuine issue of these evils, they could no longer have carried public opinion with them as they had done thirty years earlier over the abolition of slavery. In those thirty years, the Industrial Revolution had far outstripped most men's understanding of the forces governing it. The utilitarian theories of Adam Smith, of Malthus and Ricardo, of Mill and Bentham, now widely accepted, worked strongly against interference with private enterprise. The whole economic system was held to hinge upon the prevalence of cheap labour, and factory owners, loudly asserting the value of their contribution to the national economy, received a sympathetic hearing from general public and legislators alike. Reforms came

* According to Dr. Barnardo, however, a very few of these uncorrupted children did exist.

slowly. The little workers of mill and factory were not wholly liberated until past 1860. Nor did they often appear in books for children, even at that date.

One pressing cause connected with industrial cities did, however, present itself to the tract writers of the 1830's and 1840's: Temperance had lined up beside missions and was gathering as many enthusiastic supporters. The temperance campaign was particularly congenial to Victorian Evangelicals. In this field the declining doctrine of universal human depravity could be successfully revived and drunkenness could be assailed on religious grounds. As a matter of clear-cut individual choice, it was in keeping with Evangelical theory; it affected efficiency, and thus concerned the utilitarians.

Drunkenness at all ages was fearfully prevalent in the manufacturing areas. The weariness of long working hours; the lack of recreation; the miserable living conditions—all helped to fill the beer shops and gin palaces that sprang into existence following the Sale of Beer Act of 1830. According to Norman Longmate's study of the temperance movement, *The Waterdrinkers* (1968), juvenile temperance societies were formed almost immediately, the best known being the Band of Hope (1847). Educational and morally uplifting, they were an important part of the campaign for the "elevation of the masses", and their work was enthusiastically supported by tract writers and Tract Societies. Indeed the magic lantern shows, the songs and recitations, and the extremely dramatic speakers supplied on some temperance programmes must have compared favourably with music hall or stage entertainment (with which they had much in common.)[19] In tract literature temperance became a major theme.

In spite of their failure to touch upon the subject of the oppressed working child with the same pathos and concern that they brought to the cause of missions and temperance, the tract tale writers were very occupied during these years. Much of the groundwork of the Education Act of 1870 was being laid in the form of schools and missions intended to counteract the well-known wickedness of industrial cities. Before the end of the century the education that the Evangelicals put forward as the prelude to widespread conversion was to be firmly entrenched as the foundation-stone of material progress. That the Tract Societies and a number of their favourite writers should have helped to make this secularization possible is one of the ironies of the century.

CHAPTER IV

THE EIGHTEEN FORTIES:
The Early Victorians and the Elevation of the Masses

BEFORE the accession of Queen Victoria in 1837, the original Evangelical Movement was at a standstill. Its authority, the personal magnetism of its leadership, and much of its prestige had died in 1833 with Wilberforce and Hannah More. The two stirring objectives of earlier years—abolition of slavery and establishment of Indian missions—had been gained; Sunday observance was taken for granted; respectability, no longer on the defensive, was in fashion. A whole younger generation, Evangelically educated, was asserting itself: the early Victorians.

The adults of 1840 were children or grandchildren of those whose lives had been disrupted by the French Revolution and the Napoleonic Wars. Whatever their religious backgrounds, the literate among them had been educated wholly or in part according to the theories of Mrs. Trimmer, John Wesley, Hannah More, the Edgeworths, and Mrs. Sherwood, theories augmented by other works of the eighteenth century. Such a mixture of moral and religious training left most of them with a strong certainty of their own rightness. How could it be otherwise? They were a part of the reaction against violence, revolution and war; they had absorbed a disgust for the luxury and vice of the Regency; and their own energies were channelled into habits of honesty, frugality, industry, and individual effort. It had, moreover, come to be generally understood that these habits were among the hallmarks of sincere religion. (Fanny and Edmund in *Mansfield Park*, making common cause against the frivolity of Mary and Henry Crawford, illustrate perfectly this change in the social and moral outlook of their class.)

Religion itself on all sides had been disciplined to the pattern of self-examination and prayer, Bible reading and Sunday observance approved by Tractarian and Evangelical alike, by churchman and dissenter. All felt a strong sense of mission. "Everyone seemed waking up to a sense of unfulfilled duties," wrote Elizabeth Sewell in her recollections of the 1840's, "and the question constantly discussed was, which had the primary claim, home, or church services, and works and charity?"[1]

Henrietta Keddie, who with her sisters was starting a private school in those years, describes in detail the feelings of earnest early Victorians of her class:

> There had been so much stupid excess and gross extravagance in former reigns, such contemptible frippery and affectation, such folly and false pretence, leading to what was worse still, sin and wickedness. We were young to be so sensible and good, but like our liege lady, we would lead busy, useful lives, content with what we had, occupied with our duties, seeking our reward in approving conscience and the peace of well-ordered happy homes. All was to be real and lasting. We were to reckon up the use and not the show of our surroundings.[2]

Although she wrote (as "Sarah Tytler") in religious magazines, Henrietta Keddie was not an Evangelical. Nor was Jenny Lind, the Swedish singer, who renounced the stage in 1849.

> (She) had felt that the religious and the contemplative part of her character were being swamped by the glare of the footlights or the plaudits of the crowd, and the renunciation seemed essential to her if the higher part of her nature was to be saved.[3]

Indubitably the early Victorians were religious, more religious than many of their forebears. The Evangelicals were not forgotten, but their children, the Victorians, reacted differently to emotional stimuli, seeking new outlets for their energy and their enthusiasm.

Religious belief itself was undergoing modifications that earlier generations had not anticipated. The spiritual energies that animated the Evangelical—romantic fervour, revolutionary ardour, religious dedication—components, in short, of *vital religion,* had for forty years been concentrated like the rays of a burning glass upon the great evangelical causes of 1790–1830. Like a burning glass, they had generated light and heat, exposing dark corners, burning out accumulated evils. Nothing could be the same again. But now, in the 1840's, the focus had shifted with time and the rays were diverging.

After 1830, Evangelicalism separated once more into components which by then had changed both in colour and intensity. Much of the original fervour and dedication passed into Tractarianism along with the romantic passion for colour and beauty, the romantic search for the past. Short-lived because of its association with Roman Catholicism, the Tractarian Movement nevertheless left an enduring mark upon the Established Church in the forms of liturgy, music and architecture, as well as in the study of history, the recovery of tradition, and the re-examination of doctrine. A type of radical thinking within Evangelicalism became the liberal Christianity of mid-century, of which the farther edge diffused within another thirty years into scientific free-thinking. The spirit of reform remained healthy and relatively unchanged, retaining its old sense of urgency. But it changed direction. The majority of Victorian reformers turned their energies to the removal of political and social evils as much as to the purification of personal morality or the saving of individual souls.

Certainly the emotional intensity of Evangelicalism did not die out when its forms and doctrines were questioned and repudiated. It remained to enliven secular relationships. Thus politics became invested with religious fervour by the time of Gladstone, and the cause of sanitary reform was argued from the pulpit by Kingsley. Romantic intensity of emotion blossomed tropically from an Evangelical rootstock in the novels of the Brontës and the poetry of the Rossetti family.

The age produced an abundance of tracts covering the whole spectrum of political and religious belief. Although the controversial *Tracts for the Times* (1833–1845) were not for the young, they aroused a furore which was reflected in children's books for the rest of the century. Only two Evangelical tract writers of any significance wrote copiously for children between 1830 and 1840: William Carus Wilson (Charlotte Brontë's Mr. Brocklehurst) and "Charlotte Elizabeth", Mrs. Tonna. The former produced reams of tracts for his numerous publications, *The Children's Friend* (Fig. 12), *The Child's First Tales*, etc. Since all his writing demonstrated eighteenth-century Evangelical teaching for the young in its most terrifying form, it is not remarkable that his livelier and kindlier predecessors, Hannah More, Legh Richmond, Mrs. Sherwood and Mrs. Cameron, still held their places. Indeed the last two, who had taken to tract fiction since about 1830, were more popular than ever.

Mrs. Cameron, never an extreme Evangelical, was favoured by both moderate and High Church readers; Thomas Arnold and

Pusey recommended her children's tales;[4] and Charlotte Yonge in 1869 praised her "nice little practical books" and the excellence of "The Polite Little Children".[5] Mrs. Sherwood had modified her religious stand as the griefs of her Indian years faded in memory. Shaking off her earlier obsession with infant death and heathen idolatry, she began about 1825 to write tales and novels rather than tracts. The novel, so long discouraged by the Evangelicals, had begun its upward climb towards moral responsibility. Some years earlier, Maria Edgeworth, Sir Walter Scott and Jane Austen had established its value as respectable amusement, historical instruction or ironic comment upon social foibles. Mrs. Sherwood's tales after 1825 nurtured this process of literary disinfection, and created a taste for sentimental narrative with moral and religious purpose. Readers who later welcomed such novels of social purpose as *Sybil* (1845), *Mary Barton* (1848), or *Hard Times* (1854) had been accustomed in childhood to narrative with a religious lesson that required its characters to make serious moral decisions.*

Victorians of 1840 inherited many of the anxieties and problems that had plagued their parents. Napoleon had passed into history, but fear of revolution remained, fostered in the 1830's by the unlicensed radical press. The first issue of *The Poor Man's Guardian* attacked the Reform Bill as a "precious deceit" of "The 'liberal' (Ha! Ha!) WHIGS" who would never "deprive themselves of the power to plunder and persecute". It later proclaimed Robespierre "one of the most truly good and great men that ever existed"; advocated political assassination; and christened the Workhouse as set up by the New Poor Law, "a Bastille for the poor".[6] Politics of the early 1840's, highlighted by Chartist threats, the Factory Acts, and the repeal of the Corn Laws, aroused much excitement and a nervousness reflected in large printings of tracts for workers with titles like "A Dialogue between a Reformer and a Labourer", or "Advice to the Labouring Classes with Especial Reference to Tumultuous Assemblages".[7] Mrs. Sherwood was similarly apprehensive in 1829 when she wrote *Emancipation*; and in 1841 the distribution of socialist pamphlets in the factories brought an unbalanced tirade from the well-meaning "Charlotte Elizabeth" in which she defined Socialism as the supreme effort of

* For Mrs. Sherwood's part in this change of literary outlook, see Cutt, M. N.: *Mrs. Sherwood and her Books for Children*, (1974).

the devil's long experience in working evil, "the moral Gorgon", and "the last effort of Satanic venom".[8]

Since the beginning of the century, Evangelical concern over religious indifference, infidelity, and Roman Catholic encroachment had never died down. Mrs. Cameron's comment that, by the Catholic Emancipation Act of 1829, Anti-Christ reigned once more, had its counterparts later in the nation-wide torrents of bitter protest against the Government's decision in 1845 to increase the grant to Maynooth College, and again in 1850, against Cardinal Wiseman. Much within the Church of England—Tractarianism, for instance, and ritualism—infuriated Evangelicals and dissenters; and a chilling rationalism long evident in economic thought was now, in Germany, being applied to matters of religion. Known as the Higher Criticism, it seriously questioned the literal truth of the Bible, and endangered the very foundation stone of Evangelical belief.

On a worldly level there was increased realization of the conflicting elements of Victorian life. Industrial cities had swallowed up the beauties of the Midlands even as they absorbed its rural population. As the Factory Acts of 1843 testified, industrial evils flourished. The chimney-sweep still scrambled up the flue. The pauper inhabitants of the slums lived and died in the filthy courts and alleys described a generation later (for children) in *Jessica's First Prayer* (1867), or *Little Meg's Children* (1868). Thinking people asked themselves unanswerable questions. How was the vast new accumulation of knowledge about the hopeless state of the Second Nation to be reconciled with the economic theory that was credited with bringing about the national prosperity? How could either be reconciled with Christian belief?

In 1847, the Mayhew brothers presented industry allegorically in a children's book, *The Good Genius that Turns Everything to Gold*. (Industry here, as so often in Victorian writing, included both technology and hard work.) For their elders the same note was sounded in the writings of Carlyle, Macaulay and Samuel Smiles, and those of Bentham and Mill. Yet industry and the machine could flourish only in the stifling cities where much of the population had a life expectancy of less than thirty years. The railways, the arteries of English industrial life, which Dickens implied in 1850 were "not all material, but have a kind of soul in their stupendous bodies . . ." had intensified the concentration of the slums that they had revealed to the public eye. While half the nation dwelt in squalor at the mercy of every kind of disease, steamship and telegraph pushed back the geographical limits of the earth, and vast tracts of land in new dominions and colonies lay clean and empty. No wonder that

> . . . there was then in these twenty years (1830–1850) an atmosphere more heavily charged with emotion than anything we know. That emotion was potent. It had revived religion and was forming morals, it could enliven politics, it could revivify nationalism, it taught men to feel and to understand the lot of the less fortunate and to stand up for their own wrongs. . . . ("The Romantic Element, 1830–1850".)[9]

As Elizabeth Sewell and Henrietta Keddie noted, the 1840's brought an awakening. In some quarters, the rising sense of urgency was a feverish anxiety over religious strife and doubt, or political unrest and the quickening pace of life. In others, it was a stimulating awareness of a widening world and a challenge to the individual. During this decade was born the great cause of the mid-century into which the works of all the principal writers of tract fiction and many of the great novels may be fitted: *the elevation of the masses.** Conditioned by the Evangelical fervour of their youth, early Victorians responded with enthusiasm to the demands of their age.

The situation worsened daily. Exposed in the vastly-expanded press, and in reports and statistics issued by the Committee of the Reform Parliament, the extent of the dangerous rift in the nation was recognised about 1840 as never before. Within a few years, novels of social purpose, *Sybil* (1843), *Mary Barton* (1848), *Alton Locke* (1850), and *Yeast* (1848), provided the painful interpretation of these facts. What it meant to be helpless in the squalor of industrial cities, in the degradation of London slums, or in the depressed countryside, was fully revealed; laid bare too was the spiritual, mental and moral destitution of a large part of the Second Nation. The grey reproachful shadow of the Pauper dimmed the lustre of economic progress; the Workhouse loomed blackly over the lives of the poor; the gross ignorance of the masses terrified

* The phrase is used in the late 1840's by *Howitt's Journal* and similar domestic periodicals. In Dec. 1852, Wilkie Collins' second novel was criticized in an *Athenaeum* review for failing in the "proper office of art . . . to elevate and purify".

those already committed to extending the franchise again in the near future.

Victorians of 1840, educated along the lines laid down by the moralists, by Mrs. Trimmer and Mrs. Sherwood, remembering Anti-Slavery, factory reforms past and present, and other great social issues, were acutely conscious of their duty. Even those whose early Evangelicalism had worn thin and been discarded (the younger Newmans and Wilberforces, and George Eliot, for instance) could not discard their secular habits. Lacking the intense religious dedication of their parents or grandparents, they still obeyed the call of Duty, "Stern Daughter of the Voice of God". Others, intellectually or spiritually cramped by Evangelicalism, became Tractarians, High Churchmen, or Roman Catholics. A third group became free-thinkers or Liberal Christians. But the social duty of all pointed the same way.

Between 1845 and 1860 the fairly new domestic journals—*Eliza Cook's*, *Howitt's*, *The Family Economist*—and a number published by the tract societies, constantly exhorted the reader to participate in this great salvage work of the times.[10]

> In whatever we do or write, let the grand duty of humanity to succour, champion, and equalise humanity be ever before us. It is the only work worth doing. It is the only philosophy and the only religion. . . . (*Howitt's and The People's Journal*, 8 Jan. 1848, p. 16.)

By 1840 many responsible people were convinced that the illiterate poor, "the masses", must be fed, healed, housed, educated, depauperized, and restored to a sense of human dignity and worth. But the chasm between the Two Nations was not easily filled or bridged; it gaped before reformers for the rest of the century.

> How much depends upon us as to what both the Church and the world are to be in future ages!

exclaimed the writer of a sermon printed in *The Christian Cabinet*, a nonconformist religious journal, in 1859.

> Our individual existence has derived additional importance from the circumstances in which we are placed. We each of us help to mould the world and are moulded by it. . . . Never before have men had such work to do. We have useful responsibilities lying upon us. . . . (Vol. IV, Jan. 5, 1859.)

Few readers in 1859, or ten or twenty years later, would have demurred. The Victorians had found and accepted their crusade, the equivalent of the movement for the abolition of slavery and the establishment of Indian missions—the grand unifying concept of the times. Within it Evangelicals, moralists, utilitarians, High Church, Low Church, Dissenters; Radicals and Conservatives could find common ground and common purpose. They did not always choose to do so; it was inevitable that sectarian conflict should be carried over into social service as it was into education. Nevertheless, in the 1860's, Charles Knight believed that in any really important cause connected with social improvement there was an encouraging co-operation among all classes.[11]

The huge scale of the work and the very general terms in which it was described made participation acceptable to all. A term like *the elevation of the masses* was in itself a form of compromise. Avoiding the denominational implications of *education* or *conversion*, it could be interpreted as the individual saw fit. In 1843, Carlyle had expressed with the same convenient vagueness the duty of the individual:

> To shape the whole Future is not our problem; but only to shape faithfully a small part of it, according to rules already known. It is perhaps possible for each of us, who will with due earnestness inquire, to ascertain clearly what he, for his own part, ought to do; this let him, with true heart, do, and continue doing. The general issue will, as it has always done, rest well with a Higher Intelligence than ours.[12]

The Victorians faced their duty in good heart. Along with the social problems of the past, they also inherited their forebears' energy and decisiveness, and they had been disciplined by a moral or evangelical education into habits of order and industry. This unremitting industry of the Evangelicals, part of their protest against the laxness of the Regency, had helped to win and hold the approval of the rising middle class, and thus ensure a constant flow of new recruits into the Movement. Many were more attracted to the order, the industry and the respectability than to the religious dedication of the Movement: to the outward forms rather than to the inner flame. When this happened, there was a spiritual narrowing-down, sometimes with the sort of results recorded in works like Gosse's *Father and Son* (1907); William Hale White's *Autobiography of Mark Rutherford* (1881); or Kipling's recollections of his childhood years at Southsea.

Evangelical discipline was tied to a strict code of moral conduct. The Evangelical kept himself up to the mark by the constant renewal of his religious life by prayer, Bible reading, and Sunday observance, with regular attendance at church and attention to solid, lengthy sermons. He laid much stress upon soul-searching and self-examination, a practice recommended and followed by Wilberforce.[13] Lord Shaftesbury's diary entry for Dec. 25, 1851 is in the form of questions asking what he had gained for the public in the previous year, what for Christ, what for himself? It is followed by a summary of the public opinion of him.[14]

Children were similarly trained to catechise themselves upon their spiritual life. Numbers XIV and XV of the Taylors' *Hymns for Infant Minds* (1808) were long considered ideal for this purpose.

> (E)very morning must begin
> With resolutions not to sin;
> And every evening recollect
> How much you've failed in this respect.
> (XV. "The Way to Cure Pride")

Victorian writers likewise framed suitable questions in verse for easy memorising.

> Did I this morn devoutly pray
> For God's assistance through the day?
> And did I read his sacred Word,
> To make my life therewith accord?
> Did I for any purpose try
> To hide the truth and tell a lie?
> Did I my time and thoughts engage
> As fits my duty, station, age?
> Did I with care my temper guide,
> Checking ill-humour, anger, pride?[15]

The S.D.U.K. produced in the 1830's a secular and moral version of a form of self-examination for the young.[16]

All this emphasis upon moral and spiritual uplift had prepared a fertile field for the tract tale writer. "The masses", an unlimited and uncritical potential reading public, were there to be elevated, educated and reformed. Numerous domestic and religious periodicals ensured a market: between 1840 and 1849, at least thirty-eight new children's magazines began, and seven others were revived. From 1850 to 1859, forty-one new magazines for the young appeared.[17]

Fiction, no longer considered intellectually enervating or spiritually corrupting, had become respectable. It was redeemed for Evangelicals by its dedication to reform at many levels. In attacking vice, exposing social evils, and emphasizing individual duty, the novel worked for the elevation of the masses, even if not overtly religious. Two or three generations of children's tales inculcating vital religion, duty, self-sacrifice, self-discipline and self-improvement had prepared the way for the literature of social purpose.

Most Evangelical tract and tract fiction writers of Queen Victoria's reign were women who welcomed the opportunity to share in the great cause of the time. William Carus Wilson and George Mogridge ("Old Humphrey") were the chief exceptions. Even though tract fiction writing was socially acceptable at a time when writing for a living was still thought to be unladylike, most women published anonymously or, like Charlotte Tucker, under a pen-name. Of the four important tract tale writers discussed in the following chapters, only "Hesba Stretton" wrote for a living.

CHAPTER V

THE HEART OF LOVE AND THE HAND OF CHARITY

Maria Louisa Charlesworth (1819–1881) and "Ministering Children" (1854)

OF these four significant Victorian writers of tract fiction, the one who diverged least from the literary path blazed by Mrs. Sherwood and Hannah More was Maria Louisa Charlesworth, author of *Ministering Children*. Devoutly and narrowly religious, far closer in spirit to the early Evangelicals than to the Victorians, Maria Charlesworth reflects perfectly the moral fervour and concern with the Four Last Things that characterised the Reverend Legh Richmond or Mrs. Sherwood in her earliest books for the young. She did not qualify her stand in later years, showing little recognition of the changing Victorian world. Firmly rooted in the past, serenely convinced of the absolute rightness of Church and State, Miss Charlesworth presented in her works an ideal rural community closer to Goldsmith's Auburn than to the English village of her day.

She was the youngest daughter of a strongly Evangelical family. Her father, the Reverend John Charlesworth, was a graduate of St. John's College when Charles Simeon and Henry Venn were leaders of the Movement within the Church. The patron of John Charlesworth's living at Flowton, near Ipswich, was Henry Sykes Thornton, who, like Wilberforce and other wealthy Evangelicals, bought up livings to fill with dedicated young clergymen who would carry Evangelical principles to the far corners of the kingdom. Under the auspices of the Clapham reformers too, John Charlesworth moved to London about 1850 when his health failed. There, as incumbent of the small city parish of St. Mildred's, Bread Street,*

* St. Mildred's, in the heart of the wealthy financial district, was apparently a sinecure. Its charities were severely criticized in an article in *Good Words* (1879), p. 602–6. The church was destroyed in the bombing and its site is marked by a plaque.

he assisted in the committee work of numerous Evangelical societies until his death in 1865.[1]

Evangelicalism was strong in Ipswich, where the rector of Flowton took a prominent part in local religious societies. At various times he was secretary or treasurer to the Church Missionary Society, the British and Foreign Bible Society, the Religious Tract Society, and the Mission to the Jews. His name appears after 1856 in the list of subscribers to the S.P.C.K. He supported the anti-slavery campaign and worked on behalf of oppressed chimney-sweeps. He was, in short, one of the conscientious clergy of the day who had long since recognised the challenge of the times, and who, in partnership with laymen similarly fired by Evangelical fervour, turned willingly to the task of setting their world right.

In 1819, the year of Maria Louisa's birth—and that of Queen Victoria—the protracted economic depression and social unrest that followed the end of the Napoleonic Wars were well under way. In rural areas like Suffolk, the magnitude of these problems was not fully realised, and life went on, externally at least, as it had for generations. The majority of English people still lived in the country: not until 1831 would the urban population equal the rural.

Although Ipswich did not know the degradation of slums such as those of London or Manchester, it was, like other country towns, in need of improvement. Widespread poverty in town and country, and its inevitable corollary, the Workhouse, were coming under the eye of the reformer. Reform, social and religious, was in the air. Hospitals and schools were inadequate; sanitation shocking; disease rife. *Ministering Children* from this point of view gives some interesting little sidelights upon poverty in and around Ipswich.

The serious-minded Charlesworths felt their responsibility keenly. John Charlesworth was a member of the Royal College of Surgeons as well as a clergyman; his brother, Dr. Edward Parker Charlesworth of Lincoln, pioneered a system of humane care for the insane. At the time of Maria Louisa's birth, John Charlesworth held two livings, but on moving into Ipswich to further the education of his six children, he gave up the curacy of Blakenham Parva where she was born. According to his son's account, he did not abandon the flock, continuing to minister there and in neighbouring parishes, which, even in the 1820's, seldom saw their absentee incumbents.[2] It is likely that Maria Charlesworth's mention of old, worldly, careless clergymen in *Ministering Children* and *England's Yeomen* is drawn from her own memories, and that in the conscientious curate who tends neglected parishes, she pictures her own father.

The eldest of John Charlesworth's three daughters married a professor at Cambridge; the second died young. The eldest son became a scientist of some note; the second was the Reverend Samuel Charlesworth, Rector of Limpsfield, Surrey, and later, of Limehouse. The youngest son (for a short time his father's curate), died shortly after ordination.

Most of Miss Charlesworth's books were written in London. Upon arrival there around 1850, she had attempted to throw herself into the parish work, as she had done in Suffolk. In the country, this meant visiting in the villages and the local Workhouse; reading to the sick and the aged illiterate; and distributing charity. It was a pattern familiar since the Middle Ages, and in rural areas it survived until the 1880's.[3] But by 1850 charity thus administered was under fire; indeed the word itself was beginning to acquire its invidious modern connotation. Ironically, Miss Charlesworth, who wrote so much on the subject with such excellent intentions, unwittingly contributed to the general disillusionment with this personally-administered oldest form of Christian charity.

Her earliest book, *The Female Visitor to the Poor* (1846), re-issued in 1856 as *The Cottage and its Visitor*, indicates her absolute dependence upon her Evangelical predecessors. Typical chapter headings include

II. The Aged Poor—History of Nancy and her Husband
IV. The Sick Poor—The History of John
VII. The Weekly School—Alice and her Parents
X. The Bible Class

Each chapter is illustrated by a tale in the tradition of the well-known cottage tract. "Alice and her Parents" is modelled upon Hannah More's "History of Hester Wilmot"; the "History of Margaret" is but a condensed version of Legh Richmond's "The Dairyman's Daughter". The advice itself, wordy and sentimental in the extreme, contains nevertheless a core of common sense and genuine concern.

> The secret of successful intercourse with the Poor is the training your own heart in Prayer and Sympathy. . . . If a ready sympathy

> be not cultivated in the home life of every day, it will not be found on an occasional visit to the cottage. The disposition that we need for useful and pleasant intercourse with those of our own family and station, is the same that we need for useful and pleasant intercourse with the Poor . . . sympathy or fellow-feeling is the necessary groundwork of all true Charity. . . .
>
> But while we hold it our *privilege* wherever we may be, to visit the poor man's home, we have no more *right* to enter it apart from his permission, than the beggar who knocks for relief. . . .[4]

Miss Charlesworth advised the visitor to be patient, persevering, respectful to those she visited. She suggested that some cottagers would be resentful, and that a visitor might meet a cold reception. She disapproved of bribery and of injudicious efforts to argue against ignorance or superstition (unless these involved "breach of any divine command"). The book suffered from cloying sentimentality, a condescending tone, and a distressing breathlessness of style.

From the point of view of the active reformer of the 1850's and after, it was thoroughly out of date. To a generation seeking solutions to the physical and moral problems of poverty in industrial cities (now fully exposed by the Select Committee of the Reform Parliaments of the last twenty years), Miss Charlesworth offered the assurance that only the state of the individual soul really mattered. Fundamental as this is to Christian belief, it was not the answer sought by many of her contemporaries, and it was not acceptable to those she sincerely wished to help. For within five years of the publication of this book in 1846, the Great Exhibition had made clear that the future of the nation lay with the industrial cities. They might be the social cancers of the nation, but they were also its economic heart.

Living after 1850 in London, Maria Charlesworth was faced with a terrifying world in which the familiar parish patterns no longer existed. Conditions in the London slums could not parallel those in the country. The London poor were not the Poor of her books; the sharp, cynical London street children an entirely different race to the quiet, respectful Suffolk Sunday scholars. Nor could the concentrated evils of London rookeries be countered by the simple methods of an earlier period; in spite of the Ragged Schools and the work of the London City Mission since 1835, the slums remained as pagan as the African wilds to which General

Booth of the Salvation Army compared them a few years later.

Never strong (two members of her family had already died of consumption), Maria Charlesworth took to her bed and wrote. "She became a confirmed invalid," says the *Memorial*, "confined to the house, and mostly to her little bedroom, with its dull look-out on brick walls and chimneys". For the rest of her life she remained a secluded semi-invalid, living quietly with her mother in Nutfield, Surrey, after her father's death in 1865.

So far as her health permitted, she took an active interest in parish work and Sunday School activities in the village, and taught a class of men. The proceeds of *England's Yeomen* (1860) supported a Ragged School in London; it is the only book which indicates that she had ever lived there. The city, we must assume, had defeated her.

Neither in the *Memorial* nor in the account of her niece's childhood[5] is Maria Charlesworth described. The nieces found her an indulgent aunt. Her own writing reveals her to be deeply devout and sincere, limited in outlook, quite devoid of humour, and devoted to her family. The sentimentality so offensive to modern readers is usually poured out on characters who seem to represent those especially dear to her: Mary Clifford (*Ministering Children*), the sister who died young; Mabel's brother (*England's Yeomen*), her youngest brother.

Her death in 1881 passed almost unnoticed. Literary fashions had changed and a new generation of vigorous writers: Mrs. Ewing, Mrs. Molesworth, Louisa Alcott, George MacDonald—was in the ascendant. Her missionary writing was fast being superseded by that of the energetic A.L.O.E. Her books dealing with the education and conversion of villagers and servants differed little in content from those of Hannah More and Mrs. Sherwood forty years earlier, but lacked the vitality which kept the pioneer works alive in the uncongenial atmosphere of rapid social change. Like these writers, Miss Charlesworth opposed any disturbance of the social order, subjecting every facet of life to the double test of Scripture and the Evangelical conscience. But it was half a century too late to announce that

> The several classes of society are recognised in the Scriptures. Their order is of God, and every effort to overthrow that order by a general intermingling has had most baneful results. But the intermingling of spirit . . . is the result of a still higher and per-

> manent law impressed on our common humanity. (*Oliver of the Mill*, 1876, Chap. IX.)

Twenty years earlier she had entered the great Victorian debate about schools. *The Ministry of Life* (1858), a sentimental tale for young people of the upper classes, was a defence of the church-directed parish school. She had no doubts about the erroneous policy of State intervention in schools.

> . . . and so these village children, born to cultivate the land around them like some bright garden, to tend the cattle of the field, and in such occupation find a living interest; to look up to the holy Heaven above their hills and valleys, and learn from their Creator's word the path to reach that sinless home; these simple rustics must be drilled in learning's school, have every mental faculty forced, and all power and interest concentrated in rival competition; the tendency of which was to unfit them for their native calling, and to send them with a vagrant intelligence to add their counterfeit knowledge to the current market of towns and cities! (Page 211.)

She wrote much more sensibly in dealing with the nursery governess. Miss Mansfield of *Ministering Children A Sequel* (1867) turns out to be Little Jane of the earlier book. She handles her spoilt charges capably and sympathetically, and is eventually allowed a pallid romance of her own.

In all Miss Charlesworth's writing, the countryside is the type of perfection, a rural Eden. She had left Suffolk before the changes described by Jeffries[6] took place. Her young curates do not meet with coldness, nor must they leave the field to the Dissenters. The rick-burners spare the farm of Stephen, the ideal yeoman. One would never realize from Miss Charlesworth that the Labourers' Rising of 1831 was the third since 1816. She does not acknowledge the existence of the shocking rural "gang" system of female agricultural labour, very common in East Anglia.[7] Nothing tarnishes her Wordsworthian picture of seedtime and harvest. Her view is that of the clergyman who wrote in 1866, "That which is to elevate the public taste must be a little above the public taste. Popular illustration of daily life cannot be so. . . . Popular work seems to have a kind of centrifugal tendency away from beauty and nobleness . . ."[8]

Completely blind she might be to the squalor behind much of the beauty of the rural scene, but Miss Charlesworth could not ignore the seriously damaged relationship of mistress and maid. Well before the end of the eighteenth century, the tract writer and the satirist had tackled the problem, for servants were a part of every household with any pretence to gentility or financial success. Thirty years later as the social balance changed and class boundaries thinned and shifted, the servant became a status symbol. A man who was rising in the world marked his stage on the social ladder by outward signs of affluence: servants, carriage, a new house. Since servants too had ambitions of rising in the world, not many remained for years with one family. A note of lament for "the constant service of the antique world" is quite as apparent in Victorian writing as the voice of honest concern for the welfare of the young female servants who were all too easily recruited into prostitution in large cities.

In 1848, Maria Charlesworth wrote *A Book for the Cottage*. It and *The Old Looking Glass* (1878) and *The Broken Looking Glass* (1879) were her contributions to the mass of tract literature intended to instruct, warn and amuse servants, while inculcating thrift and responsibility, encouraging a moral sense, and driving out the taste for lurid literature.

The nineteenth century employer was uneasily aware that his servants' search for entertainment was the vulnerable spot in an otherwise well-defended family fortress. There was no keeping children and servants apart. Some children, like the young Beatrix Potter and her brother, saw more of the servants than they did of their own parents. Some servants were but children themselves, nursemaids often being engaged at the age of twelve. Unless the nursery were carefully supervised, the talk, actions, and reading matter of the maids engrossed the children, occasionally with distressing results.

There were also nursery maids like the one described by Dickens, whose tale of "Captain Murderer" (a character compounded of the most gruesome elements of Bluebeard, The Robber Bridegroom, and Sweeney Todd the Demon Barber), held her little charge paralysed by terror. Her other tale of Chips the Ship's Carpenter was in an even older tradition: Chips, long bedevilled by Satan reciting the ominous incantation

A lemon has pips,
And a Yard has Ships,
And *I'll* have Chips!

finally capitulated and sold his soul for copper nails.[9]

Undoubtedly the victim improved these tales in the re-telling, but this nursery spellbinder must still be credited with dramatic power and Gothic artistry. Other nursemaids with a bent in this direction were less original. Who supplied the precocious Marjory Fleming (aged seven) with details of the Newgate Calendar? ". . . very instructive, Amusing & shews us the necessity of doing good and not evil. . . . There is a book that's called the Newgate Calendar that contains all the Murders. . . ."[10]

The Newgate Calendar was periodically resuscitated throughout the nineteenth century by new renderings of favourite items, Harrison Ainsworth's *Rookwood* and *Jack Sheppard* being the most respectable. Parents, teachers, clergymen and the forces of law and order deplored these and similar histories of crime, but the popularity of Dick Turpin, Jack Sheppard and other criminal heroes never failed.

> . . . (W)e'd read stories about Jack Sheppard and Dick Turpin and all that set. . . . They told us how they used to break open the houses, and get out of Newgate, and how Dick got away to York. We used to think Jack and them very fine fellows. I wished I could be like Jack. . . .

said a young vagrant to Henry Mayhew in the 1850's.[11]

Ballad mongers and broadside presses did a roaring business in crime sheets. A glance at surviving specimens shows why so many employers tried to limit their servants' reading matter to the innocuous publications of Paternoster Row.

> . . .
> In the great town of London near Manchester Square,
> Jane Jones kept a mangle in South Street we hear,
> A gentleman's coachman oft visiting came,
> A cold-blooded monster, Dan Good was his name.
>
> As a single man under her he made love,
> And in course of time, she pregnant did prove,
> Then with false pretences he took her from home,
> To murder his victim and the babe in her womb.

Nine stanzas and many gory details later, Dan Good is

> . . . . sentenced to die
> The death of a murderer on the gallows high.

A crude block print of the hanging, well attended by a large crowd, completes the sheet. A similar broadside celebrated the execution of Emma Pitt for child-murder. The fact that she was

> A schoolmistress too, how sad to tell,
> Well known for miles around,

probably did little to further the cause of education in Dorset.[12]

In addition to the Newgate Calendar, chapbooks and broadsides, newspapers such as *The People's Gazette* gave lurid details of crime, filling columns with police court reports.

Maria Charlesworth's belated protest, uttered by Dorothy Cope, the ideal housekeeper in *The Old Looking Glass*, was unlikely to catch the attention of young servants.

> . . . in some of the low papers that got into the servants' hall there was the worst of reading for the young. . . . I spoke with our Lady, and then we were supplied with good pamphlets and a library of books. The low papers did not show themselves. . . . I was sore loth to see the young women taken up over any newspaper, even not the worst, with the tales of murder and sin. . . . (Page 136–37.)

In spirit this work belonged to the 1840's when a fairly successful effort was being made to supply respectable reading matter.[13] The "good pamphlets" and the library certainly came from a Tract Society, and included by 1860 fiction guaranteed not to inflame the passions, weaken the understanding, or swell the sentiments. For by this date, in addition to the popular literature of crime, the popular literature of romance—sentimental, Gothic or horrific—was streaming off the cheap presses. Earlier sentimental and sensational works were copiously reprinted: *Pamela*, *Fatherless Fanny*, *Ada the Betrayed*, *Varney the Vampire*, *Maria Monk*. . . . All were highly melodramatic and most were conducive to the type of daydreaming abhorred by employers, implacably hostile to the Cinderella theme in real life. Mrs. Sherwood's attempt early in the century to counter cheap romance—*The History of Susan Gray* (1802)—was only partially successful. This was a sentimental tract tale with a lesson of impeccable morality and religious resignation; its eponymous heroine was sympathetically presented and shown to have the same delicate feelings, great beauty and pure heart as any well-born lady of romance. Because of its high proportion of romance, the book often joined the ranks of sensational literature, appearing in the 1860's in a Cottager's Library Series (put out by W. Nicholson of Wakefield) in the doubtful company of *Pamela*, *Maria Monk*, and *The Lives of Highwaymen, Robbers and Traitors*, etc. But Maria Charlesworth and other Victorian tract tale writers carefully refrained from presenting servant girls in melodramatic or romantic situations.

Matters worsened as the age of compulsory education drew nearer. The 1840's and 1850's brought the torrid novels of G. W. M. Reynolds, in which the elements of crime, violence, sentiment and passion made a heady mixture. Former chapbook tales such as "The Life and Death of Jane Shore" or "The Life of a Woman of the Town", were brought up to date, expanded, and printed in the weekly penny numbers that Charles Knight described as "garbage". Reynolds, outspokenly radical and incredibly copious, ranged far and wide for subject matter, two of his favourite sources being the Newgate Calendar and the novels of Eugene Sue. Those who, like Howitt, had hoped that a general rise in literacy would bring about the "elevation (mental and moral) of the masses" were disappointed. Knight lamented that in the '60's current publishers of cheap literature were "diffusing a moral miasma" throughout the land, and admitted that his earlier certainty of the beneficial results of literacy had been ill-founded.[14] Tract publishers concurred: faced with the enormous increase in cheap fiction, they significantly expanded their own offerings to include moral and religious tales for servants and villagers. These were based on the narrative tracts of the early part of the century.* Few of the new ones were as lively as those of Hannah More and Mrs. Sherwood at their best; they blended the sentiment of Legh Richmond's *Annals of the Poor* with a condescending didacticism stressing the material advantages of industry and honesty. Very few could compel the readers' attention, for their writers refused to cater to wishful thinking or the thirst for suspense. Moreover there was stiff competition from the prolific Reynolds. *His* principal theme was that of youth, beauty and innocence pursued by a cruel and licentious aristocrat or an unscrupulous rich man. Lovely heroines who had suffered prolonged brutal treatment emerged at the end of sixty or seventy chapters, beauty unimpaired, virtue inexplicably intact, to live happily ever after upon a much higher social level than the one on which they

* For example, Miss Charlesworth's *A Book for the Cottage* and Mrs. Walton's *My Little Corner*.

began. (This point which ought to have aroused some doubts about the sincerity of Reynolds' radical and Chartist sympathies did not disturb his readers: he both championed them and amused them. And they too had every intention of rising on the social ladder.) The triple appeal of sex, sensation and wishful thinking was reinforced by a heavy top-dressing of Gothic-style romance: castles, caves and secret passages; kidnappings and pursuits; repulsive villains and gallant rescuers; lost heirs and wicked relatives; documents stolen, lost, found. Reynolds threw them all together, spicing the mixture with high-flown oratorical attacks upon Law, Church, Wealth, Privilege, Government, and employers. The undiscriminating found this kaleidoscopic treatment of the familiar matter of sensational romance irresistible.

We may assume that a number of young servants in the 1850's were presented with Miss Charlesworth's *Book for the Cottage: or the History of Mary and her Family* (1848). Undoubtedly those with opportunity purchased or borrowed the weekly instalments of Reynolds' novel, *Mary Price: The Memoirs of a Serving Maid* (1851–52). (By a happy coincidence, Miss Charlesworth's heroine is also Mary Price.) A glance at the content of the two books explains not only why Miss Charlesworth and the Tract Societies worried about reading matter for servants, but also why servants were lukewarm towards most Tract literature. Unlike employers and Tract Societies, Reynolds had recognised the utter boredom of so much nineteenth-century domestic service: no one can say that he was not stimulating.

Miss Charlesworth's Mary Price, a housemaid trained at the Rectory in quietness, cleanliness, sobriety and religion, comes from a poor but worthy family. Her brothers turn out well; her sisters give every satisfaction as domestics and later marry honest tradesmen. Events are as bland as skim milk. But Reynolds' Mary Price is one of several children of a mother whose "fine dark hair and eyes, pale countenance, and somewhat pensive if not positively melancholy expression" cast her as a romantic heroine who has come down in the world. There is a mystery about her . . .; naturally, she dies without revealing it. Her children lead spectacular lives: son Robert goes entirely to the bad in partnership with a pair of housebreakers fittingly named The Bulldog and Sawbridge; daughter Sarah (like Mary, ravishingly lovely) enters service only to be seduced at seventeen and lead thereafter a life of gilded sin.

Miss Charlesworth's Mary follows a blameless path. Her three employers are all fond of her; she leaves service only to marry another trusted servant after a pallid romance occupying about six lines. Her prosaic life for several years is described, closely linked with the cycle of the Church Year. At one point, it is true, the writer, who had lived in country villages, seems to have a qualm about the optimism of her picture.

> It is not every great family which is like this one—(i.e. Mary's employers); some are very different; nor is it every servant who is like Mary. (*A Book for the Cottage*, p. 53.)

she murmurs, and reading Reynolds, one can but agree.

The employers of *his* Mary Price number about a dozen sentimentalised or satirized types including money-grubbing and lascivious grocer; newly-made Alderman and silly wife; and idiotic young heiress. Among them too is lovely Lady Harlesdon (false to her elderly husband with handsome Sir Aubrey Clavering who is also lusting after Mary). Lady Harlesdon is strangled by her husband during an amateur performance of *Othello*, in which he plays the title rôle. Mary in the rôle of Nemesis subsequently frightens the old man into committing suicide. Twice she saves silly women from the wiles of an adventurer. Disguised as a negress, she rescues a kidnapped child from the vilest slums. Several times kidnapped herself, she is hurtled about in post-chaises, lumbered about in coaches, dragged off on horseback, tied up and bundled over a cliff by Bulldog and Sawbridge.... Incredibly, during this life of perpetual motion, she collects a lover:

> ... tall, slender and as straight as a lance; his hair was of a rich brown, very thick, glossy and naturally arranging itself in large wavy curls; his eyes were of a fine hazel, large, bright and serving as resplendent mirrors to reflect the intelligence which beamed upon his high pale forehead....

This Mary Price is far from quiet. Cottage, courtroom, and ducal drawing-room ring with her interminable flights of rhetoric.

"Rest assured," she cries to those who are holding her prisoner,

> ".... that, though for the time being, you may with impunity persecute a poor, helpless unoffending girl—an orphan who has never injured you—yet there is One above who sooner or later

will visit all this dire wickedness with a terrible retribution upon your head. Alas! I do perceive indeed that the web of a hideous treachery has been most insidiously woven around me, and that its meshes appear to me to be rapidly closing in upon me. But I cannot forget that when the mighty ship with a thousand souls on board founders or burns at sea, yet if heaven wills that only one single individual of that multitude shall be saved, a spar to which this one may cling will be wafted by the divine hand to the shore of security . . ." (*Memoirs of a Serving Maid*, p. 157.)

This appalling rubbish has something of that vitality compared by Dr. Queenie Leavis to the exudation of a manure-heap.[15] Its essential appeal was deeply rooted. Tinselled, bloated, swollen to cancerous extremes, it was still *The Tale*, beloved of children and here adapted by Reynolds to the tastes of a bored and ignorant reading public untrained as children. This is Little Heroine, out in the cold, crossing the Dark Wood of danger; these are the Wolves, the Robbers, the Helpers. There is the Fairy Prince, the Happy Ending. Its original readers had sixteen pages, double-column, fine print, every week for about two years. It catered to a grievously distorted concept of "elevation"—but who shall say that they did not get their money's worth in vicarious excitement?

Compared with contemporary romance of this calibre, Miss Charlesworth's tract tale stood no chance. Improving and elevating, religious and respectable, it was also dull and didactic. Mrs. Sherwood's sympathetic *History of Susan Gray*, Hannah More's pungent and sensible tracts still had their readers in the 1870's. But Maria Charlesworth's cottage tales showed her to be condescending and out of touch. Most of them seem to have been sold to employers to present to their servants.

Where the religious instruction of children was concerned, it was a different story. As the author of *Ministering Children* (1854) and its *Sequel* (1867), Miss Charlesworth was a brilliant success. *Ministering Children* had sold 170,000 copies in England alone at the time of the author's death in 1881; was widely reprinted on the Continent and in America; was issued piece-meal as short tracts for Sunday Schools; and was last printed about 1924.

Modern readers (adults mostly, for modern children are unlikely to see it) find it offensive; probably only *The Fairchild Family*, with which it has something in common, has had harder things said of it. With the wide-spread twentieth-century repudiation of religion and systematic religious training, the whole basis for understanding this sort of literature has gone. With *Ministering Children*, we return to early Evangelicalism but in a Victorian setting.

Miss Charlesworth's purpose in this book was, as she specified in the Introduction, to demonstrate the Christian life in action. She intended to show

> (T)he early calling forth and training the sympathies of children by personal intercourse with want and sorrow, while as yet those sympathies flow spontaneously. Let the truth be borne in mind, that the influence of the giver far exceeds that of the gift on the receiver of it . . . the best feelings of the heart, in both the giver and the receiver, is the most important object to be kept in view.

And she asserts at the end of the tale that the story "has been written to show, as in a picture, what ministering children are".

Undoubtedly this avowed religious purpose prevents the modern reader, hemmed in by educational psychology and the habit of subjecting everything to the test of reason, the assumptions of science and the desire for instant knowledge, from seeing the book justly. Equally, it was the very thing that made *Ministering Children* popular in its own day.

It was the perfect Sunday book, serious, strongly evangelical in tone, apparently as acceptable to dissenters as to churchmen. It owes something to Tractarianism: thoughts from Pusey's sermons on charity are discernible, and traces of Keble's *Christian Year* (1827). A general romanticism underlies its insistence upon spontaneity of feeling and its descriptions of nature. Mrs. Sherwood and Legh Richmond are the obvious inspiration of its deathbed scenes and its lessons of village life; and Mary Clifford's funeral is certainly derived from that of Little Nell.

The book accords with the spirit of its day in making much of the family and the community—village, town, and school. Individuals belong to groups that are themselves families in Christ. The isolated one (Patience, the deserted child; Mrs. Smith, alienated by her stubborn pride) is cause for loving concern, and is eventually brought back into the family of faith. The life of the shopkeeper's family is shown in some detail and also that of his Foreman's family. There are the very poor—the Shoemaker, the couple in the almshouse, the destitute woman in a squatter's hut on the common. The near-by country village shows a similar cross-section of society: the Squire's home, the farmhouse, the ramshackle cottages of shepherd and labourer. The community contains many classes and ages; there is sickness and health, death and recovery. It is full of children, some lovingly cared for, others half-starved or fed by charity, or sent to the workhouse. In short, the corporate whole of a largely rural community of the 1820's or 1830's is presented as the background of a story designed to show quite young children their place in a Christian society. The scale on which this is done is the really original part of the story: there are about a dozen children in all, quite well distinguished, all shown to be important members of the Christian community.

Evil is limited to that which can be cured by sincere Christian effort *initiated by children*. Modern readers must keep this fact in mind. Thus the village has no alehouse with its attendant problems; there is no mention of rick-burning by resentful, half-starved labourers; no squalid labour gangs; no illegitimate children; no village idiot. All these would be beyond the scope of children's effort for good. Miss Charlesworth gives her picture spiritual harmony at the expense of realism; but realism is a tricky problem in books for children—even today.

Granted the thesis of the corporate community, one in Christ, *Ministering Children* illustrates admirably how children fit into this sanctified whole, and take their places in the Church Militant. The book was never intended to amuse: amusement in the modern sense of entertainment was not contemplated for children's Sunday reading until near the end of the century, and often not then. *Ministering Children*, printed several years after *Agathos and Other Sunday Stories* (1840), conforms satisfactorily to Bishop Wilberforce's requirements for a Sunday story. It occupies the imagination, gives scriptural instruction, and avoids "all lowering down of holy things".[16]

Where the modern child's story usually confines itself to a hero (or a socially-acceptable group of three or four) overcoming some rational obstacle to the general satisfaction of characters and readers alike, *Ministering Children* presents many children, equal in accomplishment if not in social standing. Events are never sensational. No one finds treasure; no one is transported to a life of ease. No one travels; no colourful villain, gypsy or pedlar enters the village to disrupt the daily rhythm of a life geared to nothing faster than the changing seasons. Drunken fathers exist but are not shown. The chief sins are those of omission: the well-fed child throws away her bread-and-butter while the half-starved schoolmate looks on; the child of the rich home stands idly by while her friend sews for the poor. Judged by the standards set by Arthur Ransome, Laura Ingalls Wilder and others of today, this book is hopeless.

The fact remains that it *was* widely read, passing through about seventeen printings by five publishers in England alone. Many of its young readers liked it. Laura of Lark Rise was pleased to get it as a gift, spending pleasant hours over it (or *The Wide Wide World* or *Queechy*) with her friend, Emily Rose. And if Oswald Bastable scoffed at it, his sisters attempted to put its precepts into practice.[17]

Every page of it is a sermon for children, reminding them to read their Bibles and prayer books, to keep the Commandments, serve God, help neighbours, honour and obey parents. These duties are not presented as severe: Rose and Mercy enjoy learning their hymn to please their Sunday School teacher; their work at home is not hard. Nothing is done or shown that could possibly induce a child to take a false step. Children are flatteringly depicted as obedient, kind, willing; most of them are happy at home. At least two faulty parents repent and improve: Little Ruth's stepfather and Little Rose's impatient and intolerant mother.

Miss Charlesworth seems to have had the teachings of Pusey in mind: his sermons on "the duty of the present day", on charity, on the poor who are "Christ's Poor".[18]

What did the book offer its little readers? It has a great deal of interesting detail, beginning with little girls going to school.

> ... (A) little school girl, shutting her mother's door, came stepping down the long dark flights of stairs at the top of which she lived; she wore no shawl or cloak or bonnet; a frock of dark brown stuff, a little white linen apron tied around her waist, a white linen tippet, and a little fine linen cap with a single border crimped close around her face; this was the little school-girl's dress. Her name was Ruth; and on her arm she had hung her green baize bag with her Bible and school books. (Chapter I.)

The morning at school is described. Little Ruth is on time for school and gets a good mark for that. Lessons are from nine to eleven; Bible class from eleven to twelve. On her way to and from school, Ruth visits a sick friend in the tenement, telling her Bible stories, reading to her, sometimes sharing food with her. Details are realistic and pathetic. "There was meat and rice and potatoes in the nice hot soup . . . Ruth found a small yellow bason and a spoon; she broke up the child's dry bit of bread in the bason; poured some of the hot soup over it; folded her hands and asked a blessing in the name of Jesus; and then the two children dined together."

Scenes of country life are usually home-like and happy. Little Rose lives much outdoors, and ". . . hers were the first rosy nuts gathered from the hazel-trees when glowing autumn came to ripen the fruits; she called the wild birds all her own . . ." (Chapter III).

The book brings in animals. There is a black horse called Black Beauty (did Anna Sewell read about it?). Rose feeds the poultry and the wild birds. Children are never idle. Their work, no matter how small, is made to sound important. It may be planting grain by hand in cold wet weather, or the pleasant occupations of the kitchen. "This was baking morning; Rose peeled apples for pies and turnovers, filled little round tartlets with jam, and washed over the tops of the loaves with a feather dipped in beer, to make them brown and shining . . ." (Chapter V).

Little Jane, a small paragon of industry, learns to mend stockings, taking three days to the first pair. Later she pieces a carpet for an old woman in a cold cottage, and makes slippers for her father.

All this is fully in accord with its time in presenting religion and work going hand in hand. Children in books and in real life were being recruited into the busy Victorian world of progress and good works.

> When all things are merry and glad
> Good children should never be lazy and sad;
> For God gives us daylight, dear sister, that we
> May rejoice like the lark and may work like the bee.[19]

It is not easy to write books for children in which the young generate their own power to do things. Yet, if physically inferior, children are spiritually as good as adults, if not, on the highest Authority, better. Children in Victorian adult fiction had a high emotional significance for the reader, the inevitable result perhaps of the blending of the romantic image of the child as the unspoilt babe of Nature with the godly Puritan child whose death had been celebrated for two centuries in the obituary tract. The result suggested the ideal child of Scripture who exemplified the inhabitants of the Kingdom of Heaven. Some latent sense of guilt and responsibility for the misery of the child factory worker, chimney-sweep, parish orphan or street beggar also helped to surround the image of childhood with a cloud of sentiment. Thus George Eliot shows Silas Marner changed by the coming of Eppie; and the shades of Little Nell, Tiny Tim, Paul and Florence Dombey hovered over many a tract tale writer at this time.*

A successful combination of sentiment and spiritual values was assured of the favour of Victorian readers; it explains the longevity of *Ministering Children* as a Sunday book. Never before had so many children been so usefully employed on such good works for so many pages. All the work was directed to excellent ends: it helped others and ennobled the doer, setting up between giver and receiver an exchange of feeling which did credit to both. Little Jane, for example, gives her flowers to Little Ruth, the pale sickly child who has looked longingly at them, and Ruth in turn shares the flowers with her dying friend in the tenement. All through the book, children share: no matter how trivial the item, the action gives it worth. Love in action—kindness—charity in its Biblical sense of *caring*—is shown in terms that children understand. Miss Charlesworth seems to be following E. B. Pusey closely in this matter. Pusey had emphasized that in charity, man expressed his love for God. He specified too the various kinds of charity—forgiveness, mercy, and especially "self-denying almsgiving to Christ's poor . . ." Pusey did not consider casual almsgiving genuine charity, which consisted rather in seeking out poverty and need and relieving them by "self-denying acts of love". In seeking Christ's poor, the charitable giver seeks Christ.[20] It is essential to keep this point in mind when considering *Ministering Children* in the light of its own time.

The book illustrates children's works of charity. A little deed of love or sacrifice, like a pebble thrown into a pool, sends ripples of goodwill in all directions: the cold are warmed and clothed; the hungry fed; the friendless comforted; the ignorant taught. The good deeds of children make an endless chain, linking individuals

* Stripped of the Eppie/Little Nell stereotype, the idea still appeals: children still exert spiritual power for good, as in the *Narnia* books, or Madeleine L'Engle's *A Wrinkle in Time*. Even the inversion of the idea testifies to its strength; the shock value of books like *A High Wind in Jamaica*, *Lord of the Flies*, *Lolita* and *Our Mother's House* was considerable.

of all ages and from all levels of society. The social *order* is maintained: that is the realm of Caesar. But goodwill and Christian charity flow between the social levels.

This true meaning of charity, this person-to-person contact, explains much in Victorian writing. Here is Octavia Hill, in 1875. After paying tribute to the efficiency of committees and organisations, she notes,

> But now a new danger seems to me to be arising; a danger lest, rushing from one extreme to another, we should leave to committees, with their system of rules, the whole work of charity, and deprive this great organising movement of all aid from what I may call the personal element. . . . Charity owes all its graciousness to the sense of its coming from a real friend. We want to bring the rich and poor, the educated and uneducated, more and more into direct communion.[21]

No two women could have been more different in other ways, but both had the determination to keep "the personal element" uppermost in the work of charity.

Miss Charlesworth displays in her village two landlords, the admirable resident squire, Mr. Clifford, and the absentee businessman, Mr. Sturgeon. The contrast between them appears in their treatment of Old Willy, the retired labourer. He is Mr. Sturgeon's tenant—but the Cliffords come to his rescue.

All through the book the Christian message is passed from one individual to another. It does not depend upon the clergy (of whom there are two—the elderly, indifferent Rector and the Evangelical Curate). Little Ruth teaches her dying friend and causes her stepfather to repent; Mercy lends her hymnbook to Rose, who influences her whole family; Jane learns from her mother and her nurse; Mrs. Smith from her servant, Patience. Thus the things of the spirit are shown to be independent of age, wealth, experience, or social station: all are equal under God. Miss Charlesworth's thesis, theologically sound, is grounded on faith, not reason, and shows children precisely what is meant by "step by step" in the serious matter of leading souls to God.

The book was flattering to the childish ego, showing the child's impulse to be better at times than the adult's reason.

> After dinner, little Rose said—
>
> "Mother, widow Giles is very ill; they don't think she will ever get about again."

> Mrs. Smith only replied, "I don't know anything about those Gileses, I am sure; I only know if I had my way, they would never be at work on this farm again!"
>
> "I thought, mother, I should like to go and ask poor old widow Giles how she is!"
>
> "And what would be the use of that? She won't be any thing the better for your asking how she is."
>
> "No, mother; only then she would know we did think about her."
>
> "Think about her!" replied Mrs. Smith, "that's a family that don't deserve thinking about after all your father's done for them, and the man worked on this farm from a boy, and his father before him, and then he must turn against it all and go a-poaching!"
>
> "But if Widow Giles should die, mother, and we did not speak a word to her, she would think you had not forgiven her."
>
> "I don't know anything about forgiveness, I am sure," replied Mrs. Smith, "till people show a little sorrow for their ingratitude." (Chapter XI.)

Obviously Rose is in the right, and her mother tacitly admits as much later by going to see the dying woman and making her last days comfortable.

With no idea whatsoever of social equality, Miss Charlesworth showed at times a perceptive understanding of the poor. She might sentimentalize to the point of absurdity over Old Willy (by this time a stock character in tract, novel and on the stage) but her story of Patience, the deserted child, is told realistically and sympathetically.

> . . . (P)oor Patience never had anyone to love or comfort her. . . . She came to school every day, but she generally came late; she had learned to read there, but she hardly ever knew her lessons; and she never answered when asked the reason. She was very small and very thin; and the lady who came to the school never saw her laugh, or smile, or cry; she always looked upon the ground, her lips were pressed together, and she seldom answered when spoken to . . . nothing seemed to amuse or interest her, she looked with the same dull eyes on all. (Chapter I.)

Equally perceptive is the comment on the well-meaning teacher who lacked understanding. "She thought it was no use to go and see a child who seemed not to care for anything. . . ."

Patience is not promoted at school, remaining "small and thin . . .

silent and shrinking . . . the lowest, which she generally was in the second class . . ."

Deserted by her father, the motherless Patience is found "a place" by the landlady. (At this time—c. 1830—children of ten went into service as maids of all-work.) The teacher then sincerely regrets that she had not tried harder: "She had always been kind to Patience, she had never spoken hastily or severely to her, but she had loved her less than she loved the other children, and poor Patience had wanted more love than others—not less." (Chapter XIII.)

"More love—not less". It has a curiously modern sound. The story of Patience is worked out in full in this book, and the idea of "more love—not less" shown to be justified by results.

Miss Charlesworth in her realistic vein is again seen to advantage in the incident in which Little Jane is taken to visit an old couple in the almshouse.

> Mrs. Mansfield had known something of them in their better days, and now she hastened to visit them in their affliction; she saw the silent dejection of both, and the thought occurred to her mind that very probably it was as much owing to the loss of all active interest in life as it was to any sense of present poverty; and that to provide the old woman a little employment might prove a great help in cheering their spirits. (Chapter XIV.)

Tactfully she suggests that the old woman should teach Jane to knit. "I know that you are a superior knitter, and I want my eldest little girl to learn the art, and if you would not object to take a little pupil, I would send her to you three times a week for an hour. . . ."

Thus the old people are made to feel of use, for the old man is to teach Jane to tell the time. Mrs. Mansfield pays them a little sum weekly; Jane reads to them after she has finished her knitting lesson. In spite of their dependence upon the almshouse, the old couple feel themselves valued.

Unfortunately there is too small a proportion of this sort of writing. The reverential awe with which the writer treats the Clifford family, and the sentimentality that swamps so many episodes obscure the merits of the book. Miss Charlesworth, in fact, does not know where to stop, and *Ministering Children* by the end of the century, was severely criticized by many of its Sunday readers. From the 1850's her work was competing with that of Charlotte

Yonge and A.L.O.E., both of whom moved with the times and wrote with brisk common sense and energy.

Ineffective in her writing for servants and villagers, outdated in her educational theories, and inexplicably (from our point of view) successful with *Ministering Children*, Maria Charlesworth had few followers. Times were changing. Nevertheless, this book had some remarkably far-reaching effects, both in the field of social service and that of popular literature, as will be seen in Chapter XI.

Chapter VI

"SEVERE YET FRISKY": A.L.O.E.

(Charlotte Maria Tucker 1821–1893)

As well as being an ideal Sunday book, *Ministering Children* owed much of its contemporary popularity to the common mid-Victorian nostalgia for a vanished rural past,[1] its author having skilfully evoked an ideal country life that lay far enough in the past for some of its evils to be partly forgotten. Her rival in the field of Sunday books, Charlotte Tucker, dealt with other matters. Evangelicals both, they represented diverging aspects of the mid-Victorian Evangelical movement.

The former, born into the small, exclusive group centred on Clapham early in the century, adhered closely to its principles all her life. But Charlotte Tucker, one of a large competitive family, raised in a household reared on moral rather than Evangelical principles, had strong practical advantages over Miss Charlesworth. Having turned to Evangelicalism as an adult, she brought to it her first-hand knowledge of secular life. She was acquainted with the bustling commercial world of the 1850's and 1860's in which Work and Progress became synonymous, and in which the old concepts of religion and charity were being squeezed out of the education of the young (and of the masses) by the incursions of Useful Knowledge. Highly intelligent, brisk, unsentimental, she was, in a practical sense, better equipped to write for her time than was the shrinking Maria Charlesworth. Her moral tales in particular (*Fairy Know-a-Bit, The Crown of Success, The Story of a Needle*, etc.), fitted well to the secular philosophy of education that was making inroads into earlier theories: like many tract writers after 1850, A.L.O.E. was willing to compromise in this matter.

After 1840, Duty came to be linked with Work and Progress, and by 1860 the elevation of the masses was felt by many to depend less upon religious conversion than on sound secular education and the improvement of living conditions through industry (in the sense of Technology) and science. Moreover both industry and science (apart from the Darwinian theory) were by then considered to be as compatible with religion as work had always been. This change in attitude explains the rapid secularisation of children's books after 1850, including books published by the Tract Societies.

Technical science, the new-hatched cuckoo in the educational nest, found its voice in the Great Exhibition of 1851. Opening on May 1, the Exhibition proved from the first to be all that its organisers had hoped, and more. Carlyle, referring disparagingly to the "big Glass Soapbubble and all the gauderies spread out in it (beautiful to the fool, insignificant or even hateful to the wise)"[2] was in the minority. Most observers were enthusiastic. Macaulay was struck by the good temper of the crowd; *Punch's* reporter by that of the police and the authorities. Classes mixed freely; there was no privileged order for carriages but the order of arrival; and the Royal Family attended without special guards: "a magnificent lesson for foreigners" in the superiority of constitutional monarchy over republicanism and tyranny. Mayhew admired the impeccable conduct of the "one shilling crowds" who thronged the Crystal Palace from Monday to Thursday each week. He thought that they looked on the Exhibition as a school rather than a show and noted their interest in the machinery, particularly the power-looms.[3] These were the same power-looms that had enslaved the factory children of the 1830's; unfortunately there seems no record of what these on-lookers were thinking.

The closing of the Great Exhibition in October was marked by relief and pride. An increased confidence in the working classes was seeping upward. Chartism and the prospect of a further extension of the franchise ceased to be attended by the spectre of revolution. The national progress that had so often seemed fitful and fragmentary had been demonstrated real and solid. British confidence in the value of industry and technology was seen to be justified.

Prince Albert's speech at the Guildhall in 1849 took on overtones of prophecy when it appeared in the Exhibition Catalogue in 1851.

> So man is approaching a more complete fulfilment of that great and sacred mission which he has to perform in this world. His reason being created after the image of God, he has to use it to discover the laws by which the Almighty governs his creation, and, by making these laws his standard of action, to conquer Nature to his use—himself a divine instrument. Science discovers these laws of power, motion, and transformation; industry applies them

> to the raw matter, which the earth yields us in abundance, but which becomes valuable only by knowledge: art teaches us the immutable laws of beauty and symmetry, and gives to our productions forms in accordance with them. (Official Catalogue of the Great Exhibition, . . . p. 3.)

The success of this vast undertaking was to many tangible proof that science, industry and art were ordained to bring about Divine purpose. It was, on the surface, the happiest of compromises between religion and the world.

Maria Charlesworth, as one would expect, ignored the whole thing. But the buoyant and practical A.L.O.E. wrote all of her moral and educational books in the light of the Great Exhibition philosophy of the 1850's rather than in the spirit of early Evangelicalism. She was but one of many children's writers who did so in the next fifty years.

The Exhibition was followed by a spate of highly utilitarian children's books on industry, technology, science and trade: some might as well have been written by Bentham himself. The reader of *Little Henry's Holiday at the Great Exhibition* (1853) learned with statistics details of the construction of the Crystal Palace and of the Grand Opening. His brief glances at the displays of foreign nations were both educationally and morally instructive.

"What are the manufactures of Spain?" asks the child.

"Not such as please me," replies his omniscient father, obviously a direct descendant of Thomas Day's Mr. Barlow. And he elucidates.

> "In Toledo, the town from which this jar was sent, the hardest and sharpest of sword-blades are made. The *Government* of this country carry on the manufacture, and that of tobacco and gunpowder.
>
> "Think, Henry—wine, tobacco, gunpowder and swords! Men may learn one day to discard them all! The wine manufacture is no better than the other three, for wine may lead to drunkenness; and 'drunkenness kills more than the sword'.
>
> "Oh, when we talk of the *fruits* of this Exhibition well may we be glad! Many a Spaniard may learn in this building, from the works of other nations, what *industry* is worth,—so, should there be another Exhibition in 1951, perhaps Spain may be represented by far more noble things than this great wine-cooler!"

Published by Houlston's, the tale illustrates the secularisation of tract literature through the return of the moral tale. It informs, it inculcates temperance and industry. At one point readers are exhorted to "ever lift up your voice against the slave-trade"; at another, to compare the bloodthirsty twelfth-century crusades to this beneficient undertaking "which has for its end . . . the strengthening of the bonds of peace and friendship among all nations of the earth". Religious exhortation has been replaced by reverence for work, progress and science.

Four years earlier the moral tale with a scientific basis had been revived by the Mayhews. Of *The Good Genius that Turned Everything into Gold* (1849), a reviewer said,

> It is a fairy tale that shows the magic of patient industry, demonstrating clearly truthfully, that what sloth believes to be superhuman, industry shows to be simple cause and effect . . . thus the little bee—the type of patient industry—calls up with her magic wand the giant power, steam, and bids the roaring monster to obey man's skill. The good purpose of this is obvious; . . . It is essentially a family book; it paints no horrors, it contains no false sentiment, and it arouses no bad passions.[4]

The book was one of the many scientific allegories and "fairy tales" appearing at this time and later.

Science, long thought of as a part of the mystery of religion and formerly treated thus in Evangelical children's books, began about this time to establish itself as a serious rival. Mrs. Gatty recognised the fact early; she worried over *The Origin of Species*, and, according to her granddaughter, kept the author's signature (with that of Tom Paine and Voltaire) in the "Chamber of Horrors" of her autograph collection.[5] Her *Parables from Nature* attempts to counteract materialistic science by interpreting nature as revelation of God. Kingsley's scientific works for children do the same thing, admitting and facing boldly, as in *Glaucus* (1855), the new concepts of creation.

> Geology has disproved the old popular belief that the universe was brought into being as it now exists, by a single feat. We know that the work has been gradual; that the earth
>
> "In tracts of fluent heat began,
> The seeming prey of cyclic storms,
> The home of seeming random forms,
> Till, at the last, arose the man."

> . . .
> Such progress as experimental science actually shows us, is quite awful and beautiful enough to keep us our lives long in wonder; but it is one which perfectly agrees with, and may be perfectly explained by, the simple old belief which the Bible sets before us, of a LIVING GOD: . . . One who works in all things which have obeyed Him. (*Glaucus*, p. 71–3.)

But Mrs. Gatty and Kingsley were highly educated, and they wrote for the children of the educated. Unfortunately for the religious interpretation of nature, lesser writers lost sight of the broader view and produced pathetic fallacy; or, with the Evangelical dependence upon a literally inerrant Bible, repudiated the idea of a developing cosmos. The ultimate significance of the theories set forth in Robert Chambers' *Vestiges of Creation* (1844) and Darwin's *The Origin of Species* (1859) continued to escape readers trained in simple acceptance of the Bible as the word of God. And as literacy increased, the new scientific concepts were too abstract and complicated to grasp in a time when dramatic and long-familiar issues such as the machinations of Roman Catholicism were being dangled before an undemanding reading public. The Evangelical cast of mind, preferring as it always had done, clearly-differentiated issues, revolted at the new scientific theories.

It turned instead to a fascinated contemplation of the dazzling display of scientific achievement in material progress. "Science" to the reader of the 1850's and 1860's was synonymous with the efficient machine. No longer a grave threat to the workman, machinery had increased employment and revolutionized trade. "Science" was the railway, the steamship, the telegraph, drawing the people of the world together. Connotations of progress, prosperity and hope clung around the word. Periodicals (a very important part of lower and middle class reading of the time) accepted almost without reservation the idea that *all* scientific progress would be for the general good.[6] In 1847, an early science-fiction novel, *Sixty Years Hence*,* came up for review in *Howitt's Journal*. The reviewer, probably the optimistic Howitt himself, was shocked by the story in which a mad scientist who has gained tyrannical control of the world succeeds in poisoning earth and sea.

* "By the Author of *The White Slave*" [Richard Hildreth].

> The moral of this strange book is that the mammon-worship of the present day may bring England, nay, perhaps even the whole world to utter ruin. And so it might, perhaps, were it not that, with the mammon-worship, we have in the great heart of the nation, a conservative, healthy current of moral life, which will circulate from the greater to the lesser streams till it permeates the whole of existence. . . . (*Howitt's Journal,* II, (1847), p. 165.)

Work was assumed to have a morally disinfecting quality, bound in the long run to cure its own ills. Science and its partner, industry, were becoming sacrosanct. In children's books as elsewhere, science (manifested in transport, communication, and manufacture) was treated with respect, approval and at times, with reverence. This was the new spirit in educational theory when Charlotte Tucker, known to several generations of young readers as "A.L.O.E." ("A Lady of England"), began publishing books in 1851.

She was born at Barnet in 1821, the sixth in a family of ten. Her father was Henry St. George Tucker, whose chequered career in Indian affairs bridged the period from the times of William Hickey to those of Mrs. Sherwood. Between his arrival in Calcutta in 1786 as a boy of fifteen, and his departure in 1815, he held a number of important offices in the East India Company and the government; he was the planner of the Bank of Bengal. After his marriage in 1811 to a distant cousin of James Boswell, Tucker was re-appointed to India, retiring to England in 1815. Between 1826 and his death in 1851, he was a Director of the East India Company and twice Chairman of its influential Court of Directors. A man of strict personal honesty and great talent, he held strongly conservative opinions, often opposing popular measures of the day. He objected to the first Afghan War, to the Indian opium monopoly of the East India Company, and to Free Trade. He opposed missionary work in India, and argued against extending the freedom of the press to Indian newspapers.[7]

Henry S. Tucker's position gave him some social importance; he was friendly with the Duke of Wellington, Lord Metcalfe, and other highly-placed persons. But he discouraged his family from going much into society or seeking many outside friendships. The family entertained much on a modest scale but went very little into society. The Tucker daughters never attended school. Educated by their parents and by governesses, they in turn helped to teach the younger children: the familiar pattern of Victorian education found in the novels of Charlotte Yonge and tales by Mrs. Gatty and Mrs. Ewing as well as in A.L.O.E.'s own books—*Parliament in the Play Room, Old Friends with New Faces*, etc.

The Tuckers were clever, vigorous and highly literate. Henry St. George Tucker had two stiff eighteenth-century type plays to his credit as well as his professional and financial writings. Charlotte throughout her girlhood wrote much poetry, short plays for family acting, and tragedies in verse. She was musical; she could draw; and she showed talent for acting.

She never married. Probably the fact that she was hard-featured, gingery-haired, tall, thin and awkward had early destined her for the part of the daughter who remained at home to care for her parents in their declining years. According to her biographer, Agnes Giberne, she had decided young to be good because she knew that she could never be pretty. That she was often reminded in childhood of her plainness and her general untidiness is suggested by the tone of the family and nursery life described in many of her books. They abound in children who are painfully plain-spoken or downright malicious; one could probably reconstruct from them a fairly accurate picture of the Tucker ménage and its nursery (undoubtedly a stormy one at times). The necessity of holding her own among so many, and the domination of boys over girls in the Victorian family may account for A.L.O.E.'s blunt tactlessness and occasional ruthless determination.

"Directness to a fault was, . . . a leading characteristic of Charlotte all through life," says her biographer, quoting later a character sketch by a friend: "With all her exceeding kindness, hers could hardly be described as the true sympathetic temperament. . . . Purpose seemed woven into all her liveliness; and she tried to keep others up to her level."[8] This is precisely what she intended to do with her young readers: *elevate* them, morally and spiritually, and *keep them up* to that level.

During the 1840's, Charlotte Tucker became a practising Evangelical. Although she was raised a strict churchwoman, her education under her father's eye had been more along eighteenth-century moral lines. The influence of *Sandford and Merton* underlies her educational and didactic works; that of the Kilners is discernible in *Rambles of a Rat; Fairy Frisket* is a didactic *Butterfly's Ball*. She was obviously well acquainted too with Mrs. Sherwood's books, the only children's tales of the time with an authentic Indian background. Along with *The Pilgrim's Progress*, *The Infant's Progress* and *The Indian Pilgrim* shaped her own allegorical bent. Tales like *Little Henry*, *Little Lucy and her Ayah*, and *The Ayah and Lady* pointed the way to her own Indian writings. However opposed to Indian missions and missionaries Henry St. George Tucker might have been, his elegant home in Portland Place had produced Mrs. Sherwood's successor—a dedicated (if delayed) missionary.

Missionary work in India and the copious writing of missionary stories was, however, A.L.O.E.'s ultimate contribution to the *elevation of the masses*. She set about it in 1875 when she was fifty-four; but for many years before, she had worked like other dedicated Victorians to forward the twin causes of education and religion.

A dutiful daughter to the last, she helped to nurse her father for two years before his death in 1851. Since she was fidgety, untidy and loquacious, it may have been a time of trial for both. She always wrote of him with the deepest respect and affection, and Miss Giberne, a typically cautious Victorian biographer, never suggests that the relationship of father and daughter was anything but excellent. Nevertheless, in the forty-odd years between his death and her own, A.L.O.E. utilized the energy, intelligence and determination inherited from her father to do a number of things that he had deplored, discouraged or forbidden.

She became, for instance, a Workhouse Visitor, how successfully or for how long, we do not know. No detailed account of workhouse life is found in her books (unlike those of Maria Charlesworth and Hesba Stretton). Her comment that the workhouse was "a refuge mercifully provided for the homeless and the helpless" suggests that she did not question the justice or the necessity of the New Poor Law. One would think that her well-known tactlessness and desire to preach must have made her anything but the ideal Visitor to the Poor described by Miss Charlesworth; nevertheless, after she went to India, "one bedridden cottager . . . collected over £9 for the Church in Batala, aided by some of her Sunday scholars",* and those whom she had visited are said to have recalled her with affection.

Shortly after her father's death, too, she sent out a manuscript

* *Sunday at Home* (1894), p. 455.

to the publishers. *The Claremont Tales*, forwarded in 1851 to Chambers, was passed by them to Gall and Inglis, who printed it in 1852. It was followed in 1853 by a book of verse, *Glimpses of the Unseen*, and from then on she never looked back. Continuing to publish with Gall and Inglis and with Thomas Nelson, she became one of the best-known tract fiction writers of the century. Numbers of short tales printed in *The Children's Paper* (1855–1926) and similar magazines, were at intervals collected into hard-covered books to become Sunday School prizes until after 1920. She is credited with about one hundred and fifty titles in all, a figure almost impossible to verify.

Being financially independent, she devoted the proceeds of her writing to charity and mission work, supporting in the last years of her life, a school for Hindu boys at Batala. Many of her books were printed abroad, about forty, for example, are listed in Swedish printings.*

By the time A.L.O.E.'s books appeared, publishing directed to the elevation of the masses, including that of the Tract Societies, had separated into two distinct streams: religious and secular. The first included all the older tracts and tract fiction as well as the output of religious writers of the day. The second (which took in the publications of the S.D.U.K.) was highly factual and often geared to the demands of industry and science. Earnest Evangelicals of 1850 could no longer re-direct the national course of education as their predecessors of 1800–1820 had done, a fact that A.L.O.E. recognised and accepted. Her popular educational writing contained much factual information in the framework of instructive moral tales from which religion was often conspicuously absent. And she revealed a sense of humour and an eye for the absurd that had been missing in tract literature since the astringency of Hannah and Sarah More had been diluted by the tearful effusions of the Rev. Legh Richmond.

The allegorical *Crown of Success* or Four Heads to Furnish (1863), except for the Victorian tone of the conversation, might have been written under the guidance of the Edgeworths or the Aikins. Like Rosamond, the four children learn from their mistakes: the lazy one who refuses to climb the tricky "Ladder of Spelling"

* A figure supplied by Mrs. Mary Ørvig of the Swedish Institute of Children's Books.

can only half-decorate his Cottage of Head with its wallpaper (i.e. reading matter); his flighty sister, having selected a paper "covered with fairies", finds it soon wears thin. Pride and Folly lead two of them astray; Duty and Affection guide the one who will listen—sensible Nelly, winner of the Crown of Success. A slow but steady worker who has humbly accepted advice, she nails down her "Carpet of History" with the requisite number of dates and cultivates plants of Plain Sewing in her garden. The only mention of religion is an allusion to "a Book . . . in a cover of gold", and Affection's advice to Nelly: "However well the head may be furnished, if the highest knowledge be wanting, all other things become worthless and vain. . . ."

The same secular approach marks *Fairy Know-a-Bit* (1866) and *Fairy Frisket* (1874). Highly informative about food, textiles, medicines, paper and ink and birds, *Fairy Know-a-Bit* supplied scientific classifications and a variety of relevant statistics. Manufacturing processes were not mentioned, but readers were assured that "The cotton brought into the British Islands in the *one year* 1860, would, if woven into cloth, stretch to such a length that it could be wrapped *two hundred times* around this huge world!". A brief history of the slave trade and the cost of its abolition to the British taxpayer accompanied the section dealing with sugar.

Fairy Frisket, sister of Know-a-Bit, displayed the insect world, turning the boys briefly into ants so that they might see the wonders of the ant-heap. A.L.O.E., herself no Sluggard, and very fond of ants and bees, taught the same lesson as Adelaide O'Keeffe did sixty years before.

> My youth is but a summer's day:
> Then like the bee and ant I'll lay
> A store of learning by; . . .

Both tales were based on *Sandford and Merton*, the chief characters being two sharply-contrasted small boys and their mentor, who, in eighty years had dwindled from the omniscient Mr. Barlow of 1783 into the Fairy Know-a-Bit, ". . . not six inches high, dressed like a student in cap and gown, with wee dots of spectacles on his nose, and a grand beard nearly an inch in length. . . ."

With something of the smug self-satisfaction that pervaded much post-Great Exhibition thinking, he explains that, although he once lived in the green wood and danced on the moss by moonlight,

> . . . times have changed—and so have I. A railway now runs right through the valley . . . there are engine lights instead of the glow-worm's. . . . Education is now all the fashion, and fairies, like bigger people, are sent to learn lessons at school. . . . For more than four hundred years, ever since printing was invented, I have taken to books. . . . (Chapter I.)

From this point until the end of the book, Fairy Know-a-Bit dispenses facts almost non-stop. Neither Jeremy Bentham nor Mr. Gradgrind could possibly have found fault with him.

Religious teaching joined morality in *The Story of a Needle* (1858), in which the needle, scissors, thimble, etc. tell their stories and describe the sources and uses of various metals. The information is embedded in a sentimental account of the troubles of the Ellerslie family. Its sequel, *Old Friends with New Faces* (1858) allegorized tales like *Bluebeard* to carry moral lessons such as "Good Resolutions are excellent things, but Good Habits are a thousand times better"; or ". . . fling Pride away and drown him in the Sea of Forgetfulness for ever".

A.L.O.E.'s best known and most popular tale of this sort was, however, *The Rambles of a Rat* (1857) (Fig. 16). In the style of Dorothy Kilner's *Life and Perambulation of a Mouse* (? 1783), or Miss Sandham's *Adventures of Poor Puss* (1809), the humanized rats, Ratto, Whiskerandos, Oddity and others relate their histories and adventures. Narrative is varied by appropriate moral or religious reflections, and sprinklings of miscellaneous knowledge. A sub-plot (told as witnessed by the rats) deals with the rescue of two London street waifs by a kindly sea-captain and his little son. Placed in a Ragged School, these children are started on the way to a respectable independence. A.L.O.E.'s plea for the support of the Ragged Schools indicates that the situation in the London slums had changed very little since the 1840's. ". . . Were all the children of the middle classes in England to give each but one penny a week, no wretched boy need wander about desolate in London, to perish both here and hereafter because no one cared for his soul!" (Chapter VIII.)

The stereotyped sub-plot about the street children is far less interesting than the plausible, amusing and often exciting adventures of the rats. A.L.O.E. (always strictly honest about her sources) was inspired by an article in the *Quarterly Review* (1857). Her rats help their blind companion; they visit the Zoo by going through the sewers, a jaunt which enables her to describe other members of the rat family. A whole geography lesson on Russia is incorporated in the voyage made by Ratto and Whiskerandos to St. Petersburg. Shipwrecked on the way home, they float to land on a barrel and have some exciting moments afterwards.

Living in close association with man, the rats keep up a running comment on human beings. They approve of the sea-captain, but most of their observations are critical and ironic; those on gin-drinking, for instance.

> "Are there any creatures that lay traps for man?" said I. . . .
> "As well as I can understand," replied Furry, "man himself lays traps for man. . . . They are large and generally built of brick, with a board and gilt letters in front. They are baited with a certain drink, which has effects something like opium, which destroys slowly but surely those who give themselves up recklessly to its enjoyment."

Oddity's remark that rats are not caught twice in the same kind of trap gives his companion a chance to point out the folly of human beings.

> ". . . They walk with open eyes into the great man-trap. . . . They know that they are going the straight direct way to be worried by sickness, poverty, and shame . . . and yet they go gaily to their ruin." (Chapter II.)

Like Anna Sewell twenty years later, A.L.O.E. pleaded for kindness to animals, and by humanizing her rats, made them likable. Although in 1857, the rat had not yet come fully under the ban of medical science, she was the only children's writer to defend it, considering it a useful scavenger which ". . . by clearing away that which, if left, would poison the air . . . does good service to man".

In all her tales she was adept at supplying juvenile versions of that mid-Victorian theory of work laid down by Carlyle in *Past and Present* (1843), its "perennial nobleness and even sacredness". While not going so far as to describe the individual's knowledge of his work in the world as "the latest Gospel", she certainly approved Carlyle's dictum that the person must recognise his work, "and work at it like a Hercules".[9] This concept of work inspired Ruskin and Morris; shorn of its spiritual implications and simplified, it was popularised by Samuel Smiles and Eliza Cook, both widely read by the working classes at this time.[10]

Like respectability and the *elevation of the masses*, work was held to be a unifying element helping to close the gap between the Two Nations. In 1865 Ruskin asserted at a Working Man's Institute that

> . . . the distinction between workers and idlers, as between knaves and honest men, runs through the very heart and innermost nature of men of all ranks and in all positions. There is a working class—strong and happy—among both rich and poor; there is an idle class—weak, wicked, and miserable—among both rich and poor.[11]

"Weak, wicked, and miserable"—it is the picture of Dr. Watts' Sluggard, heightened by a touch of Victorian melodrama, for Watts did not mention wickedness. But by 1860, idleness was thought to be very close to wickedness; industry had acquired its connotation of spiritual worth, and work became intrinsically important. "All service ranks the same with God" was almost an Article of Faith. The very hymnbook emphasized the point.

> Come, labour on,
> Away with gloomy doubts and faithless fear!
> No arm so weak but may do service here. . .
> (Jane Borthwick, 1859)

Or,

> Give to each flying minute
> Something to keep in store;
> Work, for the night is coming,
> When man works no more.

Moreover, the idea that work faithfully carried out could cure the spiritual impoverishment of the worker, raise the moral level of the community, and improve the quality of life in general was completely in harmony with the Benthamite thought of the mid-century. It was, naturally, welcomed by employers; it raised production, it raised the standard of service.

All children's writers stressed the value of work. The wisest of Mrs. Gatty's Fairy Godmothers gave her little protégé *the love of employment*; Kingsley showed Tom, the Water-Baby, learning and working in the water world. By the end of the story, he emerges from the allegory to become ". . . a great man of science and can plain railroads, and steam engines, and electric telegraphs . . .". The Moral reminds the reader "to stick to hard work and cold water". Dr. Watts still proclaimed to children on Sundays that

> Satan finds some mischief still
> For idle hands to do; . . .

By the logic of the nursery, the busy hands were approved by Heaven.

Thus the revived moral tale joined the religious tract tale in encouraging children of the upper and middle classes to aid their elders in the work of education or conversion or charity and good works: to be Ministering Children or Busy Bees.

A.L.O.E. rather preferred the Busy Bees.

> "Oh, foolish children!" cries the fairy in *The Story of a Needle*, "do you think life was made only for a plaything, and time given to be thrown away in folly! There is work in the world for every one to do, and everything is created for some use. As you have never, with your wills, done any service to mankind, it is your doom to do service without them . . .; for seven long years you shall toil in humble estate, till you have learned how great is the value of time, and opportunity to do some good to others!" (Chapter XII.)

Just as the unfortunate fisherman in the allegory of "The Two Purses" only recoups his losses and becomes wealthy when he receives from the hand of Experience the iron hook of Industry (*Old Friends with New Faces*, 1858), so all the children in A.L.O.E.'s books learn the spiritual and material value of work.

This was the sort of book Charlotte Tucker was writing in the twenty-five years before she achieved her lifelong ambition to be a missionary. Every kind of improving tale was represented by these cottage tales in which honesty and thrift, patience and faith were as invariably rewarded as lying, drunkenness and ungodliness were punished. But her rural settings were contemporary; her characters, however stereotyped, were acceptable stereotypes, presented in common situations, struggling with current problems. *Sheer Off* (1867) revolved around the control of the village school—a lively issue all over England at the time; the village drunkard in this tale was a woman; the converted Jew and his grandson reflected the current interest in Old Testament themes, and supplied variation in characters. In fact A.L.O.E.'s cottage tales, less impeded with religious explication than her improving works for the upper classes, were very close to the fiction found in the domestic periodicals of the day: *The Family Friend, Eliza Cook's Journal, The Family Economist*, etc. If they contained more religion, they were also more vigorous and often more interesting.

"I liked A.L.O.E.," records George Sturt, in *A Small Boy in the Sixties* (1927). He especially liked *Ned Franks* whose eponymous hero could paint "(with one hand too . . .) all the flags of all the navies of the world;" and *The Lake of the Woods* (1867).

Like earlier Evangelicals, A.L.O.E. assumed that social station was unalterable. Her cottage tales were better geared to the taste of the times than were those of Maria Charlesworth; she played no favourites and showed no reverential awe before a title. Taking for granted that all classes of society were wanting in charity, honesty and sincere religious belief, she dealt out rewards and punishments impartially: if the poor girl lost her sight through her own folly, the spoilt heiress lost her beauty through smallpox. A dishonest servant is discharged; a dishonest agent struck down with paralysis. Village readers liked this sort of literary justice by which A.L.O.E. sought to establish the now unpopular doctrine of original sin and show the strict equality of all in the sight of God.

Tales for village children and Ragged Schools also laid emphasis upon honesty and industry, faith and prayer. The writer's approach here was direct rather than allegorical.

> Willie was a truly religious boy—his hope and trust were placed in his Saviour; but he well knew that religion gives no encouragement to idleness—that we are recommended to be *not slothful in business, fervent in spirit, serving the Lord*. The more earnestly he prayed, the harder he worked; his piety gave new impulse to his industry. (*Upwards and Downwards and Other Stories*, 1874).

She also wrote some extremely sensational religious adventure stories. *War and Peace* (1862), intended to illustrate "the power of faith to give *peace* even in the midst of tumult and *war*", held its readers by lively accounts of siege and massacre, the details of an Afghan household, the suspense of the escape from Kabul, and descriptions of a winter in the mountain hut. Elements of juvenile romance suggested by the colourful figure of Zobeide were firmly re-arranged into A.L.O.E.'s favourite brother-sister relationship.

This is Henty territory, where A.L.O.E. preceded him by several years. Of *The Lake of the Woods* (1867), George Sturt said that "the title . . . was a romance in itself"; romantic and exciting too were *The Mine* (1858) and *The Robbers' Cave* (1862).* When not heavily underlining her elevating lessons of Duty and Self-sacrifice sweetened by Faith, A.L.O.E.'s writing was as lively and highly-coloured as any in *The Boys' Own Magazine*, or the tales of Marryat, Kingston, or Ballantyne.

Take a scene like this:

> . . . Suddenly there was heard the sharp report of a pistol, which made Mrs. Cleveland start and shriek, and the next moment the horses were thrown violently back upon their haunches, and the lamplight dimly showed indistinct forms glancing like phantoms through the darkness. Then came wild fierce faces at the window; the door was forced open, and the travellers dragged out of the carriage almost before they had time to be certain that all was not some horrible dream. Horace's first impulse, however, was to defend his mother; all unarmed as he was, he struck at the man who had seized her, but received himself a sharp blow on the arm which made it drop stunned to his side. . . . There were at least five or six robbers around, most of them already busily engaged in rifling the carriage; and strange sounded their laughter and their jests as they drew forth now this thing—now that—dragging cloaks, bandboxes, dressing-case, umbrella, fan, carpet-bag, to be piled in a heap on the road. The bandit who had seized Mrs. Cleveland had already torn from her neck the gold chain, and with it, the watch which she wore. . . . (*The Robbers' Cave*, Chapter IV.)

One might suspect that she was an enthusiastic reader of boy's adventure tales; actually she probably drew the details from articles in the *Quarterly*, or *Blackwood's*.

She was certainly an avid reader of anything concerning religion, and it was a time of brisk religious controversy. Since 1850, in response to the growing demand for fiction, the Tract Societies and other publishers who supplied the Sunday books had been bringing out a host of little novels, ostensibly historical, actually strongly anti-Catholic. Stories of Wyclif and the Lollards, of the Huguenots, of victims of the Marian persecution and the Spanish Inquisition, were the popular themes. Writers such as Emma Jane Worboise,

* Also known as *Light in the Robbers' Cave*, and mentioned by "Edna Lyall" (A. E. Bayley) in *The Burges Letters* (1902) as a favourite book.

Emily S. Holt, Emma Leslie, Kate Thompson Sizer, and—inevitably—A.L.O.E. oversimplified history in the defence of Protestantism. Not all were Evangelicals, but all wrote with overt purpose, their books a part of the afterglow of the fierce blaze of religious conflict around 1850. Behind the assumption of the perfect rightness of the Lollard-Lutheran-Huguenot-Cromwellian causes lay all the fears and ill-feeling engendered by the secession of Newman and his followers to Rome in 1845, by the explosive Maynooth issue in the same year, and above all, by the "Papal Aggression" of 1850.

"I rely with confidence on the people of England . . . a nation which looks with contempt on the mummeries of superstition, and with scorn on the laborious endeavours which are now making to confine the intellect and enslave the soul," wrote Lord John Russell, in an open letter of reply to anxious representations from the Bishop of Durham, protesting Cardinal Wiseman's Pastoral Letter of 1850.[12] His confidence was quite justified: a wave of anti-Catholic feeling swept the country, and writers of tract literature until the end of the century continued to pour out a variety of sturdily Protestant children's tales exposing the "mummeries of superstition". Mrs. Sherwood's anti-Catholic tales received a new lease of life; Mrs. Hofland's *Adelaide* (1823), a Huguenot tale, was reprinted; Foxe's *Book of Martyrs*, never quite forgotten, came out again, as did Bunyan's *Holy War*. G. A. Sala noted in his *Life and Adventures* (1895) that he had co-operated around this time with the cartoonist, Alfred Forrester (known to children as the picture-book artist "Crowquill") on a set of anti-Papal cartoons, "ominous pictures" which threatened dreadful disasters to the country if Roman Catholicism and Puseyism were not opposed.[13] And even the tolerant Margaret Gatty wrote that a Roman Catholic service was "great *nonsense*", both theatrical and wicked.[14]

In Evangelical children's books, all this violent reaction resulted in domestic tales displaying the efforts of convent schools to ensnare little Protestants mistakenly committed to their care, or stories in which earnest young Protestants converted grateful Roman Catholics by explaining to them the infallibility of the New Testament and denying that of the Pope. A.L.O.E.'s *Robbers' Cave* is of this class. Even during her Indian years she wrote sensational "historical" tales such as *Driven into Exile*, a Tale of the Huguenots (1888), or *The Blacksmith of Boniface Lane* (1890) (about a Lollard martyr). However she avoided verbal sniping at High Church or Dissenters, and her books were acceptable all around. Charlotte Yonge, in *What Books to Lend and What to Give* (1887), recommended *Wings and Stings* (1855) and *The Story of a Needle*; and remarked of *The Giant Killers* (1856) that it was "Rather stilted, but has been much enjoyed by elder children . . ." and went on to observe that A.L.O.E.'s books were very religious without Church teaching, and though stiff in style, were useful. This testimony must have pleased A.L.O.E., who was extremely anxious to be useful.

She had been demonstrating her usefulness in the fields of education, both religious and practical, since 1851. But her heart was set on missionary work; restricted by home duties, she turned to Ragged Schools and the Mission to the Jews. This had begun as the Society for Promoting Christianity among the Jews (1809), and the contribution of families like the D'Israeli's and the Montifiore's to Victorian life ensured a continuing interest in Jewish life and belief. In 1839, the Committee of the General Assembly of the Church of Scotland for the Conversion of the Jews had sponsored a mission of enquiry "to see the real conditions and character of God's ancient people, and to observe whatever might contribute to interest others in their cause".[15] A.L.O.E.'s interest in the Society for Promoting Christianity among the Jews is indicated in a letter of the 1860's.

> I am going to have it (a piece of music composed by her sister) printed by converted Jews and the entire profits devoted to the Society for the Conversion of Jews.[16]

For decades, the many Sunday magazines ran articles on the Holy Land, on Old Testament characters and subjects. Novelists followed suit,[17] and children's writers picked up the theme as early as 1822, when Miss Sandham wrote *The History and Conversion of the Jewish Boy*. Mrs. Sherwood used it in *Shanty the Blacksmith* (? 1835); Maria Charlesworth in *Oliver of the Mill* (1876); and Hesba Stretton in *Carola* (1884). All these tales, like A.L.O.E.'s *Sheer Off* and *The Mine*, bring in the Jewish child (or old man) who is converted. All give, on the whole, a favourable picture of the Jews.

The theme was part of the general interest in Old Testament studies, quickened in the middle of the century by the desire to counter the emphasis placed by Tractarians upon the New Testament and upon ritual, suggestive to most dissenting Protestants of mariolatry.

But A.L.O.E.'s desire to become a missionary in the east took precedence over her other interests. Following the death of her mother in 1869, she went to live with a brother in the country. Financially independent, a very successful writer of the Christian-moral tale for the young, she was at last without family responsibilities, the orphan niece and nephews, children of Robert Tudor Tucker, being now grown up. In defiance of all advice, she began to study Hindustani. She had brothers and nephews in the Indian Army and Civil Service; her favourite brother, the Evangelically-inclined Robert Tudor Tucker, had been killed in the Mutiny of 1857. She was certain that Duty called her to India, and Inclination had long pointed in the same direction.

Late in 1875 (having made a brief visit to Canada in the spring) A.L.O.E. arrived at Amritsar to work with the Indian Female Normal School and Instruction Society. By 1878, she was at Batala, remaining there, save for yearly holidays spent elsewhere in India, for the rest of her life. At fifty-four, well over age for a missionary, she had come as a voluntary worker at her own expense, and Batala offered the greater independence. It was, moreover, a boys' boarding school, and A.L.O.E. had always preferred boys to girls.

She was as industrious, as sincere, as devoted to duty as she had ever been. Her faith was strong; like all devout Evangelicals, she knew she was right. Still determined to *keep others up* to the mark, she was, as ever, tactless and outspoken. Extremely healthy herself, almost unaffected by the tropical heat, she could not believe that others were less fortunate. A colleague retiring to her room with a sick headache was quite likely to be ministered to by A.L.O.E.: guitar in hand, she would settle herself at the invalid's bedside and sing hymns. "Though her voice was never really very good", murmurs her biographer in another connection, "she sang much . . .".

Even less appreciated in Amritsar may have been her disapproval of certain marriages of colleagues, notably those ladies who then abandoned their missionary labours. Love and sentiment did not rate highly with A.L.O.E.: pretty girls in her books suffer much humiliation. At one time she had hoped to found a "zenana" of maiden missionary ladies at Batala, but soon found that no mission station could function in India without male authority.

Living at Batala, however, in one room of the High School which had once been a Maharajah's palace, she was perfectly happy and worked harmoniously with her colleagues there. Her official position was that of Zenana Visitor, the female missionary who visited native women, talked and listened to them, read them the Gospels, taught them hymns and explained Christian belief and practice. At times she helped in the Boys' High School. She composed a school song for it evidently inspired by English public school values:

> Generous and just,
> True to his trust,
> That's what a boy of Batala should be.
> Eager to learn
> Knowledge to earn,
> That's what a boy of Batala should be. . . .
> (Quoted in E. C. Dawson; *Missionary Heroines in India*, 1908)

One year, during the missionary's absence, she presided over it very successfully. She was well liked by the boys.

Some years before her death, she endowed the school for younger boys, naming it, in her usual allegorical fashion "The Plough". More religious in its teachings than the government-sponsored school, it was to prepare the ground for the seed of the gospel. Later it was re-named the Baring-Tucker School and accommodated several hundred pupils.[18]

"Severe yet frisky" had been part of the summing-up of A.L.O.E.'s character offered by an old friend. The friskiness increased with years and the severity certainly mellowed. Missionary colleagues called her "Auntie"; tidied her up; inspected her before she went out lest she forget her cap; and insisted that she must keep *one* dress in reserve (for she was generous to a fault with her personal possessions). She died in 1893 after an illness of several months, sincerely mourned by her schoolboys and her co-workers, white and native. For over forty years, her books went marching on.

She had written copiously over those eighteen years, taking up where Mrs. Sherwood had left off. Like Mrs. Sherwood she wrote allegorical tales to be translated into the vernacular, finding it, as she explained in the Preface to *A Wreath of Indian Stories* (1876), "a way to amuse and through amusement to instruct". Her work in this line was it seems, greatly appreciated by working missionaries of the time. Indian mission education had never been the simple matter that perusal of some children's books suggests. Revealing glimpses of its difficulties, and the differences between the time of Mrs. Sherwood and that of A.L.O.E. are found in the Indian journals of Emily Eden and Helen Douglas Mackenzie.[19] Bedevilled almost from the start by internecine struggles, confounded by the variable conditions of the mission field, it was interrupted in 1857 by the Mutiny. In some quarters, missionary work was to be held responsible for this uprising. The post-Mutiny changes in government brought new complications, as did conflict among the different governing societies in Britain, and disagreements about the several systems of education transplanted from there. Thus there were in India Scottish Presbyterian missions with Unitarian leanings, and Anglican missions ranging doctrinally from Evangelical to High Church. There were Baptist and Methodist missions, among them that Danish one at Serampore so well known and highly regarded by Mrs. Sherwood. All were supported by their parent societies: the Church Missionary Society, the London Missionary Society, the S.P.C.K., the Methodist and Baptist Missionary Societies. And the work in the field was correspondingly influenced by the convictions, whims or prejudices of the leaders in Britain and on the spot.[20]

The major issues in Indian education were, first, the extent to which knowledge of Christianity should be incorporated into the teaching; and second, the relative importance to be assigned to the use of English and the use of the vernacular. Both questions had been earnestly debated since the beginning of the century. By the time A.L.O.E. reached Amritsar in 1876, the vernacular was in general use in the lower schools and English in the High Schools. Government-supported schools in the Punjab followed the policy instituted by W. D. Arnold,* Director of Public Instruction in the 1850's. He had not been a supporter of missionary schools, and opposed the introduction of Bible teaching into government schools on the grounds that Christians had no business to demand that non-Christians should support their teachings.[21]

About 1879, A.L.O.E. noted in the Preface of *Little Bullets from Batala* that "hundreds of thousands of natives have been receiving an education from Government, one from which religion is excluded, but which enables them to be reached by means of the

* A son of Thomas Arnold of Rugby.

Press". Fearing the rise of nihilism among these "sharp conceited lads whom the Government so carefully educates *without God*", she wrote her allegorical Christian tales to fill the needs of this new reading public whose minds she would train "in the first principles of morality as well as of religion". Like earlier observers of missionary education, and many missionaries, she believed in drawing close parallels between native education and that introduced by government and missionaries. Among her tales are brief accounts of the lives of the Mohammedan poet, Kabir, and the Sikh reformer Goru Nanek, both of whom were outspoken against idolatry and superstition.[22]

Closely as it followed Mrs. Sherwood in subject matter and in the use of allegory, A.L.O.E.'s writing nevertheless revealed a significant change in Evangelical outlook between 1815 and 1875. Whereas Mrs. Sherwood's acceptance of the doctrine of universal human depravity had enabled her to depict the proselytizing Christian admitting his own wicked heart, A.L.O.E.'s Evangelicalism was modified by the Victorian belief in progress and in the national destiny. Like so many of her contemporaries, she apparently assumed that most of the wickedness was on the other side.

"I have, during my life, broken God's Commandments many and many times; . . ." says Mrs. Sherwood's Lady to the Ayah she hopes to convert: "and as he that breaks one of the commandments of God deserves hell, so, if I were to receive the due reward of my deeds, I should certainly go to that dreadful place . . . you cannot look into my heart . . . the Almighty God has kept me from foul and open sins . . ." (*The Ayah and Lady*, Chap. XIV). But A.L.O.E. laid her emphasis upon the sins of the unconverted, and was careful not to expose those of her own countrymen. Her "government Sahib" who, when begged for a loan by a native convert, must admit that he too is in debt, is able to explain that on arrival in India he had been robbed of his money, and had borrowed a large sum from a wealthy man to help his needy father at home: a debt which he has been paying ever since. A converted pupil at boarding school who backslides, has to be brought to a sense of her spiritual danger by her devoted missionary teacher,[23] but the latter has nothing to say about her own spiritual failings.

By A.L.O.E.'s time, memories of the Indian Mutiny had heightened the barriers between the British and those they governed, and the white man's awareness of his industrial and scientific knowledge further strengthened the paternalism of which later generations of Indians complained. That missionaries in 1875 were not exempt from this sense of moral and racial superiority is discernible in A.L.O.E.'s tales in spite of their Christian morality and their attempts to give due credit to native converts. She loved India and was genuinely attached to her pupils and those she worked with; on the other hand she would have supported convictions expressed in a Religious Tract publication of 1884:

> England has not yet been duly impressed by the thought that . . . possession of India gives her greater facilities civilizing and elevating others than have ever been entrusted to a nation . . .(T)o take any part in the overthrow of such stupendous forms of superstition . . . is a supreme honour as honours are truly estimated in the sight of God.[24]

This attitude was an unfortunate outgrowth of the education policy laid down for India in the 1830's by Macaulay and John Stuart Mill (who had himself been brought up to believe in the unlimited possibilities of human improvement through education). Indians were to be educated towards an eventual position of responsibility in their own government; but on the assumption that they would fit into the pattern of British and Western European culture. Eastern philosophy and literature had no place in this theory; they were not progressive.[25]

Undoubtedly the Victorian missionary movement helped to disrupt traditional values, break down native culture, and make commercial exploitation easier. Yet it should not be forgotten that these missionaries and the government behind them helped to put down the slave trade and discourage the caste system. Missions supplied the nucleus of schools and colleges which educated leaders and followers for the twentieth-century movement towards national independence.

And A.L.O.E., "severe yet frisky", at times almost a missionary for a comic opera: did she make any real mark on Indian history? Possibly, yes—but indirectly. Determined, dedicated, and brave, she represented something very much larger than her strongly opinionated self. She publicized; she was one of many women, who by their single-hearted devotion to the work of school and hospital, first opened the doors of opportunity to the women of India, Africa and China. With the establishment of mission schools and hospitals came the training of thousands of women of the Orient who have helped to bring their own people into the twentieth century.

Fig. 1 Thomas Day, the author of *Sandford and Merton*, one of those "enduring classics . . . solid with practical information" (Chapter I)

Fig. 2 The young Mrs. Trimmer at about the time she began to write for children

THE
NEWTONIAN SYSTEM
OF
PHILOSOPHY.
Adapted to the Capacities of
YOUNG LADIES AND GENTLEMEN,
And familiarized and made entertaining,
By Objects with which they are intimately acquainted:
Being the Subftance of Six Lectures,
Read to a Select Company of Friends,
BY TOM TELESCOPE, A. M.

First collected and methodized by the late Mr. Newberry, for the Inftruction and rational Entertainment of the Youth of thefe Kingdoms.

Illuftrated with Copperplates.

A NEW EDITION,
[illegible]vifed and enriched by an Account of the late new Philofophical Difcoveries,
BY WILLIAM MAGNET, F. L. S.

LONDON:
Printed for OGILVY and SPEARE, Middle-Row Holborn. 1794.
Price One Shilling and Sixpence bound.

Fig. 3 Isaac Newton (1642–1727), physicist and mathematician, was the author of *Philosophia Naturalis Principia Mathematica* (1687), in which he expressed his conviction that God is th Supreme Being and Maker of the ordered universe. Although a conforming churchmar Newton denied the doctrine of the Trinity; educational works based on his scientific discoverie were therefore carefully edited for schools governed by Evangelicals. This work was probabl free from such editing.

Fig. 4 A schoolroom of the 1820's from *In School or Out of School*, or The History of William and John (Dean & Munday, 1827)

Fig. 5 Hannah More in 1786, three years before she started her Sunday Schools at Cheddar

PARTICULARS OF
William Honeyman, *alias* Innes,
THE

YOUNG SWINDLER.

James Danes, a Smuggler,
FOR ROBBING

The Rev. Mr. Andrews.

S. CLARKE, alias HAGGER,
Who said he was an

Innocent Sufferer.

JOHN STAINES,
FOR

STEALING CATTLE.

And an Account of all the
PRISONERS TRIED in MAIDSTONE,
AT THE MARCH ASSIZES, 1806.
Among whom were some Companions to the late
HELL FIRE JACK.
To which are added
THE PRINCIPAL

LAW CAUSES.

LONDON:
Published by Mr. Hughes, Stationer's-court; Mr. Tegg,
Cheapside; Mrs. Kemmish, Borough;
And Sold by all other Booksellers.

R. Pocock, Printer, Gravesend.

Fig. 6 Woodcut and title page from a chapbook assortment published around 1810

Fig. 7 Mrs. Sherwood

Fig. 8 Little Henry explaining the scriptures to Boosy from the 1867 edition of Mrs. Sherwood's *The Story of Little Henry and his Bearer Boosy*

THE NEW TEMPERANCE PRIMER.

Q

Stands for the Question common sense will decide,
That a drunkard's curse cannot be denied;
To prove it you see is so easy a task,
Then who would be a drunkard I kindly ask.

Stands for Rags, which the drunkard is in,
When he finds he's no money for Brandy or Gin;
He's just like a madman without self control,
He is bought by the Devil, body and soul.

Stands for Vultures the great worthy host,
Who praise the man who can spend the most;
Should his wife starve does not care a pin,
So long as he plies them with whisky or gin,

Stands for Workhouse, where in anguish and strife,
Dwell the poor wretched sot and heart-broken wife
And those he's supported will not try to save
The poor dying wretch from a damp pauper's grave

Fig. 9 Inculcating total abstinence (*c.* 1890)

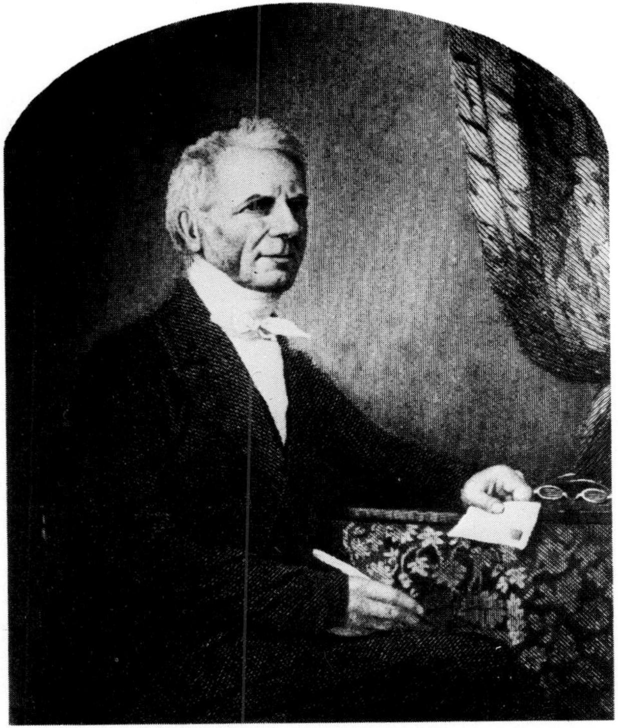

Fig. 10 George Mogridge (1787–1854) was a spurious "Peter Parley" and the author of numerous tract tales for six or seven publishers.

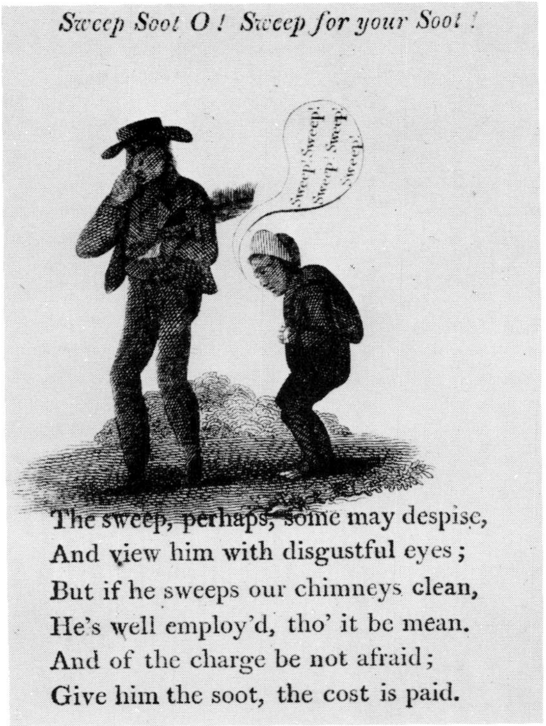

Sweep Soot O! Sweep for your Soot!
Sweep! Sweep! Sweep! Sweep! Sweep!
The sweep, perhaps, some may despise,
And view him with disgustful eyes;
But if he sweeps our chimneys clean,
He's well employ'd, tho' it be mean.
And of the charge be not afraid;
Give him the soot, the cost is paid.

Fig. 11 The chimney sweep in children's books. The moralist's view as depicted in *London Cries* (Darton, 1820)

Fig. 13 William Carus Wilson (1791–1859)

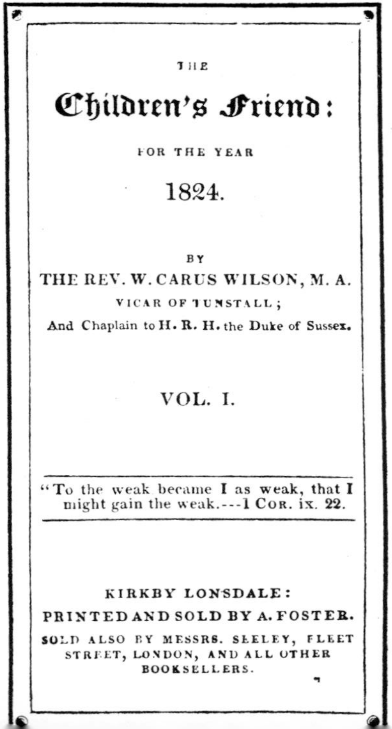

THE

Children's Friend:

FOR THE YEAR

1824.

BY

THE REV. W. CARUS WILSON, M. A.

VICAR OF TUNSTALL;

And Chaplain to H. R. H. the Duke of Sussex.

VOL. I.

"To the weak became I as weak, that I might gain the weak.---1 Cor. ix. 22.

KIRKBY LONSDALE:

PRINTED AND SOLD BY A. FOSTER.

SOLD ALSO BY MESSRS. SEELEY, FLEET STREET, LONDON, AND ALL OTHER BOOKSELLERS.

CHAPTER VII:

POVERTY IN TRACT LITERATURE: PATHOS AND THE POOR LAW

THE 1860's was a stimulating decade of undeniable progress in politics and science. The Reform Bill of 1867 was ushered in with little of the political anxiety evident in 1832; colonies were quietly becoming dominions. Scientific achievement had fulfilled the promise of 1851. The London Underground was opened in 1863; the Atlantic Cable laid in 1865. Darwin's *Origin of Species* continued to trouble religious thought, but the practical message heard by the average mid-Victorian was voiced by Samuel Smiles, who pointed out at the beginning of *Self-Help* (1859) that, since the nation was but the total of individual conditions, civilization could be attained through personal improvement of the individuals comprising the nation. "National progress", he concluded "is the sum of individual industry, energy and uprightness".

This sort of optimism, however, came to be qualified in the 1860's by a growing realization of the other side of the picture. Urgent voices pointed out with statistical proof certain circumstances that no individual effort could possibly improve. However encouraging the national progress, the elevation of the masses had not kept pace. More middle-class people were more prosperous; but the slums belied the optimistic assertion of national achievement. Their challenge to the reformer resulted in tensions both stimulating and depressing, many of which were directly traceable to the Benthamite policies of the New Poor Law.

For the Poor Law of 1834, having in thirty years destroyed much of the traditional concept of charity, had also deepened the rift between rich and poor. Dissociated from voluntary giving in a religious context, charity as organised in 1834 became for the well-to-do an unpleasant matter of rising tax rates and for the poor, in Dr. Arnold's words, "economy by terror".[1] Fear and hatred of the Workhouse and its officials runs like a refrain through much mid-

Victorian writing. Dickens, having taken a half-humorous critical look at the parish workhouse in *Sketches by Boz* in the early 1830's, warmed up to the famous denunciation in *Oliver Twist* (1838–39), and in 1864 represented the effect of the New Poor Law at that date by the pathetic figure of Betty Higden, wandering across the country,

> driven away by her awakened horror of falling into the hands of Charity. It is a remarkable Christian improvement, to have made a pursuing Fury of the Good Samaritan; but it was so in this case, and it is a type of many, many, many. (*Our Mutual Friend*, Book III, Chapter 8.)

He never dropped the matter. His magazines and novels alike kept the condition of the poor before the public eye and protested the inhumanity of the Poor Law.

The voice of Dickens was but one in a chorus of complaint that ranged all the way from the factory inspector's report blaming the Poor Law for the high illegitimacy rate among the nailers of South Staffordshire[2] to the bitter humour of the music halls:

. . .
It is a splendid thing, I'm sure,
(Tho' some it may be fun for,)
That we has Unions, where the poor
Are *taken in* and *done for*!

CHORUS Don't speak ill
Of such a precious, holy, blessed, Poor Law Bill!

By living in the work'us, none
From paupers money axes,
We 'scapes all them wot t'others dun
For rent, and tithes, and taxes;
'Tis true, we're starved to death, by goles!
Which some say sorry fate is,
But then they takes care of our souls,
And sends us to heaven *gratis*[3]

Many workhouses were run with as much efficiency and humanity as the system permitted. But the sudden change in 1834 had allowed no period of adjustment to the new, impersonal regulations. These specified that relief was to be given *inside the workhouse only* (with exceptions for the ill, the very old, and the very young); and that inmates were to be segregated by ages and sex. Thus, as Hesba Stretton pointed out in *The King's Servants* (1873), and *Under the Old Roof* (1882), couples and families were separated: Old Transome and his wife are together for only half an hour on Sundays and half a day once a month. The law specified too that conditions within the institution were to be less comfortable than those outside, thus, in theory, forcing the poor to make every effort to help themselves before applying for parish aid. But as Dr. Arnold protested, "economy" implies some kind of an income—the destitute cannot economize out of nothing. And for those who have an income to demand economy of those who have none, seemed "very like mockery".[4]

As mockery it was construed by many of the hardworking poor who were reduced to parish aid. Their sojourn in the workhouse could mean complete and permanent loss of respectability and of self-respect. Much was written in the periodicals of the 1850's and 1860's of "the pauper taint" which clung to the children raised in the workhouse, or long domiciled there. Since a large Union could accommodate over a thousand children in its great orphanage and school, the concern of the writers is obviously justified. The "taint" (the word comprehended apathy, moral paralysis, corruption, and adverse psychological effects) of such an upbringing became more apparent with every year's output of children. By fourteen they were expected to earn their own livings. But girls, usually put to domestic service, were so inadequately trained that a horrifying proportion of them ended on the streets.[5]

Most tract tale writers of the 1850's and 1860's acknowledge the presence of the Workhouse, but none spoke against it so strongly as Hesba Stretton. A.L.O.E. touched lightly on it in her village tales; Maria Charlesworth and Hesba Stretton showed it from inside as well as outside. Read in the context of their own times and in the light of the bitterness, resentment and fear aroused by the New Poor Law, tract tales which appear trite and sentimental today must have had sharp emotional impact and far greater significance than any modern reader can appreciate.

According to many, the Workhouse was as deeply dreaded as the prison (which, in its austerity, compulsion and harsh discipline, it strongly resembled). In popular periodicals, it was still "the Bastille". Hesba Stretton, by far the best-informed of the tract tale writers, asserted that for children it was worse: a boy under prison sentence might, with luck, be salvaged (as Roger Blackett is in her tale *In Prison and Out*, 1878) by a term on a training ship or in a trade school. But the child raised in the Workhouse because it was abandoned, or had criminal parents, could turn into a Rosie Trevor, who when her mother came to claim her,

> . . . crept in timidly out of the darkness! It was no merry laughing little darling. This thin, long-armed girl of seven, with short clipped hair and dull, pale face! This frightened-looking child had her face half-hidden by an ugly green shade over her eyes, and she crept about carefully like one nearly blind. . . .
>
> (*The Storm of Life*, Chapter III.)[6]

Poor Rosie had contracted the prevalent ophthalmia; dull and apathetic, she does not respond to her mother's affection for a long time. There had been no ill-treatment (there rarely was), merely soul-chilling indifference. Mrs. Walton's picture of the overworked Betsy Ann shows what such children could become later. Appearing as "a girl about fifteen years old, with a miserable, careworn face, and dressed in an untidy torn frock", she tells Rosalie that she was given her name "in the workhouse", adding, "I was born there, and my mother died when I was born, and I've never had a bit of pleasure in all my life; I wish I was dead". (*A Peep Behind the Scenes*, Chapter XIV.)

Maria Charlesworth, however, had shown a child's happier experience of workhouse life; but the workhouses in question were the old-style pre-1834 local variety like that managed by Samuel Bamford's father.[7]

In the tract fiction of the 1860's and 1870's, child characters show an unchildish dread of the workhouse that testifies eloquently to their parents' feelings.

> "You'll be forced to go into the house," said Mrs. Blossom.
>
> "Oh, no, no, no!" cried Little Meg, drawing Robin to her, and with a great effort lifting him on to her lap, where he almost eclipsed her. "I couldn't ever do that. We'll get along somehow till father comes home." (*Little Meg's Children*, 1868, p. 90.)

Little Meg at ten is certainly aware of the disgrace attached to workhouse life, but her terrified reaction is provoked by the thought of separation from Robin. Similarly the street waif, Tony, of *Alone in London* (1869) protests the sending of little Dolly, apparently abandoned, to the workhouse.

"Don't you go to give her up to the p'lice," he says to Old Oliver. "They'd take her to the house, and that's worse than the jail."

The 1848 scandal of the cholera outbreak at the squalid baby-farm at Tooting was long remembered. So were the facts that in the 1840's, workhouse children had been sent in droves to the cotton factories; that many had been apprenticed at the age of five or six to master chimney-sweeps; and that, in 1860, they were still being hired out in the country to agricultural "gang-masters". A dying woman like the mother in Mrs. Sewell's ballad, "Mother's Last Words" (1860), who bids her little boys

> ". . . don't go to the workhouse, dears,
> But try for work, and always pray."

might well feel that they stood a better chance on their own, with the certainty of staying together, than as units on the parish rolls.

The penurious relief accorded to the sick who formed a very large proportion of those drawing out-relief (Gregg suggests 30%) was another grievance against the system in its early days (though we must remember that workhouse infirmaries improved wonderfully within the century, becoming at last the hospitals of the poor).* Treatment varied, some parishes giving good care, others little or none. Hesba Stretton depicts a London parish relieving officer estimating the minimum amount required to maintain in her poor lodgings a woman dying of cancer.

> Four or five shillings a week would cost the parish less than taking the woman and her girl, even if the boy was left to care for himself, into the house, and provide for her the necessaries and comforts the medical officer would certainly pronounce indispensible. He advised a carefully-reckoned dole of four and eight-pence a week. (*In Prison and Out*, 1878, Chapter I.)

The result of this calculated economy is that the money covers only rent and the minimum of food for two. Nothing is allowed for

* Silas Hocking's tract tale, *Ivy*, A Tale of Cottage Life (1881) gives interesting glimpses of the workhouse infirmary and the attitude towards it. The care is adequate to good; the doctor very good; the nurses, untrained, included the dreadful Mrs. Squibbles—a sort of Sairy Gamp—and the angelic Ivy. The book is a plea for improved sanitation in country places, and brings in a cholera epidemic, probably that of the year 1866.

medicine; nothing for the boy, who, arrested for begging, never manages to struggle back into a decent self-supporting life.

Against this depressing picture of the 1870's can be set another of 1898 in which the workhouse infirmary authorities do everything possible to help a woman dying of cancer at home, including medical assistance and "a quite irregular amount of liberality".[8]

A minimum subsistence was given to the aged outside the institution. In Mrs. Walton's tale, *Nobody Loves Me* (1883), the old pauper collects her "weekly allowance of half-a-crown and two loaves of bread" from the workhouse. The dole had gone up by a shilling in the thirty years since a crippled bird-seller told Mayhew that while his old father was alive the parish provided them with one-and-six and a quartern loaf a week. But ". . . after he was buried, they'd allow me nothing; they'd only admit me to the house . . .".[9]

Faced with this degree of poverty, the child of the tract tale whose wages help to keep his sick or widowed mother and his little brothers and sisters off parish relief is not just a sentimental little helper. He is a genuine hero or heroine, holding the Parish Overseer at bay, and keeping the respectability of the family brightly burnished. Little Meg is such a child; Mrs. Sewell's water-cress seller another.

> "Yes, Sir" replied Nelly, "I'm cold, it is true,
> But then I have plenty of work now to do,
> So I never trouble to think of the cold,
> For I am just turned of my eight years old;
> My father is ill in the hospital, Sir,
> My mother's in bed, and too weakly to stir."
> Then lifting her basket she cheerily said—
> "So I am the woman that works for the bread."
>
> ("Our Father's Care". *Ballads for Children*, 1861)

Like Maria Charlesworth, Mrs. Sewell advocated the old system of private and personal charity; Nelly and her family are rescued by a generous customer:

> And he became their comforter,
> He wiped away their tears,
> He softened all their poverty,
> Through many coming years.

It is kindly, humane, scriptural; the feeling heart and the open hand are there. On the surface (perhaps, indeed, in fact), it is charity in the best traditions of the past, an example of the point made by Maria Charlesworth and Mrs. Sherwood that God puts it into the hearts of others to help the needy who pray in faith.

Unfortunately the personal charity that often worked well in the stable society of a rural community where every face was known did not bear its spiritual fruits in the industrial city where it could not be followed up by practical action. Instead of being a manifestation of the oneness of the community in Christ, such giving became very often an occasion on the one hand to get rid of a nuisance or a reproach (Old Nurse Brame's treatment of Patience in *Ministering Children* is an example), and on the other, an opportunity to defraud. Thus there was serious and justified objection to this form of charity in Victorian times. Hesba Stretton was among those who vigorously protested it, giving in *The Lord's Purse Bearers* (1883) a gruesome picture of the exploitation of children by beggars.

Hundreds of impostors preyed on indiscriminate givers of charity. Mayhew's wonderful catalogue in *London Labour and the London Poor* (Vol. IV) reveals them as he found them in the 1850's. Infinitely skilled in the production of ingeniously faked epileptic fits or ulcerated limbs, they took a cynical pride in the pathos of their circumstantially-detailed tales of woe and disaster, in their persuasive begging letters and their artistically-forged certificates to impress gullible givers. Mayhew's concluding advice to charitable readers was to remember that "there is a duty of the head as well as of the heart"; to use their common sense; and above all, not to waste their funds on "beings that will . . . never return a moral profit" on what they receive as charity. Dickens struck a similar note in his warnings against fraud. The greatest charitable benefactor of the age, Angela Burdett-Coutts, enlisted his aid in her tremendous projects, and Dickens' effort on behalf of Ragged Schools, Children's Hospitals, impoverished retired actors, and a host of other causes is at variance with the criticism of organised charities in many of his writings.[10] Like most of his contemporaries, he had difficulty in deciding what to do about charity and how best to do it.

By 1870 a vast number of organised charities existed—hospitals, refuges, almshouses, schools and others whose work overlapped with that carried on under the Poor Law. Their administrators attempted (as Mayhew had recommended) to sort out the poor into the deserving and the undeserving. This was the purpose of "ticketed" charities mentioned by Maria Charlesworth and others.

Most writers for children avoid discussion of the complicated difficulties of organised charity. Instead they show the children of the well-to-do dispensing charity in the time-honoured fashion: visiting Ragged Schools, entertaining village and Sunday School children, giving little gifts or prizes, teaching Sunday classes, or contributing to the upkeep of a hospital cot. A.L.O.E.'s Temple children in *Dora's Mistake*, or The Children's Tabernacle (1871) make their model Tabernacle for the Christmas entertainment of the Ragged School in Chester. The Charity school, training school, or training ship often becomes the happy ending to such a tale of street life as Hesba Stretton's *Pilgrim Street* (1866), or Mrs. Walton's *Christie's Old Organ* (1874). "I should like him to go to school for a year or two," writes Christie's benefactor, "and then I intend, if the boy desires to serve Christ, to bring him up to work as a Scripture-reader among the lowest class of the people in your neighbourhood." (Chapter XII.)

Hesba Stretton gives a balanced and realistic picture of organised charity and its limitations at this time, showing the workhouse as it affected old and young, the refuge with its pitiful inmates. Margery Beade, ill and alone, becomes an almswoman of Bede's Charity, only to be summarily ejected some years later when a new administrator finds a flaw in the circumstances of her admission.* The inadequacy of hospital space is pointed up with less restraint in *Alone in London* (1869) (Fig. 17). At the same time she continued to write stories showing private and personal charity at work: like Dickens she could not abandon one viewpoint or the other, for the dilemma was part of the world they lived in.

Poverty then is one of the great themes of the tract tale in the 1860's even as it had been earlier. But there was a difference: "Christ's Poor" were becoming Society's poor. They supplied tract literature with an enduring excuse for the display of pathos and sentiment as well as with causes to support.

At this date, the offerings of the tract societies had been greatly expanded to include much secular material: books of factual information for school use, volumes of advice (*Enquire Within Upon*

* *Bede's Charity* (1872).

Everything)*, tales of travel, biographies of missionaries, explorers, inventors. There was, however, little change in the subject matter of tract fiction. The demands of Sunday reading still called for Sunday books that were sober in content and spiritually instructive, invariably including a death and a conversion.

Emotion in fiction had been intensively cultivated for three-quarters of a century. The sensibility of the eighteenth-century novel, the religious fervour of the Methodist and Evangelical movements, and the emotional aspects of romanticism combined to create a literary climate in which pathos flourished. Stage sentiment included much pathos; cheap popular fiction utilized pathos to catch and hold a reader's sympathy.[11] Passing into the Victorian novel as a matter of course, it soon filtered down into books for children, into which the tract tales of Mrs. Sherwood and other early Evangelical writers had already introduced much feeling.

There was, however, a difference in the treatment of sentiment by the 1860's. The rational reserve governing the expression of emotion in the novels of Jane Austen or Maria Edgeworth was interpreted by the Victorians from about 1850 as heartlessness or indifference. "People complain that there is an element of matter-of-fact in most of Miss Edgeworth's writing," noted Anne Thackeray Ritchie late in the century. For young readers she favoured "Rosanna" and "Simple Susan", making her choice on obviously sentimental grounds.

> . . . how pretty the scene is where Susan, working in her arbour, hears the sound of her friend Philip's pipe and tabor; the children come across the green with their garlands, leading up Susan's lamb tied up with ribbons, the wicked agent skulks away; innocence and beauty triumph over wrong . . .[12]

Sentimental and pastoral, dashed with melodrama for excitement, virtue rewarded and villainy punished—her selection accords perfectly with the Victorian taste for pathos and sentiment. It had been apparent since the 1850's. "I am glad that you liked *Ruth* properly, and cried over it," wrote Catherine Winkworth to a friend in 1853.[13]

Sensible, humorous and cultured, she typified one large section of the educated reading public. Gladstone found *Nicholas Nickleby*

* One of twenty-five volumes of useful knowledge published by Houlston's in the 1860's.

"most happy in touches of natural pathos"; Kingsley wept over *Heartsease*; and Macaulay over Florence Dombey. Anxious readers implored Dickens to spare Little Nell, Smike, Paul Dombey and others in his long parade of the frail and the doomed. George Du Maurier confided to Lewis Carroll that he had "cried pints" while he illustrated Florence Montgomery's *Misunderstood* (1869).[14]

Like their elders, young Victorians enjoyed a good cry, nor did writers deny them opportunity. Mrs. Ewing, for instance, well aware of the value of restraint, could still write *The Story of a Short Life* (1885). Writers of tract fiction, secure in their religious purpose which had been strengthened by the demand for elevating and instructive books, had the full approval of most of the reading public when they produced reams of overflowing sentiment and pathos. The reception accorded several famous trans-Atlantic works also encouraged them. Of *Uncle Tom's Cabin* (1852), Susan Ferrier, then an old woman wrote "I was never so stirred by any book, and I'm glad to hear the whole world is the same". Although in her youth she had admired *Coelebs* and scoffed at sentimental tales, by 1851 she was praising *The Wide Wide World* (1850) for "beautiful passages and . . . sweet genuine piety".[15]

Succeeding generations of nineteenth-century tract fiction writers who looked back upon their predecessors saw an unbroken line of successful children's stories, beginning with *The History of Margaret Whyte*, *Little Henry*, and *The Dairyman's Daughter*, in which elements of religious tract, moral tale and sentimental novel were so blended as to arouse the immediate sympathy of the reader. Today as one surveys the development of pathos in the late Victorian tract tale, it is impossible to escape the conclusion that the course for its writers after 1850 was really laid out by Dickens. How much of the art of the pathetic *he* had learned from the early tract fiction writers seems not to have been discovered.

With a sure touch, Dickens exposed and intensified the emotional content of ordinary situations, and dramatized the pathos inherent in the everyday life of the poor, the aged, the neglected and unloved. His inexhaustible talent for inventing characters who are at once individual and universal enabled him to create a lifelike world of fiction. And since he wrote to hasten social reform and had an enormous reading public, he became a model for the aspiring writer with social purpose. He trained the reading taste of his day to expect certain pathetic characters in universally appealing situations—neglected or abused orphans, homeless people, the crippled and the helpless—and continued for many years to supply such characters and feed the taste he had helped to form. Dramatically presented, Dickens' pathetic characters appeared with an infinite number of subtle variations that prevented his art from wearing thin.

The simplified conventions of sentiment used earlier by Mrs. Cameron, Mrs. Sherwood or Legh Richmond soon merged with the more exciting formulae of Dickens. The faceless child of the Juvenile Obituary had, with these three writers, already become an individual Margaret Whyte or Little Henry; but with the arrival of Little Nell and Oliver Twist on the literary scene, the whole pattern of pathos surrounding the figures of children was enlarged. Dickens set his pathetic childish figures against the contemporary background of industrial cities. Little Henry was still ideal for missionary purposes; Margaret Whyte, confined to her village, remained strictly subject to the domestic laws governing the child; but Little Nell moved freely from place to place between the familiar and the unfamiliar, a perfect blend of the blameless child of the tract tales with the Little Heroine of the traditional Tale. Her appearance coincided with the depressing revelations of Parliamentary Committees about working children. A feeling of collective guilt may have contributed to the intensity of emotion aroused by Dickens' pathetic child characters.

One of the great conventions of the pathetic mode was thus strengthened by Dickens' use of it: the isolated child figure with an instant and compelling appeal to the reader's sympathy. Often this child was accompanied by a contrasting auxiliary figure pathetic in its own right. Mrs. Sherwood's Little Henry with "delicate complexion, light hair and blue eyes" is a striking contrast to the swarthy native bearer, Boosy. In 1840, Dickens displayed Little Nell and her grandfather, that irresistible combination of youth and age, physical frailty, moral strength and weakness, putting them at the centre of a sensational tale. The effect produced by these two was not lost on the tract fiction writers, who later took note of the reception accorded Silas Marner and Eppie in 1861. Thus Maria Charlesworth in 1854 gave young readers Little Ruth and her sick friend; Herbert Clifford and Old Willie; and in *Sequel to Ministering Children*, Little Sue and her blind father.

In the next decade, Hesba Stretton used the device with some originality and depth. Although Old Oliver and Dolly (*Alone in London*) exemplify only the conventional pathetic appeal, a number of her other "pairs" point up a universal problem as well. Daniel, who represents money as an obstacle to faith, is as important to the religious lesson of *Jessica's First Prayer* as Jessica herself. When Cassy and Simon are together, *Cassy*, a tale of overt social purpose, is given new dimensions of faith and doubt.

Mrs. Walton who began to write in the 1870's, adopted the device, with Christie and Old Treffy, Little Dot and Solomon the gravedigger. But it was by then somewhat overworked, and the pathos at times looked contrived.

Ironically, as pathos in tract fiction increased in intensity and quantity, religion lost ground. The religious teaching of the early tract or the Juvenile Obituary never lost sight of the importance of repentance, salvation, and resurrection. But after 1850 it was all sentimentalized into a sort of worship of the dying child and a frank indulgence in grief. Mrs. Cameron could control the emotion and show Margaret Whyte as a shining example of religious faith. Dickens so presented Little Nell that she became *in herself* the object of sentimental devotion (as does Miss Charlesworth's Mary Clifford).

> When death strikes down the innocent and young, for every fragile form from which he lets the panting spirit free, a hundred virtues rise, in shapes of mercy, charity and love, to walk the world and bless it! (*Old Curiosity Shop*, Chapter LXII.)

Mrs. Sherwood, Mrs. Cameron and Legh Richmond had intended only to dignify their dying heroes or heroines and to point up the aura of sanctity which surrounds a Christian death, but they had, nevertheless, gone far towards establishing a theatrical atmosphere around the deathbed by setting Little Henry, Margaret Whyte and Little Jane before the reader, by showing them surrounded by family and friends, and then inviting emotional participation in the scene that followed.

Early tracts kept the deathbed scene to spotlight the idea of life eternal:

> See the guardian angels nigh
> Wait to waft my soul on high!
> See the golden gates displayed!
> See the crown to grace my head! (Philip Dodderidge, 1702–1751)

Death was a joyful occasion for the Christian: a reflection to limit the grief of the survivors and to restrain the expression of sentiment.

Victorian writers on the other hand laid stress on the emotions of the living, thus breaking down the religious discipline and hindering concentration upon life hereafter. Little Nell's death and funeral, drawn out to great length, were never surpassed as sentimentality by later writers, though thought to be equalled by the death of Little Eva in *Uncle Tom's Cabin*. Both scenes were successfully staged, and often imitated. It is not surprising that within two generations, many pathetic passages in tract fiction sounded very much alike. A young reader who had wept over Little Nell's funeral,

> Decrepit age, and vigorous life, and blooming youth, and helpless infancy, poured forth—on crutches, in the pride of strength and health, in the full blush of promise, in the mere dawn of life—to gather round her tomb. Old men were there whose eyes were dim and senses failing—grandmothers who might have died ten years ago, and still been old—the deaf, the blind, the lame, the palsied, the living dead of many shapes and forms, to see the closing of that early grave. . . . (*The Old Curiosity Shop*, Chapter LXXII.)

would certainly feel that Miss Charlesworth's account of Mary Clifford's funeral was covering familiar territory.

> The day of the funeral came, and the whole village gathered to the grave—there came the old and feeble, whom her hands had clothed and fed, her lips had taught and comforted: there came the dark transgressor, whose chains of sin had melted under her fervent utterance of Heavenly truth and love; there came the strong-built labourer, whose dull mind had gathered light under her teaching . . .; there came the village children. . . .—all came to see the form they had loved laid to its rest. . . . (*Ministering Children*, Chapter XV.)

Mrs. Walton transposes Dickens to an exceedingly minor key in her tale, *Little Dot* (1873). Like Little Nell, Little Dot spends her time around the graveyard and holds long conversations with the gravedigger. Little Nell makes the churchyard her garden; Little Dot picks daisies for the graves. Those who read Hesba Stretton's *Lost Gip* (1873) might have been interested to see that she gave the graveyard setting a new twist: it was all demolished to make room for the railway, and the melancholy gravedigger emigrated to Canada and became a pioneer.

Dickens also used the industrial city as a background to pathos. Oliver Twist in Fagin's school; Nell's flight from the city; the night spent on the ash-heap of the furnaces, stay in the reader's mind; the helplessness of children in these grim situations strengthens the emotional impact. Hesba Stretton, who had written for Dickens, utilized this sort of background very effectively in *Pilgrim Street*, *Little Meg's Children*, *Cassy*, and others. Mrs. Walton's pathos was at its best in *A Peep Behind the Scenes*, partly because of the garish fairground and theatre setting. The poetess of tract literature, Mrs. Mary Sewell,[16] was very careful to give her pathetic slum waifs a background that immediately aroused the reader's sympathy:

> . . .
> The heavy, stagnant stifling fog,
> Crept here, and there, and everywhere.
>
> Down seven steep and broken stairs,
> Its chill, unwelcome way it found,
> And darkened with a deeper gloom,
> A low, damp chamber underground.
>
> A glimmering light was burning there,
> Beside a woman on a bed;
> A worn-out woman, ghastly pale,
> Departing to the peaceful dead.
>
> Two little boys in threadbare clothes,
> Stood white and trembling by her side. . . .
>
> ("Mother's Last Words", 1860)

Other and older devices much in use on the stage were adopted by the tract fiction writers of the 1850's and later. Their pathetic figures impress by contrast: sharply outlined against dark and evil backgrounds are the very young, the very old, the very weak. All are innocent (and in the tales of the 1880's and 1890's, many are beautiful). Ahead of them lies the plot of the story, its journeys and episodes recalling those of the traditional fairy tale. Orphans, widows, dispossessed heirs are as common as in melodrama; parents and relatives believed dead reappear to save the situation. A clear link with Biblical themes is apparent: unjust stewards (i.e. grasping landlords, wicked guardians, malicious superiors) are eventually found out and punished; faithful servants are rewarded; prodigals repent; and the lost (or stolen) are found. Readers were rarely confused by the unexpected.

Style and language also played their part in trapping the reader's sympathy and bringing tears to the eye. Hesba Stretton's restraint and Mrs. Walton's hypnotic repetition of evocative simple words were equally effective in arousing "the gentle tears that flowed when these books were read".[17] But the two women directed their pathos to different ends. Mrs. Walton was always primarily concerned with the spiritual salvation of the reader; Hesba Stretton wished to arouse him to action against prevailing social injustices and evils.

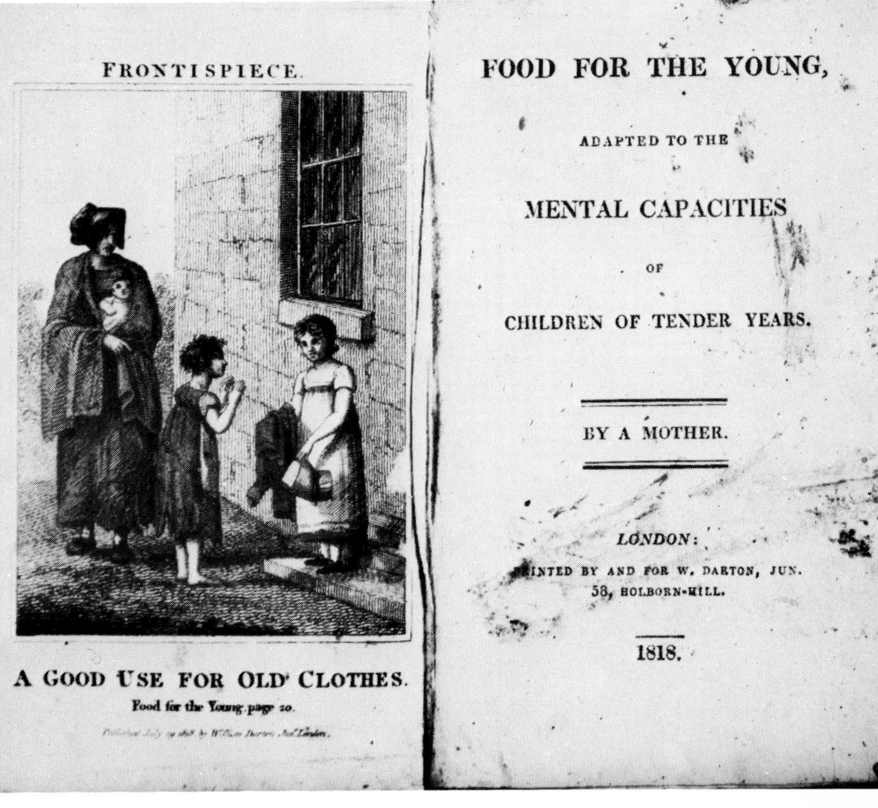

FRONTISPIECE.

A GOOD USE FOR OLD CLOTHES.

Food for the Young page 20.

FOOD FOR THE YOUNG,

ADAPTED TO THE

MENTAL CAPACITIES

OF

CHILDREN OF TENDER YEARS.

BY A MOTHER.

LONDON:

PRINTED BY AND FOR W. DARTON, JUN.

58, HOLBORN-HILL.

1818.

ig. 14 A moral tale inculcating, among other virtues, that of charity. Unlike similar charitable orts in *Ministering Children*, no effort or sacrifice is demanded of the child: these are *old* clothes.

Fig. 15 Charlotte Tucker, "A Lady of England"

Fig. 16 Plate from an 1870's edition of Charlotte Tucker's *The Rambles of a Rat* which was first published in 1857. The street child watches the rats lead their blind companion to the food

Fig. 17 Illustration by A. W. Bayes for Hesba Stretton's *Alone in London* (*c*. 1880)

Fig. 18 Illustration by John Gilbert from Richard Newton's *The Giants and How to Fight Them* (*c*, 1863)

Fig. 19 Hesba Stretton (Sarah Smith) in her sixties

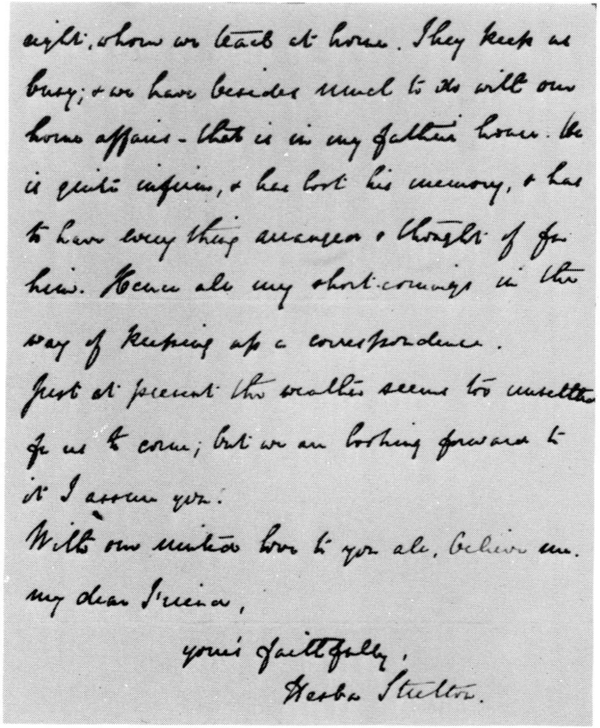

eight; whom we teach at home. They keep us
busy; & we have besides much to do with our
home affairs - that is in my father's house. He
is quite infirm, & has lost his memory, & has
to have every thing arranged & thought of for
him. Hence all my short-comings in the
way of keeping up a correspondence.
Just at present the weather seems too unsettled
for us to come; but we are looking forward to
it I assure you.
With our united love to you all, believe me
my dear friend,

yours faithfully,
Hesba Stretton.

Fig. 20 Facsimile of letter quoted on p. 129

Fig. 21 The rescue worker seeks out the young street-walker. From Hesba Stretton's *The King's Servants*

Fig. 22 Illustration by A. W. Bayes for Hesba Stretton's *Pilgrim Street* (*c.* 1870)

Fig. 23 Illustration by A. W. Bayes for Hesba Stretton's *Jessica's First Prayer* (1867)

Fig. 24 Illustration from Mrs. Walton's *Little Faith*, an edition of 1905

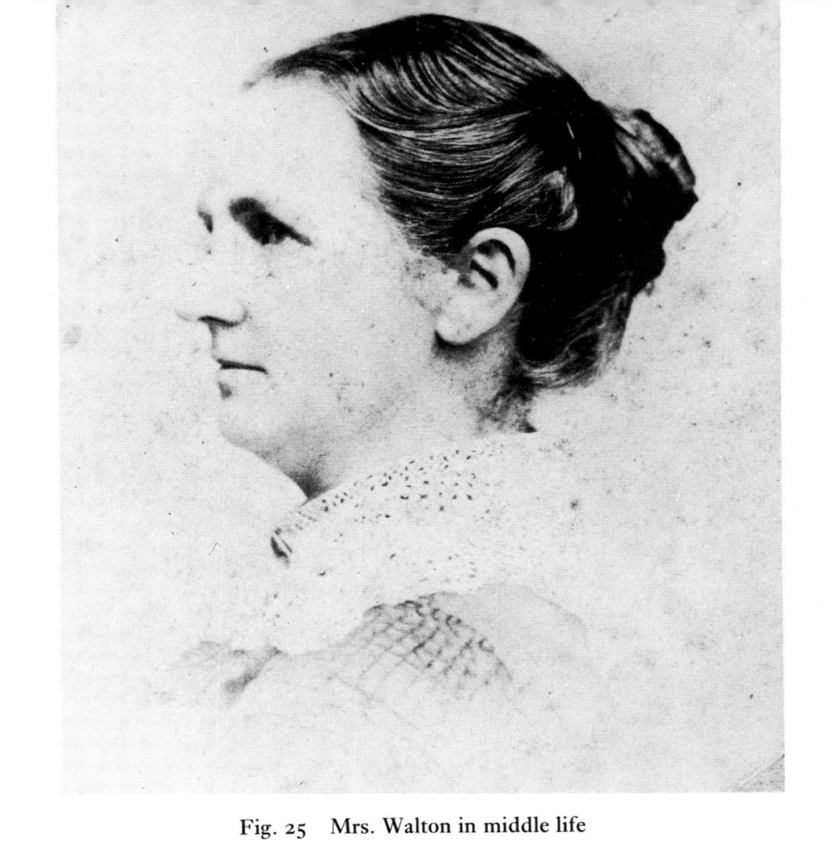

Fig. 25 Mrs. Walton in middle life

1878-9.

SERVICES OF SONG FOR SUNDAY SCHOOLS.

"CHRISTIE'S OLD ORGAN."

(BY SPECIAL PERMISSION).

A musically Illustrated Service, Compiled by TALBOT ERLE.

Published in both Notations, 4d.

"NOTHING TO NOBODY."

BY BRENDA. (By special permission of Messrs. SHAW & Co.)

Compiled as an Illustrated Service by ALFRED WELLS AND C. H. PURDAY.

Price Fourpence.

"JESSICA'S FIRST PRAYER,"

(BY SPECIAL PERMISSION),

With Musical Illustrations, COMPILED BY H. C. FREEMAN, and C. H. PURDAY.

Price Fourpence, in both Notations.

"THE SPRING MORNING;"

An Allegory from "Agathos" and other Sunday Stories,

BY THE LATE BISHOP WILBERFORCE,

Condensed and Interspersed with SACRED SONG, by A. AND D. HONE.

Price Fourpence; Published in both Notations.

"THE MUSICAL ROBINSON CRUSOE,"

(Suitable for Week Evening Entertainments),

Illustrated with Original Songs, adapted to well-known Melodies,

BY TALBOT ERLE.

Price Fourpence. Published also in Tonic Sol-fa Notation.

"JONAH,"

A MUSICALLY ILLUSTRATED SERVICE.

BY TALBOT ERLE.

Price Fourpence.

"EVA,"

A Musically Illustrated Service, compiled and arranged from

"UNCLE TOM'S CABIN,"

BY JAMES TIPTON.

Price Fourpence, also in Tonic-Sol-fa Notation, Fourpence.

"CREATION,"

BY REV. J. WILKINS.

Price Fourpence.

"CROSS & CROWN,"

BY GEORGE S. WEEKS.

Price Fourpence.

"SONGS ABOUT THE SAVIOUR:"

A Collection of Sacred Melodies for Evangelistic Services.

COMPILED AND PARTLY COMPOSED BY WALTER J. MAYERS.

The Collection contains Twenty-two Pieces of New Music. Price Fourpence.

"SONGS OF THE SEA:"

ILLUSTRATIVE OF INCIDENTS IN THE CHRISTIAN LIFE.

Being the Words and Music of an Evening of Sacred Song.

GIVEN BY WALTER J. MAYERS.

Price Fourpence,

For grants of 100 or more at Half Price, apply to

WEEKES & CO., 16, Hanover Street, Regent Street, London.

[*Specimen Copies Post Free for Fourpence each.*]

Fig. 26 An advertisement for Services of Song . . . 1878

Chapter VIII

"HESBA STRETTON": HER LIFE AND LEGEND

Of all Mrs. Sherwood's followers in the writing of Evangelical tract fiction, Sarah Smith (Hesba Stretton to her large reading public), in some ways the least Evangelical, was the most successful. Her sales reached astronomical levels, her works, widely translated, were part of Sunday School libraries all over the world.[1] She wrote with literary skill: her narrative moved quickly; her style at its best was plain and dignified. Contemporaries admired her deft touch with sentiment; the modern reader, impatient with pathos, must admit her sincerity and lack of condescension. Lord Shaftesbury thought *Jessica's First Prayer* an incomparable picture of slum life, and Herbert Read has paid tribute to the poignancy of *Little Meg's Children*, a tale in Hesba Stretton's best style—clear, bare, illuminated by telling detail and a few vivid contrasts.

Before the end of her life, a sentimental legend grew up about her, which she did nothing to dispel. It may even have amused her (as in 1867, did the compliment from her French dentist who "hoped I should have a place next to Lord Byron in the next world!"). Rarely seen save at meetings of the National Society for the Prevention of Cruelty to Children, she travelled a great deal after 1870, favouring Italy and Switzerland. For the last eighteen years of her life she lived quietly with her lifelong companion, her sister Elizabeth,* on the outskirts of London. From Ivy Croft on Ham Common, she emerged on Sundays, and according to a former neighbour, ". . . Dressed in dolman cloak and small bonnet, she used to attend our church, St. Andrew's, but never stayed for the sermon". A street in the vicinity is named after her.[2]

Her inaccessibility contributed to the legend. A reporter who interviewed her in 1892 described her as having "a grave sweet face, large grey eyes and silvering curls", and wearing a picturesque

* Elizabeth also adopted the name of Stretton, as did their nephews, Gilbert and Philip Smith.

foreign-looking cap. She spoke gently and firmly, answered questions straightforwardly, and discouraged the reporter from venturing upon a character sketch on the sensible grounds that they did not know each other. Undeterred, the interviewer produced a gushing description of "so truly good and strong and womanly a woman, who, notwithstanding a world-wide reputation of over thirty years as one of the most talented and most helpful writers of the time has remained so perfectly natural and sincere". The article also gave a rather garbled account of Hesba Stretton's life and background. In spite of its errors, the Strettons did not attempt to set the record straight: privacy was almost a mania with them.[3]

The legend was firmly established by the Memoir published by the Religious Tract Society in *Sunday at Home* (1911). Appended to it is the "Personal Note" by a niece.[4] Presumably accurate as far as it goes, it suffers from the general insipidity of so much Victorian biography contributed by the subject's own family, a notable example (oddly linked to the life of Hesba Stretton) being the biography of Mrs. Henry Wood by her son, Charles W. Wood.

On the evidence of her own *Log Books* (her journal from 1859 to 1871–72), the notes by her grand-nephew, and a number of her own tales and novels, the legend is incomplete and often inaccurate. A much more complex and interesting woman—tough-minded, determined, at once sardonic and sentimental—emerges from the laconic entries in these half-dozen little notebooks begun after the sale of her first story to Dickens. In twelve years she became the chief writer of tract fiction for the Religious Tract Society. She had hoped however, to be the female Dickens, a second Mrs. Gaskell, or even a rival to Mrs. Henry Wood (as, indeed she was, but not as a writer). But her experience was limited, and her judgment, unerring when it came to factual articles or tract fiction for the young and the unsophisticated, failed in the matter of two- or three-volume novels with upper-class characters. She insisted on writing Christian melodrama. Arguments among the congregations of small dissenting chapels, the speech and actions of unlovable eccentrics like David Lloyd, or Miss Waldron of *Hester Morley's Promise* (1873)—sister under the skin to Lady Catherine de Brough or Mrs. Proudie—these she represented with skill. Unfortunately her passion for extremely involved plots and for melodrama, as well as her determination to write at times from a masculine viewpoint* obscured a real talent. Few of her longer works are better than fourth-rate.

Practical and romantic, penny-pinching and generous, hard-headed and soft-hearted, Hesba Stretton was as good an example of Victorian stubbornness, inconsistency and idealism as the old Queen herself. This comparison would have annoyed her. "You know I am thoroughly a Radical, even a Republican; and I am quite sorry that Cromwell's scheme of a United States of Europe had not been founded by him," she wrote around 1886.[5]

The legend has nothing to say about this. It does not show her (at age 28) sleeping with a "dreamer" under her head† doing the night-work of the Post Office with efficiency and speed, quarrelling periodically with her brother-in-law, or keeping far too sharp an eye upon the outgoing letters of young men who visited the Smith family. Nor does it breathe a hint that in 1861 she was reported to Head Office in London for "insolence to a man at the Post Office window". Was she insolent? Very likely: she was certainly critical, short-tempered, volatile, often unreasonable, a woman who "demanded *much* more from frail humans than one can possibly get".[6]

The legend announces that the Misses Hesba and Elizabeth Stretton were universally beloved, "spreading around them much that is good, in the best sense of the word"; founding "a branch of the Popular Book Club at Ham, with the object of circulating among the working classes good books, and of awakening new interests in the minds of those whose lives are otherwise not over bright".[7]

This was undoubtedly truer of the elderly, independent and well-to-do Misses Stretton in 1894 than of the Misses Sarah and Elizabeth Smith around 1860. Caged behind the Post Office wicket in New Street, Wellington, watching the relentless approach of middle age (Sarah was twenty-eight, Lizzie thirty, in 1860), they were notably irritable, impatient, bored and censorious. And, it must be admitted, not without reason. They were intelligent, reasonably well-educated, good-looking, with dark curly hair, fine grey eyes, and the lovely complexions of the rain-washed Shropshire countryside. And, like so many women of their generation,

* As in *The Doctor's Dilemma*.

† "Dreamer": fortune-telling device unlikely to be approved in her strict Methodist circle. (She eventually dreamed of two babies.)

they were fettered by family duty. Without the work of his three daughters in the Post Office, Benjamin Smith could not have remained in charge of this increasingly important central office.

He had come to Wellington from Horsehay in the industrial district of Shropshire in 1808 to apprentice with the firm of F. Houlston & Son, then in the third year of a long and successful publishing life.[8] He must have helped to print the first editions of the tales of Mrs. Cameron and Mrs. Sherwood and the other Evangelical writers who were at the time rapidly changing the whole concept of education and literature for the young. His apprenticeship doubtless gave his daughter the details for *Enoch Roden's Training*, for which the Religious Tract Society paid her thirty-five guineas in 1864.

Benjamin Smith prospered during those years when the demand for the printed word was outstripping production, for he became in succession printer, Master Printer, bookseller, and in the 1840's, first Postmaster of Wellington. His wife, Anne Bakewell, was a strict Methodist; their family was raised in habits of austerity, sobriety and strict economy. In 1862 Sarah recorded with amusement that her father had "rebuked Hannah for levity", Hannah, the oldest child, housekeeper since her mother's death in 1842, being then about forty.

Of eight children born, four daughters and a son survived.* The younger Benjamin emigrated to Canada about 1851, married there in 1860, and settled near Brantford, Ontario, moving to Kansas about 1887. In keeping with Methodist practice, Benjamin Smith, a pillar of the chapel and a noted lay preacher, had given his daughters the best education available. Annie, the youngest, was married to a local artist† and out of the home circle by the time Sarah began writing in earnest, but she remained an object of the tenderest solicitude to the family, and they adored her children. Indeed the appearance of nephews and nieces in any of their Aunt Sarah's books (e.g. *The Children of Cloverley*) is the signal for an uninhibited gush of sentiment.

The second and third daughters, the inseparable Lizzie and Sarah, went to school at the Old Hall (in the 1840's a school for

* The initial letters of their names in order of age gave her HESBA; she added STRETTON from the local valley and village of that name.

† "Artie" was the landscape artist, John Halphead Smith, son of John Home Smith of Worcester. Both men painted for Coalport as well.

girls) near Shrewsbury. Both qualified as governesses. Sarah's teaching seems to have been restricted to Sunday School; but Lizzie, with a wage of £70 in 1867, was apparently very well paid.

Sarah wrote a beautiful clear hand and was extremely fluent—the result of unlimited browsing in the bookshop in the 1840's and 1850's. Reading matter was unrestricted in this family.[9] She was also businesslike and industrious, qualities inculcated by her background, essential in the work of the Post Office, and displayed throughout her career as a writer. The Post Office was part of their house at 14 New Street,[10] a big building which had probably once housed the print shop, bindery and bookstore (given up before 1859). The actual workings of this big post office are described in the article Sarah wrote for Dickens in 1863.[11] It also forms the background for several short stories, the print shop and bindery likewise appearing in her works.[12]

As strict Methodists and daughters of a tradesman, the Smith sisters were not considered part of county society: the snobbishness by which the rising social class of wealthy industrialists protected itself was very strong about 1860. In her light fiction, Sarah had a good deal to say about similar situations. Past snubs evidently rankled.[13] Judging by the *Log Books*, her appearances in Wellington society were few and strained.

> . . . Mrs. Baddely invited two of the family to a quiet party of country people to the infinite dismay of the crew.* Mrs. Williams says it is to be quite a ball.
>
> Lizzie and Sara† went to a regular Wellington party where they were regarded as natural curiosities in the animal kingdom; Chas. Lewis, John Shaney & Teddy Webb attentive. Solemn dancing with intervals of stupidity was the entertainment of the evening. Acted the word *plaintiff*, and won the admiration of all the men & spleen of the women, one of whom spoke of "cheek" & not making oneself conspicuous. Came home at 12:30.
>
> Decided dissipated sensations. . . .
>
> (*Log Book*, Dec. 18, 19, 20, 1860.)

It was never easy to entertain the unsociable, censorious, and easily-bored Sarah, who disapproved of most modes of amusement and was especially intolerant of those inaugurated by women.

* The crew: her term for the whole female household at the Post Office.

† Sara: She spells her name thus in the *Log Books*, writing always in the third person.

> . . . Sara enduring agonies from Miss Price's amiability.
> N.B. It ought to be felony to invite guests without being able to entertain them. (*Log Book*, Aug. 1, 1860.)

She loathed small talk and teas and female gatherings, complaining of "wooden women" or "stiff ladies" who attended the annual Dorcas Society meeting at their home. That the stiffness of their neighbours might have been uneasiness engendered by her own picture of a Dorcas meeting in her story "The Lucky Leg" does not seem to have occurred to her. Her own tastes varied from the simple and countrified to the downright intellectual: there was little in between. She loved a picnic in the company of children; a concert (since she lacked appreciation of music, a Ragged School Band draws her highest praise, and she liked recitations and comic turns if not not vulgar); a lecture, especially if the lecturer would answer questions from the audience. She thoroughly enjoyed a good sermon and a conversation with an intelligent man. And one of her chief pleasures seems to have been a few hours watching a court in session, for she was deeply interested in the workings of the law. In fact, her idea of entertaining guests was to take them along to the Assize Court in Manchester for a morning.

Wellington offered very little to keep her amused. Women were all too plentiful, but friends were few. Sarah Smith, unlike her *alter ego*, Hesba Stretton, had a low opinion of women, as indeed, of most adults.

Brief entries in the *Log Books* 1860–63 suggest that at intervals both Sarah and Lizzie made some effort to capture an eligible young man. Lizzie had hopes of C.W.P.,* son of a local ironmaster, "a very remarkable young man, too wary", but it came to nothing. The legend is properly silent upon Sarah's flirtation with his brother, Horace (some years her junior), whose father "objected to him seeing Sara"; with the Chapel Visitor (much her senior, and as she later discovered, unhappily married); and with the glib young Irishman who came to supervise the take-over of the Post Office when Benjamin Smith retired. He was excellent company, but within a month or two was found to be walking out with the barmaid at the spirit vaults of the local pub.

It was just as well that neither Lizzie nor Sarah ever married. Touchy, jealous, possessive, they were far from domestic. The *Log*

* Perhaps C. W. Pearce of Madeley.

Book is tart about Hannah's passion for house cleaning before Dorcas meetings; mocking about someone's description of "a marriageable young lady; one who would lay her head on a young man's lap, look up in his face, say 'dearest' & quote a text of scripture". Under no circumstances could Sarah and Lizzie ever have done such a thing. In spite of their flirtations, a profound distrust of men (save the old and the very young) permeated the whole household. Hannah defined marriage as "committing an imprudence"; Lizzie wrote pages describing a cousin's wedding without once mentioning the groom; and Sarah's wish "for a young man available on high days and holidays to make her feel more like other people" stopped right there. Critical and competitive, she never achieved more than a briefly happy relationship with a man during these twelve years. Her bent towards romance (obviously formed by novel reading and especially by *Jane Eyre*) found its outlet in her romantic tales and novels. These are full of melodramatic situations and misguided heroes who are invariably salvaged by devoted women. Her favourite word for the human male—father, editor or admirer—was *curious*; and a moment of acute irritation with editors in London brought to the surface the scathing generalization "Truly all men are cheats, especially publishers".

The shadow of Benjamin Smith the younger hangs heavy over his sister's writing. *Log Book* entries about his Canadian wife and his marriage in America are revealing; the bride's portrait "gave great dissatisfaction"; news of the wedding is indicated by "heard that the dreadful day is over for Ben". Many of her books depict that intense and possessive brother-and-sister relationship fostered within the close-knit Victorian family, and the relationship of lovers is often shown as the extension of an earlier close boy-and-girl friendship. Women in her early stories lecture their lovers in dictatorial elder-sister fashion, a domesticated blend of evangelical sermon and melodramatic oratory. Undoubtedly her first novel, *The Clives of Burcot* (1867) foundered upon the character of its heroine as much as upon its hopelessly complicated plot. In real life as in her writing, Sarah thought the boyish younger man charming.

Considering that within six years "Hesba Stretton" would overtake Mrs. Sherwood as chief supplier of Evangelical Sunday reading for children, Sarah Smith of Wellington took an incongruously disillusioned view of current evangelicalism. "The state of religion in Wellington is awful" she confided to the *Log Book* in 1860; it never, apparently, improved. The great revival movement of 1860–62 offended her strong sense of decorum.

> Revival meeting at the Town Hall, very powerful smells from a dense crowd and only one window open; obliged to go before the conclusion. Can not understand the secret of these meetings. (*Log Book*, Oct. 1, 1861.)

Her acid pen touches on various evangelists: "very burly, brawny and animal looking", "very coarse in thought, ranting, roaring, stentorian . . .". Assembled crowds fare no better.

> . . . a large congregation. Henry stormed and ranted and bawled. The Ministers in disgust and despair that such a man should attract crowds while they preach to empty benches. The masses understand and love coarseness. (*Log Book*, Oct. 28, 1861.)

She was excessively annoyed at the end of the year when her article upon the revival (presumably more favourably worded than *Log Book* entries), which had been requested by a religious magazine, was printed without payment. And the last straw may well have been the meeting at the Town Hall on Jan. 31, 1862, where Lizzie, the family representative that evening, "heard three sisters prayed for, supposed to be ourselves".

She remained nonetheless a Dissenter at heart. Lacking an ear for music, she disapproved of ritual and liturgy; for her, the church service was the sermon, its argument, its delivery. An inveterate sermon-taster (her own term), she found in the twelve years of the *Log Books* only three preachers who measured up to her ideal: the noted Scottish Baptist, Alexander McLaren;* the Congregationalist, George Macdonald; and an unidentified Mr. A. of Islington. The Unitarian Mr. Gaskell, husband of the novelist, she rated very good. Her strong prejudice against the Church of England and its adherents appears in 1861–62 entries about a newly-founded night school for poor children, a joint Church-Chapel venture in which Sarah and Lizzie had volunteered to teach.

> . . . (W)ent for the first time to the girls' school, were entirely put down by the two teachers, who were evidently appointed as spies;

* She always spells his name thus, though it appears elsewhere "Maclaren". He used both spellings himself.

> consider time wasted as they can do no real good. Not a single effort to give the poor children any notion of religion, & the reading & writing failure. (*Log Book*, Nov. 28, 1861.)

This educational venture, apparently entered upon in a thoroughly belligerent spirit on both sides, went from bad to worse.

> . . . All went to the night schools; only 40 children and four spies; rather unpleasant. (*Log Book*, Dec. 26, 1861.)

There was trouble on Jan. 4, and a meeting on Jan. 7: "unmitigated stupidity, neither fun nor profit. Mrs. I. K. Jones, aged 50 and plain, objected to being out at night". By February, the night schools cease to appear in the *Log Book*. If the degree of co-operation in Wellington was representative of that throughout the country, it is easy to see why a national system of education in Britain was so long delayed.

In later years, Sarah Smith was less censorious. She had seen for herself the Church of England mission work in the slums, and her anti-Catholic prejudice moderated somewhat after she had lived abroad.

The whole tone of her novels suggests that her religious convictions centred around rebellion against authority. Thus she favoured the extremes of Protestantism: Moravian, Primitive Methodist, Quaker or Baptist tenets were about equally appealing to her, and all are at some time favourably presented in her writings. Her children's tales for the Religious Tract Society emphasized the Evangelical fundamentals of repentance and faith, Bible reading and prayer. More and more in the tales after 1870, the individual is seen reaching his belief through these, the organised churches and their representatives often being eliminated completely.

In 1863, Benjamin Smith having finally retired from the Wellington Post Office, Sarah and Lizzie moved to Manchester. Lizzie had a position as governess; Sarah, by then a regular contributor to *All the Year Round*, had already sold articles to *Chambers's Journal*; stories to *Temple Bar* and *The Welcome Guest*; and *Fern's Hollow* to the R.T.S. She was well paid, averaging eight or ten guineas for a story or article, thirty or more for her children's books.[14]

The sisters settled into lodgings, moving frequently. The *Log Book* is eloquent on this subject, typical Manchester entries indicating that they were difficult lodgers and also that their bitter complaints were abundantly justified.

> Moved into new abode on the 26th . . . 21 packages in the cab besides things brought over by hand . . .

And two sets of lodgings later:

> Gave Mrs. Duckworth notice as we have been devoured by bugs . . .
> . . . new rooms . . . large handsome rooms.
> Sarah was bitten twice by bugs. . . . Resolved . . . never to tell any lodging house people that they have bugs in their houses. . . .
> (*Log Book*, Sept. 1864; Aug. 21, 1865; Sept. 1 & Sept. 10, 1865.)

Lodgings apart, they were happy in Manchester, enjoying their freedom to the full. They joined the congregation of Union Chapel, listened approvingly to Dr. Alexander McLaren, and in their second year, became friendly with him and his wife.[15] For a few months in 1866, Sarah was governess to his children. She taught a Bible class, and deplored the fact that some of the Sunday scholars were "found *dancing* in one of the class rooms" and others got drunk on the Sunday School excursion. True to her upbringing, she was a strong Temperance supporter, writing later on its behalf *Nellie's Dark Days* (1870), and *Brought Home* (1875), both of which were published by the Scottish Temperance League. And she exercised to the full her opportunities to attend lectures or watch the workings of the law courts during the Assizes, using her knowledge of the latter in her Manchester story, *Pilgrim Street* (1867).

The three years in Manchester established the religious viewpoint of Hesba Stretton's tales for the young. Like many clever women of the time, she rebelled against the limitations of her upbringing, and her sympathy with rigid Evangelicalism had been stretched to the breaking point before she left Wellington. She welcomed the opportunity to join the mixed congregation of Union Chapel, which included Presbyterians, Methodists, Congregationalists and Baptists. Here the Rev. Alexander McLaren (1826–1910) conducted a plain and lucid service, preaching largely extempore his famous expository sermons, models of clarity and simplicity. He was not concerned with doctrinal argument or the New Criticism, stressing instead the qualities of Christian life, the divine grace, and the needs and duties of the individual. "God's truth is not too great to rule the smallest duties," he pointed out. "The true field for religion is the field of common life."[16] His sermon on "The Christian Attitude to Social Sins" may have guided or encouraged Hesba Stretton's choice of subjects for her R.T.S. tales and strengthened her determination to write for social reform. The Christian does not live in a vacuum, he warns, "and therefore friction and atmosphere have to be taken account of".

> ... There is a Christian duty of vigorous protest ... Let us remember Paul's exhortation and reprove because the things are too bad to be spoken about. ... And if Christian people would only hold up the mirror of Christian principle to the hosts of evil things that afflict our city and our country, they would vanish like ghosts at sunrise. ... (L)et us cast the light upon them.

And he concludes this sermon by a warning against "a sense of our own superiority ... we patronize when we should sympathize ...".[17]

It reads in part like a blueprint for many of Hesba Stretton's R.T.S. tales thereafter: she "held up the mirror of Christian principle", made her vigorous protest, and reproved certain things which many people thought "too bad to be spoken about".

Evidently feeling after three years that they had exhausted the possibilities of Manchester, the Smith sisters spent the winter of 1866–67 in France (ostensibly to improve Lizzie's French) returning to England in June, 1867, and settling in London in the autumn. Sarah had already made an exploratory eight-day visit there in March, 1866. With typical energy and curiosity, she called on all the R.T.S. editors; visited the National Gallery, Westminster, Somerset House, Kensington Museum and the Crystal Palace; went to a service at St. Paul's (disappointing sermon, naturally) and to Boucicault's play, *The Streets of London*, on which she expressed no opinion.* She called on Mr. Wills at *All the Year Round*, and was invited to tea with him and his wife, the other guests being Mrs. Charles Dickens, six years separated from her famous husband, and Mrs. Henry Wood.[18] It was not surprising that on her return to Manchester, she felt "very seedy".

She said nothing in the *Log Book* about this tea-party beyond

* The legend says that she never attended a play in her life. The *Log Book* specifies two: this one, and *A Midsummer Night's Dream* in 1865 in Manchester: "we liked it better than a concert & felt none the worse for going". Possibly this visit to a London theatre suggested to her the character of Jessica's mother.

the fact that it took place. She did not meet Dickens. The legend here breaks down completely: on the evidence of her own *Log Book*, Sarah Smith *never did meet Dickens*. The closest she ever came to him was attending his reading in Manchester in April, 1866. Dickens was adept at dodging difficult or potentially-difficult lady authors. It is quite true that his photograph graced the sitting-room at Ivy Croft along with that of Victor Hugo (whom Sarah never met either).

The explanation is simple: an inveterate collector of photographs in this age of pioneer photography, she wrote to the two authors asking for a "portrait". Each responded with a courteously-inscribed likeness. If in later years visitors assumed that Hesba Stretton had been a close friend of all rather than a few of the celebrities whose "portraits" she displayed, the sisters did not explain. Doubtless they recalled certain social snubs inflicted upon the Postmaster's daughters long ago in Wellington. Thus the legend grew.

The winter of 1866–67 was passed pleasantly in Honfleur. Sarah acquired a set of false teeth ("horrible discomfort"), and wrote a great deal. She was corresponding with Charles Wood, son of the novelist, whom they had visited briefly on their way from Manchester in November, 1866. This was the beginning of that curious five-year relationship which may have been her one serious love affair. Mrs. Wood had been instrumental in getting *The Clives of Burcot* published by Tinsley during the winter. In this book, bad as it is, she must have recognised a hand that could blend passion, propriety and sentiment in a ratio close to that of her own formulae for success; but she did not recognize on sight a rival to her influence over her favourite son. During the winter, Charles Wood sent Sarah reviews of her book; copies of the book; his "portrait"; and an offer to publish *Paul's Courtship*, her second long novel. Early in June the sisters returned to England, stayed with Mrs. Wood for several days, and went out with Charles Wood. After a summer in Wellington of the type invariably recorded as "prolonged calm", or "stagnation", they rented a cottage on the edge of Epping Forest. Within a month, Charles Wood was a frequent visitor. After October, when he reported that he had bought *The Argosy*,* he appears in the *Log Book* as "Jason".

* The fiction that the *Argosy* venture was his was carefully maintained to begin with.

In October too, the friendship between Mrs. Wood and the Smith sisters began to cool, the acidity of *Log Book* entries betraying the end of yet another female friendship.

> Mrs. W. very little in her and can talk only of her own affairs. C.W.W. very quiet. We think we will not spend another Sunday there. (*Log Book*, Oct. 20, 1867.)

Mrs. Wood was certainly a talker of domestic trivia, and her son must have felt the strain of a subtle tug-of-war. "Slight symptom of a 'mother' influence" noted Sarah sourly the next week. "C.W.W. is gone to Paris without coming or writing."

One wonders what stage this friendship reached. The *Log Book* is silent on feelings. Did Charles Wood, the "drole", fluent (and mother-dominated), arouse expectations? or did Sarah, emotional, dramatic, susceptible to clever, talkative young men, jump to unjustified conclusions? Perhaps a bit of both.

Whatever the truth of it, Charles Wood called regularly through 1867 and 1868. Sometimes he escorted the sisters to visit a refuge or a children's hospital. There was no open break with Mrs. Wood. In his mother's presence, Sarah found him "queer" or "quiet"; she was ill at ease there herself, critical of her hostess, and doubtful of the Woods' fashionable friends who "went against the grain" with her.

Gradually they drew apart. The relationship withered under the sisters' prolonged visit to Wellington between April, 1869 and Jan. 1870. "Letters very dismal", Sarah recorded in June, adding cryptically, "he wishes for the impossible". By October, however, he was engaged to be married, "never having mentioned the girl at all. Such is Man!" Just after New Year she was back in London, and called informally several times at Charles Wood's office for morning coffee. In February she accompanied him to buy the wedding bouquet. "He seemed very low and said he felt as if he should like to run away; curious state of mind."

Meeting his wife a few weeks later, Sarah found her "very plain but very pleasant and unaffected", and thought that Jason "took no pride in her". When he asked what they thought of her, the sisters (who had recovered something of the old fighting spirit) replied promptly and to the point.

> We said she was much too good for him, and he did not deserve his luck. (*Log Book*, March 8 (?), 1870).

And a week later Sarah had coffee at the office "for the very last time".

There is a Postscript to this faded friendship. When Mrs. Henry Wood died in 1887, her son received among other letters of sympathy (all quoted without identification in his *Memorials* of his mother), one containing the following: "We have heard, with great sorrow for you, of the irreparable loss you are now suffering. I do not know anything I can say that could comfort you; but I pray that the consolations of God may be great . . ."[19] The facts that the writer is concerned chiefly for him, that she avoids eulogy of Mrs. Henry Wood, and that she refers later to the death of a sister (Hannah had died in 1886), all point to this being Hesba Stretton's letter. Her lapse into the first person singular, very rare indeed, seems to acknowledge the old tenderness so long disciplined into submission. Dare one suggest that she had not forgiven Mrs. Henry Wood?

Having in 1870 lost "Jason" (or handed him over?) to a rich wife, Sarah found life growing flat and stale once more. She was always easily bored. In 1871 she wrote

> (O)ur dislike to London ways, London religion and London society has been steadily increasing. . . . I have had another and I think my last disturbance with the Tract Society. Mrs. Manning* is turning the cold shoulder upon us. Mr. Lynch is dead and we have no preacher we care much about. (*Log Book*, May 27, 1871.)

At the end of June she laid the *Log Books* aside for some years. Five years of literary life in London had brought both material rewards and personal disappointments. Charles Dickens had died in June, 1870; within two years she ceased to contribute to *All the Year Round*.† Within the next decade, Sarah Smith was gradually submerged in "Hesba Stretton", and the woman of the legend took shape.

Thanks to *Little Meg's Children* (1868) and her own skill in bargaining†† she was financially independent. Lodgings, landladies

* Mrs. Manning, wife of the Rev. S. Manning, one of the R.T.S. editors, seems to have been a distant cousin. In spite of not liking her much, the sisters visited their home a good deal.

† Her last work to be published in *All the Year Round* was "Lord Westbourne's Heir" (1872).

††See next chapter for this episode.

and bugs faded into the past, and the sisters were able to take a house. Lizzie gave up working to become housekeeper and the buffer to keep the world at bay. Their lives fell into the pleasant routine of the next thirty-five years. It included much travel and holidays in Devon and Cornwall, in the Channel Isles, in France, Germany, Italy and Switzerland. In 1878, Benjamin Smith died after a long illness during which his daughters went home to Wellington. Annie's children spent much time with them, as a letter around 1877 indicates:

> Gilbert is gone to business in Mr. King's office; and Dora and Philip have entered the Art School at South Kensington. We have Elsie with us, a child of eight, whom we teach at home. They keep us busy; & we have besides much to do with our home affairs—that is in my father's house. He is quite infirm, & has lost his memory & has to have everything arranged & thought of for him. . . . (Letter to Mrs. Stoughton, Nov. 15, 1877 (?), see fig. 19.)

In 1884, their brother Ben's daughter, Alice Annie Bakewell Smith, came from Ontario to spend the next three years with her aunts and attend finishing school.[20]

All domestic arrangements revolved around Sarah's writing. She allowed herself the luxury of breakfast in bed, then arose and went for a walk. At ten o'clock she settled down to write and worked for three hours, the rest of the day being free for visits or reading.

The tension and irritability so often revealed in *Log Book* entries, and shown too by the tight, hard mouth of the face looking out of a photograph of the early '70's,[21] turned over the next twenty years into a state described by her grand-nephew as one of "serene disillusionment". At the age of sixty, she wrote "I have lived ten years longer than I fixed for myself when I was young, and thought life would not be worth living after fifty. The last ten years have been more interesting, more peaceful, and I think more useful than any other ten years".[22]

The 1880's had brought, or at least begun, the reform of various laws and institutions that she had been criticizing for years. She celebrated the passage of the Married Woman's Property Act in 1881 by writing *Under the Old Roof*. In 1884 she helped to found the London Branch of the National Society for the Prevention of Cruelty to Children, resigning from it in 1894 as a protest against the administration of its funds.* She had seen loopholes in the Education Act of 1870 being gradually closed; and the passage of the Public Health Act of 1875. The franchise was extended in 1884; a Royal Commission on Housing was set up in 1884–85. The Barnardo Homes, even in the 1870's, were providing a better than institutional care for the children they took off the streets; Hesba Stretton wrote an Introduction to G. H. Pike's *Children Reclaimed for Life* . . . (1875), an account of Dr. Barnardo's work in London. Although the Workhouse still terrified the aged poor, its former bad reputation was now offset by the excellent work being done by the Workhouse Infirmaries, the hospitals for the poor.

Watching so many of the evils she had protested being gradually done away with, she could feel with some justice that her own books had helped to awaken the public conscience and point out areas of specific need.

About 1892, she purchased Ivy Croft on Ham Common, which was her home for the rest of her life. Around this time she may have been a little bored in her comfortable surroundings, for she enthusiastically adopted a group of Russian political exiles known as "The Friends of Russian Freedom". She attended the lectures of Peter Kropotkin, and was friendly with Volkhovsky and Sergius Stepniak.[23] The legend informs us that she collected around £900 for the Russian Famine Fund that she started in 1891; and points approvingly to her sympathetic championship of the persecuted Russian Stundists† on whose behalf she wrote *The Highway of Sorrow* (1894), and *In the Hollow of His Hand* (1897). It does not make so clear that, since her chief if not only source of information was the aforesaid group of exiles, she was to some extent supporting the cause of nihilism. She assisted Stepniak with the writing of *Paul Rodents* (1894), and used her influence to get it published. The chief reason for the continued banning of *Jessica's First Prayer* in Russia after its earlier enthusiastic reception was this assistance given by its author to nihilists and revolutionaries. The Russian authorities could not believe that she was essentially concerned

* As early as 1869 she noted in the *Log Book*, "I am disheartened by the waste in London Charities." (March 3, 1869.)

† This sect, closely akin to the Baptists, arose in the 1840's. They were severely persecuted in Czarist times, their Evangelical principles bringing them into conflict with Russian Orthodoxy, and they have not been well used under Communism.

with persecuted Russian Protestants rather than with revolutionary politics.

After 1900, Hesba Stretton wrote little. In 1905 or 1906, George Bernard Shaw asked and received her permission to use the title of her novel, *The Doctor's Dilemma* (1872) for his own play. She must have approved of his theme, for she was adept in putting the characters in her own works into just such distressing moral predicaments. It would be interesting to know what she had to say about his secular approach.*

She died on Oct. 8, 1911 after an illness of some months. Lizzie had predeceased her earlier in the year. Although all the causes she sought to draw to public attention have been dealt with by law, and usually as she advocated, she would not have been in the least surprised that the same evils rise anew in every generation.

* Interviewed in 1906 for *Girls' Realm*, she was asked what advice she would give aspiring writers. Sensibly (perhaps a trifle cantankerously) she replied that no young writer should rush into print: one must write from experience.

CHAPTER IX

THE TRACT TALE AS CRITIC OF THE LAW:
The Works of Hesba Stretton

NO tract tale writer was better informed upon her subject matter than Hesba Stretton, or more closely in touch with current social problems. No works of this kind give a juster picture of the whole social scene than hers. Unlike Maria Charlesworth's, her tales do not float loose in an ideal past; nor are they restricted to upper and middle-class home and nursery. Firmly rooted in the harsh realities of the day, they are written from the viewpoint of the submerged and suffering rather than from that of the reformer or educator who was trying to elevate the masses. E. Nesbit's comment on the success of Hesba Stretton's "pathetic simplicity"[1] has helped to obscure the fact that since 1863 she had written to expose the same social evils that the Fabians (including E. Nesbit) hoped to cure through political action. Twenty years earlier than Charles Booth, she was pointing out that destitution did not necessarily result from idleness, extravagance or vice, but was all too often the consequence of illness or lack of opportunity.

From 1863, the date of her first children's book, Hesba Stretton held up (as Mr. McLaren had suggested) Christian principle in protest against specific social evils. The religious element in her books is largely a religion of works, directed to the righting of social and legal wrongs. She pointed out the lack of children's hospitals and of institutions to rehabilitate young offenders. She protested the exploitation of children as beggars, servants, entertainers; the lack of legal protection for woman and child of any class; and the blank-faced indifference of the Poor Law. Nor did she confine herself to one problem per book, nor sentimentalize for a hundred pages over a single forlorn child. Every child in her tales is part of a whole society; every problem part of a wide-scale national problem, often of a universal problem.

Her first book for children was a well-constructed little novel of the Shropshire collieries: *Fern's Hollow* (1864). This was the area in which Benjamin Smith was born, and where Mrs. Cameron had lived and written before Sarah was born. The book, which purports to be set in the 1840's, nevertheless imposes its religious message upon several live social issues of the 1860's: the legality of squatter's rights; the neglect of safety measures in working or worked-out pit areas; abuses of the New Poor Law. Miserly James Wyley, the pit owner is brother to the relieving officer of the local Union workhouse: their unhallowed partnership, paralleling similar situations in Dickens, is a threat to all local workers. James Wyley extends his landholdings at the expense of former common, and squatters stand to lose their poor homes. This accelerated process of enclosure was a live issue consequent upon the rapid growth of towns and the spread of railways. It was particularly active outside London, where in 1851, William Howitt had protested the seizure of Epping and Hainault Forests by rapacious landholders. But by 1870, Hainault was lost and Epping only saved by a legal technicality which brought the Corporation of the City of London into conflict with the landgrabbers and established the forest as perpetual common.[2]

In *Fern's Hollow*, James Wyley is not only encroaching on common land, but like greater industrialists of the day, he neglects the regulations requiring worked-out pit shafts to be safely closed off.[3] This miser's lust for money, and the consequent shrivelling of his own soul is the other serious theme of the book.

Obviously *Fern's Hollow* is overloaded with serious social problems. The same may be said of the better-known *Pilgrim Street* (1867), a protest against some crying evils of industrial Manchester, and a plea for the protection of children against a criminal parent. Hesba Stretton (in this respect true to Evangelical practice) never wrote down to the young. Like Mrs. Sherwood and Mrs. Cameron, she saw the child as a *soul*, and felt justified in making him as important as an adult and equally capable of spiritual understanding. Because her natural romanticism, unlike Mrs. Sherwood's, was not controlled by a rational eighteenth-century upbringing and a first-generation Evangelical conviction of original sin, Hesba Stretton presented the child romantically, often sentimentally. Her children are intrinsically better and purer than adults, and their flashes of insight and incomplete but clear vision point a spiritual path unseen by their elders.

In *Fern's Hollow* (written 1862–63), she had not completely developed this theory. As in earlier tract tales, the religious message is brought to the children by kindly adult mentors—the miser's niece, a benevolent clergyman. Two years later, her theological position had shifted. In *The Children of Cloverley* (1865), the child Annie, an unconvincingly angelic character, brings the religious message. This tale too had a contemporary background, the children's father being a soldier in the Union forces in the American Civil War, and they being sent back to relatives in a Shropshire mining village made idle by the depression of the 1860's and failure of the mine. A weak plot is padded out with details of a school started for village children, and descriptions of an artist's household. The book lacks emotional restraint, presumably because its writer identifies all the children with the nieces and nephews she doted upon. All bear the Smith family names: Dora and Gilbert (for Annie's children); Annie and Ben Bakewell (Ben's little daughter in Ontario Annie Bakewell Smith, had died there in 1865).

In her later books, the child is the religious mentor carrying the Christian message to his elders. Thus Jessica is a spiritual guide to both Daniel and the minister, and Little Meg bolsters the sagging faith of all the adults she encounters. The extreme Protestant view is surely reached in *Cassy*, where there is not the slightest sign of organised religion. Cassy, Simon, and old Mr. Tilley seek their spiritual assurance largely from *The Pilgrim's Progress*, and the Bible only appears near the end of the book.

In July, 1866, *Jessica's First Prayer* began in *Sunday at Home*, and was published as a book early in 1867. Never again was anything written by Hesba Stretton to be so enthusiastically received. Two million copies are said to have been printed by the time of her death in 1911, and within five years of publication, the tale was in translation all over the world. "Met with a missionary from Feejee (sic) and a black man from Liberia who both knew my books", she recorded in 1871. Along with its sequel, *Jessica's Mother* (1867), it was distributed by Temperance Societies for the next half century. Its most striking scenes depicted on sets of coloured slides for magic lantern, and bolstered by a talk on "Fire Water", it made a highly suitable programme for entertaining Bands of Hope. It likewise became a Service of Song.[4] Copies in Braille went all over the world. One still being read at the Blind School in Brantford, Ontario in the 1930's was a favourite with the children there.

The figure of Jessica in a green dress is to be seen in a stained glass window in the village church at Stretton, near Wellington. For three generations of children, she was, like Little Eva, Little Nell and Cinderella, part of the mythology of the nursery. She appealed to readers of the 1860's on several counts other than the pathos of her ragged little figure: pathos was less important in 1867 than it became by 1885. She was honest, she kept her promise, and as Daniel noted with approval, she did not beg. Tested by both Daniel and the minister, neither complaining nor self-pitying, she rings true. Her honesty and independence appealed to those middle-class and rising lower-class readers, who, having attained some degree of respectability and independence by their own efforts, were inclined to agree with the Northern Farmer that "the poor in a loomp is bad". But Jessica, being willing to work, suited them (Fig. 23).

Hesba Stretton's picture of slum life in *Jessica's First Prayer*, tiny in scale, is essentially true. Surrounding the situation in the book was the whole complex matter of slum poverty, worst in Manchester, Liverpool and London—the poverty described by Engels and Mayhew, interpreted by Dickens and Mrs. Gaskell, analysed by Charles Booth. Into it at different times went Octavia Hill to found a little island of decent housing in a sea of squalor, Thomas Barnardo to rescue the children, those vigorous Evangelicals, William and Catherine Booth to save souls. Jessica's lodging in the donkey stable, "the miserable loft, where the tiles were falling in, and the broken window-panes were stuffed with rags and paper", furnished with "an old rusty stove" and "a short board laid across some bricks" is comparable to the houses that Octavia Hill took over and renovated; Jessica's mother, the drunken pantomime actress who has abandoned any attempt to lead a decent life, is one of thousands who had sunk to the lowest level of slum existence.

The book indicates that the writer was preoccupied with the theme of money that runs through most Victorian writing. Jessica appears in two main settings—around the coffee-stall where penny-pinching Daniel is accumulating his little fortune; and around the chapel. Daniel's customers are workmen, and on the edge of the crowd, Jessica shivers in her rags, one of the utterly destitute. Her encounter with Daniel ("You're a very good man, aren't you, Mr. Daniel?") exposes his poverty of spirit and the limitations of his cherished respectability. Her presence at the door of the chapel and inside it reveals the hollowness of the religion of the wealthy congregation who must not be offended by the sight of her. The minister himself (can he be based on Mr. McLaren?) stands the test well: he takes her by the hand "in the face of all the congregation", leads her into the vestry, and tries to help her. But in the light of her simple faith and naïve questions, he acknowledges the failure of his own message to his rich congregation, and understands in humility that Christianity is best communicated on an individual basis.

Whereas Maria Charlesworth blandly ignored the existence of juvenile crime, and A.L.O.E. treated it like an awful warning in a moral tale, Hesba Stretton not only recognised the complexity of the problem, but showed sympathetic understanding of the waste and human suffering involved. A.L.O.E. represents a bad boy on his downward course as "the sluggard who would not work, whom idleness had driven to want, and whom want had driven to crime". The woman he had robbed had the last word about him: "He's a reg'lar jail-bird; he'll come to the gallows at last, . . . that's the end of the course of such as he!" (*Upwards and Downwards*. 1890. p. 7–28). In brief, he has brought his troubles on himself, and his author has contrived him to make her point.

Hesba Stretton's *In Prison and Out* (1878) is in marked contrast to this tale. David Fell, a decent boy, well brought up, gets into trouble through following his good impulses; poverty in his family comes from illness, not idleness. Because the boy cannot get a job, and the workhouse dole is restricted to his young sister and his sick mother, he takes to begging, is caught, and given a short jail term. After his release, having struck the foul-mouthed pawnbroker who had insulted his mother, he is again jailed. Thereafter, unemployable with two convictions, he throws in his lot with a petty thief. His own misery and shame, the grief of his family are made clear; the book shows real insight into the difficulties of the young offender after his release. It recommends the training-ship as a constructive alternative to prison for young offenders, a way to detach them from their bad backgrounds and provide them with a hopeful future.[5]

At no time did Hesba Stretton's work avoid mention of the crime, illegitimacy and prostitution that were part of the London scene. Considering her field, she was perhaps the most explicit of contemporary writers, able to make the distressing facts clear to adult readers yet veiling them from children. How, for instance, did Jessica's mother, the gin-sodden ex-actress, get money to buy gin? The little-known sequel, *Jessica's Mother*, gives the answer. Reappearing after a three-year absence, the woman forces herself into Daniel's little home. Told that she cannot stay, she replies, "And why not? . . . I suppose I'm as good as my daughter. Ah, she'll never be the woman I've been! I rode in my carriage, once, man, I can tell you. . . ." " I rode in my carriage!" The Victorian reader above nursery level would grasp the significance: she had been the kept mistress of a wealthy man; she is now on the streets. Mayhew quotes several such women at various stages in their career of vice using this very phrase.

Several of Hesba Stretton's books warn of the dangers facing ignorant and unprotected girls in big cities. She was greatly concerned with the criminal parent's influence on the child. Bess (*In Prison and Out*) is befriended by old Euclid and Victoria in time to save her from the evil clutches of Blackett, who, having set his own sons to thieving, begins "to speak kindly" to the pretty girl of thirteen. Although Rachel Trevor (*The Storm of Life* 1876), when discovered by her ex-convict husband goes with him, she refuses to tell the whereabouts of their eleven-year-old daughter, knowing his plans for the child.

Death haunts the slums in these little books, much as in the novels of Dickens and the daily press. People starve; the desperate die in suicide leaps; some are injured in street accidents; disease takes heavy toll. Yet Hesba Stretton's London is not all gloomy; there is goodness and honesty, human kindness and generosity. People keep faith and hope. Dreadful hovels like Jessica's attic and the horrors of Angel Court are offset by Daniel's neat little cottage or Mrs. Blossom's shop with loaves in the window and warm firelight dancing across the shining red tiles of the kitchen floor.

Economically it is a London of little shops and tiny businesses. Mrs. Blossom and Mrs. Linnett keep little shops with bread, sweets, vegetables; Old Oliver sells papers and journals; Mrs. Clack has an old clothes shop. Rachel Trevor finds refuge with the approved chimney-sweep, Sylvanus Croft, who uses the best machinery and sweeps the chimneys for the members of the Society for the Suppression of Climbing Boys. (This evil was finally eliminated in 1875.) The unfortunate Cassy, on the other hand, finds her "little place" in the slovenly household of an unsuccessful and bibulous barber. Pawnbrokers, honest and dishonest, play their part in the economic pattern of the slums; tiny sums are lent and scrupulously returned among impoverished people too often unemployed to make the regular saving of a penny or a three-penny bit every week in the Penny Bank or Savings Bank. In such circumstances, Self-Help* simply cannot get started: this is destitution, and behind it stands the grim wall of the Union.

Those who start with a little money can make more. Penny-pinching Daniel sets up his coffee-stall under the railway arches and accumulates four hundred pounds. The coffee-stall was common in the 1860's, and highly approved as a harmless alternative to the gin-vaults. Daniel is thus an admirable example of Self-Help: his fault lies in making money the centre of his life. So it is with Simon, the dwarf, in *Cassy*. Both men must balance their money against their spiritual welfare when circumstances force them to choose between their own miserly habits and the responsibility for a starving child.

Money, however, is not always the major concern. There is the matter of *respectability*. Like other Victorian novelists, Hesba Stretton made much of respectability: it was indeed built into her Methodist upbringing. The term implied infinitely more to readers between 1860 and 1900 than it ever could to the average person today. The Victorian who was rising in the world felt that his respectability was part of his achievement as well as the badge of his success.

> To be respectable is to emerge from the anonymous amorphous mass: to be a personality, to live by a standard, actually, perhaps, the standard of the class just above that into which you had been born and in which your fellows were content to live. . . . (T)he respectable man is not only bettering himself, he is bettering his family . . . improving the race. So viewed, social progress is a microcosmic section of the evolution of the world under the guidance of that Providence whose purpose, in the great words of Malthus, is ever to bring a mind out of the clod, . . .[6]

* Title and theme of book by Samuel Smiles, printed 1859, which did much to popularise the Carlylean gospel of work. In children's books, it was to find its expression in the works of the popular American writer, Horatio Alger (1832–1899). See Asa Briggs: *Victorian People* (1954).

The unfortunate characters in her books either lose their respectability—perhaps forced into the workhouse by poverty in old age, or into petty crime by accident or sheer need—or they have never enjoyed it. Those who end happily are invariably lifted out of their poverty, moving out of their early working-class background to become (like Dickens' Marchioness and Susan Nipper) safely embedded at a higher social level. Thus the otherwise nameless Jessica, illegitimate child of a brutal drunkard, is first adopted by Daniel Standring, the Chapel-keeper, a person of impeccable respectability with a prosperous sideline. When in the sequel, *Jessica's Mother*, Daniel dies in an attempt to prevent the drunkard's suicide, Jessica is not left on her own. Having in this book again proved her superior worth by her willingness to take charge of her mother, she is again rewarded:

> "There's one thing still I want to say," said Daniel. I've made my will, and left all I had to Jessica; but I don't know where she'll find a home. If you'd look out for her—"
>
> "Jessica shall come home to me," interrupted the minister, laying his hand upon hers and Daniel's and clasping them both warmly.

Since Jessica has been comforting the minister's children in elder-sister fashion during their father's illness, the implication seems to be that she will join the family as companion or adopted daughter rather than as a little servant.

Similarly in the earlier *Pilgrim Street*, the younger of two brothers, the bright, attractive Philip Haslam, is sent to a good school by a charitable benefactor, and the older and rougher Tom is aided towards the purchase of a donkey and cart so that he may become an independent peddler of fish and firewood (Fig. 22).

In other tales, young people who have run foul of the law are helped towards a renewed respectability conditional upon genuine repentance. Roger Blackett, in *In Prison and Out*, is sentenced on his offence to a term on a training-ship; thus removed from the control of his criminal father, he becomes a merchant sailor. Rosie Trevor, in *The Storm of Life*, child of parents who have served prison terms, is given a home (along with her repentant mother) by respectable people. Regarded by them as a grandchild, Rosie will grow up after her mother's death without social stigma.

Like Dickens, Hesba Stretton presented emigration as a panacea for both poverty and loss of respectability, a chance to leave behind forever the grim shadow of workhouse or gaol. At the end of *Little Meg's Children*, Little Meg, Robin and their father embark for a new world, accompanied by the reformed Kitty and her mother. In Part III of *The King's Servants* (1873), a whole group of rehabilitated streetwalkers set sail for respectable homes in New York.* Lost Gip and her brother, Sandy, are taken to Canada with "a hundred other children from the streets of our large cities"; and "before the autumn came, they were settled in a log house . . . within sound of the lapping of the waves of the Lake Huron". And Ishmael Medway (*No Place Like Home*, 1881), imprisoned for a petty offence against the game laws, is salvaged by his old teacher who takes him to America, where "ten years after . . . he owned a farm of his own and was prospering in every way".

Into these tales the author poured a good deal of first-hand knowledge. She had visited refuges and orphanages; she had met Maria Rye and seen her sail with her flock of gutter children for Canada.[7] The settling of orphans and workhouse children in the countries of the New World was a favourite topic with Dickens also; did he not send that most unlikely pioneer, Mr. Micawber, with his family and Little Em'ly to Australia where they prospered exceedingly? It must be admitted that Hesba Stretton's idea of what made a suitable settler for the wilds was rather the more practical. She had, of course, the experience of her brother Benjamin in Ontario to guide her.

Next to *Jessica's First Prayer*, the most popular of Hesba Stretton's tales were *Little Meg's Children* and *Alone in London*. *Little Meg* marked a turning point in its author's relations with her chief publisher, the Religious Tract Society. Finding on her return from France in 1867 that *Jessica* had made her a best-selling author for the young, she demanded, and eventually got, a higher rate of payment. According to the rates of the day, she had little cause for complaint. The R.T.S. paid generously for manuscripts, but a sale meant relinquishment of copyright. Profits thus accrued to the Society, which recognised a very successful book by a little bonus of £5 or £10. Hesba Stretton's rates had risen from thirty guineas in 1863 for *Fern's Hollow* to £44 for *The Children of Cloverley*; she

* I have not, to date, discovered the original (if there was any) of this interesting venture. The Baroness Burdett-Coutts?

did not note down what she got for *Jessica* or *Pilgrim Street*, but she indignantly rejected £50 for *Little Meg*. One can safely assume £40 or £45, and for *Jessica* she got two early bonuses totalling £15, and in 1873 (after her "disturbance with the Tract Society" in March, 1871) she was given a bonus of £200. The Minute Book records it as for *Jessica* "and other works for which she has only received ordinary payments". The £50 she received from *The Leisure Hour* for *David Lloyd's Last Will* is more than she records for her three-volume novels from Tinsley and Charles Wood; possibly there were other payments unrecorded.

With a sound head for business and a good deal of inside knowledge of printing and publishing, Sarah Smith, with the manuscript of *Little Meg* in hand, "resolved upon asking so much a thousand for the tale". She may have asked advice from Mr. Wills; she must have known that Mrs. Henry Wood sold only one book, *Danesbury House*, outright. Her action was tantamount to raising the red flag in Paternoster Row. The shocked editors did not know whether to bid against one another for a certain best-seller, or to close ranks against the rebel, whose exasperation with them was compounded by extreme irritation with the wives of at least two. "Mrs. Manning, our cousin" was "a wet blanket"; Mrs. Stevens ("very gushing") was involved in a disagreement which probably concerned Lizzie, at the time, governess to her children. Whatever the circumstances, Mr. Stevens, sub-editor of *The Leisure Hour*, was certainly to be pitied, caught in the cross-fire between his angry wife and the touchy Smith sisters, and bound for the sake of the Tract Society's interests to pacify this popular and prickly author.

After two months of hawking *Little Meg* around Paternoster Row, she settled with the Tract Society for £6. 5s. per thousand.[8] The story was a great success; within the year, she got a cheque for £131, and, presumably established a precedent for her other tales. In April, 1868, the Tract Society recorded payment of a £10 bonus on *Pilgrim Street* and £50 on *Little Meg*. In 1869, *Alone in London* appeared, and in 1870 she collected £370. But relations with the Tract Society were strained and chilly; and in 1873 she began to publish with H. S. King. By 1880, sales were falling off, and she made a new arrangement with the Tract Society. This resulted in a general reprinting of earlier books, and in 1898 she negotiated an agreement by which she received an annuity of £200 per annum for the rest of her life. This was carried over (on a sliding scale) to her estate, the agreement being periodically revised up to the 1930's or later. Many of her books were reissued up to World War I and later.* The interviewer of 1894 noted that from a short story on which Hesba Stretton got a penny in the shilling, she had realized £400.

Prior to writing *Little Meg's Children*, the author had visited Temple Gardens with Charles Wood; and, accompanied by a policeman, had investigated the East End slums.

> . . . (P)assed through some disgusting streets and looked over two homes and one ragged school. I think London is a horrible place. (*Log Book*, Feb. 17, 1868.)

The impressions received during this visit formed the background of the story. Angel Court near Rosemary Lane actually existed.† Henry Mayhew described Rosemary Lane as being full of old clothes dealers and pawnshops. Little Meg's attic, not the worst of its kind, was a familiar part of slum life. The building of the railway through London in the 1830's and 1840's had caused a great slum clearance in parts, and as the occupants of demolished housing crowded into neighbouring districts, the notorious "rookeries" of St. Giles, Holborn, Seven Dials, etc. were formed. Just four years before *Little Meg's Children* was written, Octavia Hill had begun her work to improve housing, an experiment watched with interest by all social workers and reformers of the time.[9]

Of all Hesba Stretton's tales for children, *Little Meg's Children* has worn best perhaps for the same reasons that Herbert Read remembered it with affection.[10] He speaks of its "grim pathos" which had, he felt, prepared him for the shock of a death impending in his own family. He cites the deathbed scene as possessing real merit, and analyses the story's appeal as being akin to that of fairy tale in that it involves both emotion and imagination. Its setting was "a strange country" to him; its heroine, like Little Red Riding-

* The forty-second imprint of *Little Meg's Children* came out in 1921. It was brought out by Johnson Reprints in 1968 in agreement with the Osborne Collection.

† There were at different times, sixteen Angel Courts, two being demolished to make room for John and Vine Streets, two more for Holborn Viaduct Station. (Harben, H: *A Dictionary of London*, 1918.)

Hood, was "Little", and she survived the dangers of her fictional journey.

Herbert Read was one of many who read the book in childhood and came under its spell. One of Little Meg's contemporaries who did so was the child, Ada, occupant of an "Aunt Judy's Magazine Cot" at Great Ormond Street Hospital, who enthusiastically shared her delight in the book and its illustrations with a visitor. ". . . I can't wait till I get to the end . . . Ain't she a dear little girl? Wouldn't you have loved her? Shall I show you the pictures? . . ."*

It was essentially The Tale: its little heroine overcame great difficulties; her helpers appeared in time of need; there was a happy ending. Meg defends the attic rooms, keeps the secret, battles enemies of hunger, loneliness and doubt. Her hardships are real and concrete, and the harsh surroundings come sharply to the mind's eye—the attic room, reached by a ladder (that detail alone impresses a child); the locked box; the make-shift bath dripping into the room below; the pawning of bedding and clothes. The reader can visualize the forlorn children sitting sadly on their high window-sill looking over the roofs, and he feels their terrors and their pleasure on the journey through the traffic into Temple Gardens.

The book is subtly flattering to childhood. Meg may be only ten, but like adults she does important things and does them well: cares for the children, plans and works to keep them fed and lodged. Grown-ups trust her and she meets them on almost equal terms, advising Kitty, sympathizing with Mrs. Blossom.

Like the rest of Hesba Stretton's little books, the tale was principally intended for children and newly-literate adults. It was a Sunday book to edify, instruct and elevate, both morally and spiritually. It dealt with a subject of widespread concern—the slums.

The children themselves are to some degree typical of little slum dwellers. Meg is "a small, spare, stunted girl of London growth" with a careworn face and "small bony hands . . . hard with work". That party of little servants whom Anne Thackeray interviewed in 1877 at a Sunday School treat included several like her: ". . . little shabby, pale-faced grinning, stunted creatures . . . grown-up girls

* Report of the "Aunt Judy's Magazine Cots", *Aunt Judy's Christmas Volume for 1877*, p. 511.

for the most part, but they looked like school children of eleven and twelve years old. . . ."[11] They too were examples of "London growth", victims, as were the two or three generations before them, of semi-starvation, of illness, neglect, bad air: children of the industrial city. Only the hardiest like Jessica and Little Meg and Robin survived. The sickly succumbed in infancy, or later from tuberculosis or one of the "fevers" carried by impure water and favoured by lack of sanitation.

Meg's attic is more sanitary than others simply because less crowded, and because the mother had been able to stay with her children. The family is better off than most. When the children spend a day and a night with the body of their mother, they are but following the common practice of their place and time. Nearly twenty years before, Dr. John Simon had complained about delayed funerals.

> For some days the coffin is unclosed. The bare corpse lies there amid the living. On an average, there would probably be lying within the City at any moment, from thirty to forty dead bodies in rooms tenanted by living persons. . . . (City of London Medical Reports, 1852. Special Report on Intramural Interments.)

In the light of the 1852 report, it seems that Little Meg's mother is buried with the minimum of delay, if not, in the eyes of her neighbours, with indecent haste. Indeed, Dr. Simon himself would have been quite satisfied with a funeral within three days of death.[12]

Repulsive as this situation seems today, it was not so in the context of its own times. It was pathetic, as was the similar situation in Mrs. Sewell's ballad, "Mother's Last Words" (1860). The Victorians were not squeamish about death, and *Little Meg's Children* is far less morbid than Mrs. Walton's *Little Dot*, and *Nobody Loves Me*. Meg and Robin accept the sadness and separation of death and grieve at intervals. The writer's treatment of the situation is well in keeping with some of the findings of modern psychology, which argues that death must be recognized, accepted and grieved for if the bereaved are not to suffer severe emotional disturbance later.[13]

Children identifying with Little Meg could hardly brood over death: there is far too much going on, and the emphasis of the book is on life. Meg shows an outgoing concern for the little children and for Kitty. The dying mother plans for her children's life when she is gone; Kitty, the young prostitute is brought back into the stream of decent useful life; both families make a new life for themselves at the end.

In spite of the Religious Tract Society's concern for the truth of the reading matter it disseminated, much truth was still omitted, glossed over, or disproportioned to pass muster with editors and readers alike. Authors were disciplined for style as well as content; Sarah Smith had much to thank it for in this respect. Her natural style, as displayed in earlier short stories and *The Clives of Burcot*, was prolix, exaggerated, sententious and often grossly sentimental: the natural outcome of a girlhood devoted to magazine reading.[14] Writing by the strict R.T.S. rules, she learned to curb emotion, choose detail with care, and reduce the wealth of incident that renders her three-volume novels a gruelling test of reader endurance. On the whole she comes out well. In the matter of truth to life, no other tract fiction writer of the time can compare to her.

Attempting to drive out the cheap literature of crime and sensation and replace it by wholesome, elevating and instructive reading, the R.T.S. over these years favoured tales about slum life. These were intended to arouse the concern and sympathy of the well-to-do and at the same time to show the slum reader where the right road of life lay for him. In trying to hold these two different reading publics, the Tract Societies to some extent defeated their original purpose. It was impossible to write about the poor *as they were* without offending the delicacy of the other class of reader. Thus by about 1880, characters in most tract tales became idealized; emotion turned into sentimentality; language and situation were tiresomely stereotyped; and many readers were bored by "street arab" tales with their inevitable assumption that all worked out for the best.

Hesba Stretton had begun writing twenty years before this deadening conformity was established. Too individual, too talented and too stubborn to be swamped by the R.T.S. regulations, she carefully adhered to them in theory and stretched them to the limit in practice. By careful selection of character and circumstance and meticulous use of language, she could give realistic though limited pictures of slum life without offending too many of her middle-class readers.

In *Little Meg's Children*, for instance, in spite of its genuine setting, the *real* slum children with their dreadful language, their thieving ways, their appalling sexual precocity, are never discernible save for Meg's dying mother's warning against "... a bad crew downstairs, a very bad crew". Later, Meg and Robin sit on their attic windowsill, symbolically and actually high above Angel Court, "the quarrelling children and the drunken men and women staggering about in the yard below". What happens in Angel Court is put into general inoffensive terms, and the squalor of Meg's lodging is similarly softened. The houses are "gloomy", "dismal", "grimy"; concrete details accurate but limited. We are shown the yard "... with its interlacing rows of clothes-lines stretched from window to window, upon which hung the yellow, half-washed rags of the inhabitants". There is no mention of the disgusting realities of the filth in the gutters where the children played; of the slop-pail carried up and down the stairs or emptied out of the window; of the bugs that crept in regiments out of every crack when the light was extinguished.

No child of Meg's age living in Angel Court in the 1860's could have remained in ignorance of Kitty's part-time occupation, and worse. But Little Meg, innocent and detached, concentrates upon her children's welfare and carries young readers with her.

On its publication, the book was defended by the R.T.S. against severe criticism. This, oddly enough, was not based upon the inclusion of Kitty in the tale. The objection was

> ... on the ground that the father and mother are made to tell a falsehood, and that no censure of it is expressed. It may, however be replied that the father is described as a profane and godless profligate, and that, on being brought to repentance ... he ... express(es) shame and sorrow for this sin. The mother likewise is an ignorant and ungodly woman. ...[15]

This version of her intentions may have silenced these particular critics, but undoubtedly annoyed the author. When she meant to portray bad parents, they were unmistakably bad: Jessica's mother, Tom Haslam's father in *Pilgrim Street*, Blackett of *In Prison and Out*. Little Meg's parents are neither good nor bad, merely human. The father had provided well for the family under ordinary circumstances; his children love him and look forward to his return. The mother makes the best possible arrangements for them, showing affection and a genuine and pathetic faith. Unlike many of their class, both are literate, and so is Little Meg.

Taken in conjunction with the criticism it purports to answer, the R.T.S. defence sheds an interesting light upon the moral outlook of the day. Did critics and readers and editors miss the painful significance of the book's secondary theme—the reclamation of Kitty? Certainly all were silent on the whole delicate matter of her presence in a book for children. Chastised for not giving the dying mother some dogmatically-correct utterance and for not censuring the father's lie, Hesba Stretton, as usual, ignored the critics. Her tales for the R.T.S., like her novels and short stories, continued to treat the streetwalker, the adulteress and several criminal types with understanding and sympathy. The Tract Society in supporting her showed itself considerably more broadminded on these matters than, for instance, *The Athenaeum*, which, in 1873, rebuked the writer for her picture of a rescue mission in *The King's Servants* (Fig. 21). This book describes a project on the style of the "Urania Cottage" scheme sponsored by Angela Burdett-Coutts in the 1840's, and administered in part by Dickens.[16]

> We object strongly to the specific form of sin and wretchedness being revealed to young creatures, who ought not to have their minds darkened by the shadow of such knowledge . . . the terrible social problem involved is not to be handled a sentimental episode in a story, nor to be made the subject of entertaining reading. We must regret that Hesba Stretton has committed what we consider a very grave error in judgment. . . . *The King's Servants* is not a book we should put into the hands of young people. (*Athenaeum*, 13 Dec., 1873.)

Little Meg's Children was followed by the morbidly sentimental *Alone in London* (1869), which underlined the grave need for hospitals for children. Facts which Hesba Stretton had established earlier were fitted into pathetic episodes such as the one in which the matron turns the sick Dolly away.

> "We have only seventy-five cots," she answered sobbing, "and in a winter like this, they're always full."
>
> "Only seventy-five!" repeated the old man, very sorrowfully. "Only seventy-five, and there are hundreds and hundreds of little children ill in houses like mine, where the sun never shines. Is there no other place like this we could take our little love to?"
>
> "There are two or three other hospitals," she answered, "but they are a long way off, and none of them as large as ours. I think there are not more than a hundred and fifty cots in all London for sick children." (*Alone in London*, p. 119.)

The book was very favourably received, standing next in popularity to *Jessica* and *Little Meg.** In its own way, it was as compelling as Dickens' dramatic statement on the same subject several years before:

> In London alone there die in a year young children enough to make an unbroken line of corpses, lying head to foot, along the kerb-stone on each side of the way from Bow Church down the Bow-road, through Mile-end, and down the Mile-end road, Whitechapel road, Whitechapel, Aldgate, and on through Leadenhall-street, the Poultry, Cheapside, and on still through Newgate-street and Skinner-street, to line with dead children both sides of the whole length of Holborn and Oxford-street to beyond Kensington-gardens.[17]

Other writers were more restrained, but all said the same thing. In aid of the Victoria Hospital, founded in 1866 with six beds and extended in the 1870's, Florence Montgomery wrote *Wild Mike* (1874). *The Cornhill* (1869) carried Anne Thackeray's moving description of London hospitals for children, which tallies closely with *Alone in London.*[18] Mrs. Gatty and Mrs. Ewing, collecting contributions from young readers (many of whom must have read *Alone in London*) and giving generously themselves, maintained over these years the *Aunt Judy's Magazine* cots at Great Ormond Street, reporting on them at intervals in the magazine.

> Charlie S— (after being under treatment for nearly twelve months) has recovered so far as to be able to leave the hospital for the convalescent wards at Cromwell House. . . . The cot is now filled by another Charlie—a sweet little boy of about six. . . .[19]

The Christian World Magazine (edited by Emma Jane Worboise, a noted tract fiction writer) likewise supported a cot, as did *The Quiver*, and many other papers, charitable groups and societies.

All these hospitals, one large, several smaller, were still at this date maintained largely by charitable donations and bequests, and staffed by dedicated workers, many of them volunteers. All showed encouraging cures like that of Tony in *Alone in London.* All were quite inadequate to the need, as the public came to recognise in the

* "I took her *Alone in London* as a Sunday School prize, and wrote her name in it. Her delight was unbounded. . . ." (Francis Kilvert: *Diary*, March 3–4, 1870.)

next few years, and the workhouse infirmaries were greatly improved to become the hospitals of the poor.

With the narrowing and seclusion of her private life after 1870, Hesba Stretton's interest focused more sharply than ever upon serious social problems: the status of women, the lack of protection for children under the law. Her longer novels dealt with runaway or victimized wives (*Hester Morley's Promise*, 1873; *The Doctor's Dilemma*, 1872); with the misuse of money and the demoralising effects of greed. Her later children's stories too were gloomier in atmosphere than earlier works, their characters less individual and often contrived to fit the cause. *Max Kromer* (1871) was written after her first journey to Switzerland, during which she saw some of the results of the siege of Strasbourg.

> "At every stage I saw how children were involved in the keen sufferings of the war . . ." she wrote in the Preface. "Thus vividly impressed with the great and sad share which falls to the lot of children, in all the misery produced by the crimes and mistakes of men, I wrote the story of Max Kromer, softening down, rather than heightening, the horrors of the siege. . . ."

Her temperance tales, *Brought Home* (1875), *Nellie's Dark Days* (1870) *Lost Gip* (1873), belong to this period. In them all a strong sentimentality is combined with the painful details which show how liquor fortifies the other social evils. In *Nellie's Dark Days*, the child's doll is pawned, her mother's funeral flowers sold by the father to buy gin, and the child herself injured in a fire. The drunkard's conversion is attributed to a noted Liverpool preacher to whom the Smith sisters were apparently related. His appearance at the Wellington revival in 1861–62 had been heralded by Sarah with an exasperated *Log Book* entry that Hannah was "cleaning for Radford as though he were Christmas" *Lost Gip* added to the temperance theme a plea for adoption of orphans, and drew flattering attention to the work of Maria Rye, who, like Miss Macpherson, Dr. Barnardo, William Quarrier, and others, worked to settle slum orphans in Canadian, Australian, or New Zealand homes.

In the 1870's, Hesba Stretton was friendly for a time with Henrietta Synnot, the niece of Marianne Thornton, who was, according to her cousin, E. M. Forster, a genuine but unpredictable reformer, "always taking people up and dropping them. . . ."[20] But Henrietta Synnot was sincerely interested in London street children. Her article in *The Contemporary Review* (1875), "Institutions", lively, sensible and sympathetic, advocated a foster home system for orphans on the grounds that "artificial life is inferior to natural life". It sounds as though Hesba Stretton may have advised the writer; she was herself a very successful writer of articles for periodicals.[21]

Henrietta Keddie, who had met Hesba Stretton about this time and admired her, wrote of her work:

> Her books for the young—*Jessica's First Prayer, Meg and her Children* (sic) etc.—had a wonderful fascination. I can bear witness to their influence on what appeared to me a hopeless subject—a child-servant, seemingly wholly ignorant and incorrigible. I am sorry to say that I shrank from contact with the small savage next door. A wiser and kinder woman in the neighbourhood, finding, I suppose, that the disturber of her peace could read, handed her a story by Hesba Stretton, and there was an almost instant transformation. How that poor little soul was interested! how she paced up and down the small suburban garden of the house left to her charge for the Sunday, still as a mouse, her eyes fixed on the printed page, heart, soul and mind absorbed in its contents. I cannot tell how long the spell lasted, but surely it was something to have thus arrested and impressed the girl, perhaps with an impulse given to the empty, neglected child's soul—vacant for the wild growth of every evil weed, which might bear fruit after many days.[22]

Into *Cassy* (1874), Hesba Stretton distilled some gruesome findings from the lengthy list of articles, reports and publications upon the servant problem of the 1860's and 1870's and after. Few people pretended by then that Miss Charlesworth's picture of the harmonious relationship of mistress and maid was anything but Sunday fiction: according to many periodicals and all cartoons of the day, it was rather a state of unremitting domestic guerilla warfare. The problem was a tremendous one, about a million girls and women being in domestic service at the time, and only about a seventh of them on farms.[23] As far back as 1849, Prince Albert had noted the unduly large proportion of aged servants found in workhouses, called public attention to the matter, and given his support to the Servants' Provident Society. Thirteen years later, *The Edinburgh Review* painted a cheerless picture of the servant's prospects:

> . . . few have more than £10 a year, and many . . . no more than £8. It is absurd to talk of their laying by money. . . . What can her savings amount to when she grows old? Certainly nothing that she can live on . . . we find a large proportion of them in the workhouse at last.[24]

For thirty years Dickens had supplied a large fictional portrait gallery of servants, making clear that he had an eye to their welfare. A study of servant and master in his novels would certainly show the former to better advantage, Sam Weller, for instance, practically taking over *The Pickwick Papers*, and the indestructible Marchioness floating triumphantly to the top of a situation that daunts her elders and betters.

The official document upon the state of affairs described in *Cassy* was Mrs. Nassau Senior's* Report upon Pauper girls and their training as maids-of-all-work, to which Anne Thackeray refers in her *Cornhill* article in 1874. Detailed and convincing, the Report presented irrefutable evidence that the workhouse upbringing of pauper girls was the worst possible preparation for sending them out at fourteen to earn their own livings as servants. Emotionally stunted and intellectually dull, they were completely ignorant of the ways a normal family live and of the domestic arrangements in a small household.

> "Oh, I've been a servant for years!" said the little thing. . . . "I learnt ironing off the lady; I didn't know nothing about it. I didn't know nothing about anything. . . ."
>
> "They wasn't particularly kind to me in my first place. I had plenty to eat. . . . I had to do all the work. I'd no one to go to: Oh! I cried the first night. I used to cry so . . . there I was all alone, and this was a great big house . . . I got to break everything, I was so frightened. . . . Then I got a place in a family where there was nine children. I was about fourteen then. I earned two shillings a week. I used to get up and light the fire, bath them and dress them and get their breakfast . . . sometimes I had the baby too, and it couldn't be left, and had to be fed. . . . There was one a cripple . . . about nine year old. I used to carry her on my back. . . . I wasn't in bed till twelve and I'd be up by six. . . ." ("Maids of-All-Work and Blue Books".)

* Wife of the noted economist, she was for some time Lady Inspector of Workhouse Schools for Girls.

Compared with poor shadowy Cassy, lost in the jungle of misery and misfortune where she started her "pilgrimage", this little servant was lucky. Hesba Stretton's book carried too heavy a load of social evils: Cassy illustrates the ignorance of the children of the floating population; her flight from a cruel, drunken father leads to her exploitation by a callous employer. Barely able to read, she stumbles through *The Pilgrim's Progress* with the aid of a dying old man, and comes to some confused but consoling ideas of Christian faith; overworked and underfed through a bitter winter, she eventually dies of tuberculosis.

Like *Jessica's First Prayer* and *Little Meg's Children*, the book also shows an adult character coming to a firm religious belief through the child's example. The dwarf, Simon, living in his forest caravan, seems in his loneliness and doubt more real than Cassy does.

> . . . (W)hat have I to thank Him for? And now there's Cassy. She'd only got her mother, as kept her father tolerably decent, and He's taken her away, for no reason as I can see except to leave that girl without any friend to care for her, if it's true as He meddles with us at all. There's nothing lying afore that girl save bad; very bad, as far as I can see. There's the workhouse, the jail, and the river . . . jail, workhouse or river; and the river's the best. . . . (*Cassy*, p. 20.)

This struggle between faith and doubt, or between religious profession and expediency is a major theme in Hesba Stretton's novels for adults. She puts her characters to the severest of tests, the usual touchstone being money, for like most Victorian novelists, she saw the fierce competition of the industrial world eroding integrity and destroying human dignity. Her plots depend upon the overworked devices of embezzlement of funds, financial crashes,* or concealment of a will to motivate plots, and she often presented incident sensationally.

The theme of wealth was always complicated in her books by the legal disabilities of women of all classes, a current issue as the demand for a Married Women's Property Act and for legal protection of women and children strengthened. In *The Doctor's*

* There were, however, some very spectacular financial crashes around this time such as that of Overend and Gurney, the great Quaker bankers.

Dilemma (1872), *The Soul of Honour* (1898), and others, Hesba Stretton displayed women ill-used, abandoned, or stripped of their money and property by unscrupulous husbands or guardians. Her Doctor's dilemma is particularly painful: if the new treatment he is pioneering cures his patient, the latter will (without legal interference) rob his young wife of the last vestiges of her once-comfortable inheritance and desert her. If the Doctor (who is in love with the wife) lets the husband die, he is betraying his Hippocratic oath.

Undoubtedly these books carry too heavy a weight of religious moralizing for the taste of the modern reader, but there is nothing trivial in their statement of serious social wrongs of the day, or, as in *David Lloyd's Last Will* (1869), her best novel, in the questions raised about individual duty and conduct. These were works of genuine social purpose, and their writer was a genuine social reformer.

CHAPTER X

"A TENDENCY MOST PERNICIOUS": THE TRACT TALE AND THE THEATRE

Mrs. Walton and "A Peep Behind the Scenes"

WITH Mrs. O. F. Walton (1850–1939), author of *Little Dot*, *Christie's Old Organ*, and *A Peep Behind the Scenes*, the line of serious Evangelical writing for children begun by Hannah More and Mrs. Sherwood came to an end. This did not happen suddenly: many nineteenth-century tract tales were reprinted until the first World War; some are still in print.[1] But after 1880 no *new* Evangelical writer made a first appearance with an enduring religious work for the young, whereas almost every previous decade since 1800 had produced at least one. Since the 1840's the religious stiffening of the tract tale had been progressively weakened by the advance of fiction in which religious elements were presented with trappings of sentiment, sensation or adventure. The later works of Mrs. Sherwood had displayed this tendency; it was reinforced by the books of Susan Warner with their interesting detail of surroundings and action, and by the lively tales of W. H. G. Kingston and R. M. Ballantyne. All three of these authors were copiously printed by tract societies. Around 1850 the revival of the moral tale directed to secular instruction had further eroded the proportion of religious teaching in children's books. What remained of serious Evangelical doctrine in the tract tale was finally washed away in a flood of sentimentality that reached its peak in the 1880's and 1890's in the works of Mrs. Walton, Amy Le Feuvre, and kindred authors. By then, too, the works of Mrs. Ewing, Mrs. Molesworth, Mrs. Frances Hodgson Burnett and L. T. Meade were in demand. Unobtrusively religious or moral, their sentiment balanced by restraint and humour, their well-written works were directed to children of the upper and middle classes. Few suggested the *elevation of the masses* though all showed sympathy for the individual living in poverty and ignorance.

By 1880, some articulate observers had become highly critical of Sunday and cottage reading offered by tract societies.[2] Eliza Keary wrote disparagingly of "... filling little heads with sensational stories of ragged London depravity". Admitting that "Mrs. O. F. Walton is at home in half the nurseries in England", Edward Salmon in 1888 complained of three prime favourites, *Little Faith* (Fig. 24), *Little Dot*, and *Angel's Christmas*, that "Such stories, however praiseworthy their aim, can be of little moral help to small children, and may easily be of harm".[3] A year earlier, Charlotte Yonge, in *What Books to Lend and What to Give* had listed *A Peep Behind the Scenes* without comment other than the terse admission, "A great favourite". It still was over thirty years later when a Sunday School librarian found among little girls "quite a number" who "like 'em sad, miss". "This type," wrote the librarian, "can easily be made happy with ... Mrs. Walton's *A Peep Behind the Scenes*, and *Jessica's First Prayer*, *Jessica's Mother*, *Alone in London*, etc. by Hesba Stretton."*

Mrs. Walton's name appeared in Charles Welsh's survey of 1884 as one of the nine top favourites of girls aged eleven and up, an honour shared with Dickens, Kingsley, Charlotte Yonge and Hesba Stretton. In spite of her wide popularity and the fact that she had a writing career of at least forty-six years, little is known of her personal life, and confusion has arisen about her very name.

According to the British Museum Catalogue, there were *two* Mrs. O. F. Waltons, contemporaries. Probably Mrs. Oriel Farnell Walton was the *Catherine Augusta* whose Christian names have somehow been attached to Mrs. Octavius Frank Walton, pious author of tales for the Religious Tract Society. Available facts are as follows:

In February of 1875, the Rev. Octavius Frank Walton, curate of St. Stephen's, Spring Street, Hull, married his vicar's daughter, *Amy Catherine Deck*. He was then thirty years of age, she, twenty-five and charmingly pretty. The Decks (like the Charlesworths) belonged to the strongly Evangelical branch of the Church of England; they were a family of clergymen. Amy Catherine's father, the Rev. John Deck, a graduate of Cambridge, wrote several sermons and tracts condemning Puseyism and ritualism. An

* Tongue, Mary E.: "The Books They Read". *Girls' Own Annual*, Vol. 43, no 10, p. 531.

exhibition of church vestments in Hull in the 1860's, for instance, inspired a pamphlet with the resounding title "Priestly Eucharistic Vestments: Ignored for Three Hundred Years in the Church of England: Are they now Desirable? Canonical? Legal?" In her father's arguments that vestments are "essentially Romish in character" and that such innovations sap "that Uniformity of Public Worship which it was the very object of the Prayer Book to preserve" can be detected the ring of fervent early Evangelical Protestantism so noticeable in the writings of Mrs. Walton. Indeed, her first recorded work was sent to the R.T.S. under her father's name—*My Mates and I* was bought in 1870 for £24.

From St. Stephen's, where he had served for three years, the Rev. O. F. Walton was appointed incumbent of Christ Church, Jerusalem (1875–76). This would seem to have been immediately after his marriage; but before the end of 1876 he was Chaplain at Cally, Kirkcudbright, where he remained until 1883. Of his brief sojourn in the Holy Land, little evidence can be found in Mrs. Walton's books. Possibly a few chapters in *Was I Right?* (1879) dealing with events in Brindisi and Jerusalem and describing a Sunday on Mount Zion refer to these months. Since she was already an R.T.S. author and very popular (*Little Dot, Christie's Old Organ*, and some cottage tales being in print before 1875), it is odd that she wrote so little about the Holy Land. She may have had religious scruples about using such material in fiction, and presented it instead in her Biblical explications such as *Unbeaten Paths in Sacred History* (1906), *The King's Cup-Bearer* (1890), and the like.

There could not have been much to occupy a clergyman in Cally at the time. "A chapel and Academy" had been built for the benefit of the English workers and their children who had been imported to work in a textile mill established there two generations earlier; but this business, a casualty of the cotton famine of the 1860's, was represented in the 1870's only by a bobbin mill. However, there was still a chapel; and doubtless the Waltons occupied the Old Vicarage on the estate (which belonged to the Murray family).[4]

Most of Mrs. Walton's best-known books were written either before her marriage or during the seven years at Cally. In 1877, *Angel's Christmas* and *A Peep Behind the Scenes* came out; by 1883 she had added, *Little Faith*, *Saved at Sea*, and *Was I Right?* She was, on the whole, well paid for these works. Although the copyright of *Christie's Old Organ* (first published in 1874 as *Home Sweet*

Home) was originally sold for £15 with a bonus of £6.60, Mrs. Walton was later given generous gratuities upon her early works totalling by 1919, £492 in all.

In 1883, the Rev. O. F. Walton became the vicar of St. Thomas, York, where he remained for ten years, St. Thomas (a new church was built in 1886) stood in Lowther Street, where it served a neighbourhood of tradesmen. A Girls' and Infants' School was attached to the church, and the vicarage stood in Haxby Road. It was not a stylish part of the old city, its presence testifying rather to the rapid industrial growth of York in the 1880's. From York, the Waltons moved to Wolverhampton, where from 1893 to 1906, the Rev. O. F. Walton was vicar of St. Jude's. His next parish was at Leigh, near Tonbridge, where, in 1906, Mrs. Walton was interviewed by a writer for *The Quiver*.* For a time, after the first World War, the Waltons were at Shamly Green near Guildford. On Mr. Walton's retirement, the family returned to Leigh, where he died in 1933.

Mrs. Walton wrote little after 1900, though her books were constantly reprinted. Perhaps the recollections of an elderly inhabitant of Leigh who remembered her give the reason.

> "I was quite a small girl when the Rev. and Mrs. O. F. Walton came to the Vicarage in Leigh from Wolverhampton (I believe). Mrs. Walton took a great interest in all activities in the village. A large Sunday School, also Mothers' Union for young mothers, and a sewing class for teenage girls at the Vicarage and articles made were sold to help anyone in need. After leaving Leigh they went to live at Guildford (I think), later returning to live at Great Barnetts among old friends."[5]

An extremely conscientious parish worker, Mrs. Walton must also have thrown herself into various kinds of war work between 1914 and 1918. Her last book, *Strange Diana* (1919), indicates that her powers had failed greatly in the forty years since she wrote *A Peep Behind the Scenes*.

Her death at the age of ninety in July, 1939, passed quite unnoticed in the shadow of the coming war. It was the snapping of the last link between books for children and the Evangelical theory of the age of Wilberforce and Hannah More. It was fitting that Mrs. Walton should have taken the stand that she did, for she was a native of Yorkshire and of Hull, the city which had elected William

* *The Quiver* (1906), p. 677.

Wilberforce to Parliament in 1780. In 1787, he had written to his sister in Hull,

> ... In one word, ... I think the tendency of the theatre most pernicious. This is my decided sentiment, not taken up lightly, but on mature consideration. ... It would be an affectation of humility to deny that your authority has very great weight in the town of Hull, ... Will not, then, your presence at the amusements of the theatre sanction them in the minds of all who see you there? ... (M)ay not the players have to allege [i.e. at Judgment Day] that by your attendance they were countenanced in their exercise of a profession, which must be allowed to be highly unfavourable to their future happiness? May not the same be said by some young unguarded people, who, forgetting the Scripture precept to avoid the beginnings of evil, there ... acquired habits, which terminated in a dissolution of the moral principle, and finally in their irrecoverable ruin.[6]

In the same spirit, almost a century later, Mrs. Walton was to write *A Peep Behind the Scenes*, perhaps the last of the genuine Evangelical tract tales for children.

In addition to several sentimental novels for older readers—*Winter's Folly* (1889), *Dr. Forrester* (1906)—Mrs. Walton's works fall into three groupings. Her Bible instruction books, simple re-tellings of Old Testament stories, include *Elisha, the Man of Abel-Meholah* (1897), *The King's Cup-Bearer* (1891), and *Unbeaten Paths in Sacred History* (1906). Among the cottage tales for Mothers' Meetings and the like are *My Little Corner* (1872); *My Mates and I* (1873); and *Taken or Left* (1885). All have contemporary settings, much overt sentimentality, and are as strict in religious doctrine as the Cheap Repository Tracts. Each demonstrates that the way of the transgressor and that of the religiously indifferent lead alike to punishment, and that punishment brings about spiritual improvement. Thus the boy who follows bad company into the alehouse falls seriously ill, repents, and is converted. The neglectful mother loses her little child, burnt to death while the women are gossiping next door. Another village woman, wearied with the household cares, fails to attend church. She must watch four of her eleven children die of scarlet fever. Neither Hannah More nor Elizabeth Turner could devise a cautionary tale with swifter retribution for sins of omission and commission than could gentle Mrs. Walton.

Her tales were equally well supplied all around with Special Providences, that peculiarly Evangelical explanation of events that the theatre knows as *deus ex machina*. Lost relatives appear unexpectedly to help the deserving; the kind clergyman happens to visit Christie at the moment he is ill and alone; stranded in a strange town at nightfall, little Rosalie rediscovers an old friend from the fairground—the kindly dwarf, Mother Manikin, who again helps her. As in the chapbook, fairy tale and play, the Little Hero or Heroine can count on finding a helper at the moment when all seems lost.

A Peep Behind the Scenes (1877) was, in its time, almost every little girl's favourite book. It was also in the history of children's books the last battleground of the war between the world of the stage and the forces of Evangelical religion. By 1877, circus, pantomime and amateur theatricals had become acceptable juvenile entertainment. As early as 1846, *Memoirs of a London Doll* by Richard Hengist Horne had shown a very happy peep behind the scenes of a pantomime in which the little Columbine's grandmother takes the part of the Dragon. Thackeray in 1855 modelled *The Rose and the Ring* upon pantomime; in the same decade Julia Corner was turning fairy tales into children's plays on the assumption that, since children *will* invent imaginary situations and characters, there can be no real objections to plays that "convey some useful or moral lesson".[7] Mrs. Ewing wrote "Hints for Private Theatricals" for inclusion in *Aunt Judy's Magazine* (1875–76), and adapted the mummer's play of Saint George for nursery theatricals. All these writers, however, represented the tolerant upper-class view of the Established Church.

Tract fiction on the other hand had always opposed such amusement. Strict Evangelicals saw stage, circus, pantomime and acrobatic performance alike shadowed by the sulphurous cloud of the Pit. Actors, acrobats, dancers and magicians were all represented in Evangelical literature as hawking the trash of Vanity Fair to lure the weak and the young into the broad way of destruction. Protestant suspicion of the "mummery" of the Church's miracle and mystery plays, Puritan abhorrence of the stage, lay behind this attitude. That Methodists and Evangelicals alike were of one mind with William Prynne that "the devils . . . did recreate and exhilarate themselves with stage plays" is indicated by the recollections of the converted Samuel Kelly, who mentions that in his unregenerate days (*c.* 1788) he went to "two places of public resort", one being Allhallows Church to hear Mr. Wesley; the other, Covent Garden Theatre, "to worship the Prince of this world" and "countenance immorality, profaneness and dissipation".[8]

Bunyan's warning against Vanity Fair, where there was ". . . at all times to be seen juggling, cheats, games, plays, fools, apes, knaves and rogues and that of every kind", is the starting point of the Evangelical writers, "Charlotte Elizabeth", Mrs. Sherwood, A.L.O.E., Hesba Stretton and Mrs. Walton. The religious authority of *The Pilgrim's Progress* was reinforced in the eighteenth century by the rational seriousness of *Sandford and Merton.*

". . . (I)t seemed to me," says Harry Sandford of the fashionable play, *The Marriage of Figaro*, "to be full of nothing but cheating and dissimulation; and the people who went out and in did nothing but impose upon each other, and lie and trick and deceive . . .". Pressed later to subscribe to a collection on behalf of an actor, he refuses. ". . . (T)he person you have been talking of gains more than fifty poor families in the country have to maintain themselves; and therefore, if I had any money to give away, I should certainly give it to those that want it most."[9]

Victorian tract tales brought in both arguments, labelling stage and circus as spiritually harmful, physically dangerous, and wasteful of time and money. A.L.O.E.'s cottage tale, "The Great Plague",* emphasized that one way to the Pit led through the penny theatre. A group of schoolboys plan to play theatre, one outlining a play which he had seen "about a clever thief robbing a judge". The thief gets drunk, is taken by the policeman, and "calls out a great oath . . .". Finally the teacher intervenes, protesting that "Penny theatres are one of the most fruitful sources of vice and ruin to those who attend them".

A.L.O.E.'s attitude is understandable on the evidence of other, more impartial observers including Mayhew, and Gustav Doré and Blanchard Jerrold (whose account of this cheapest of theatres as they found it in London began "The true penny gaff is the place where juvenile Poverty meets juvenile Crime".)[10] She was writing from the true Puritan viewpoint that even childish imitation of sin was intrinsically wicked, and to make sin a source of amusement endangered the soul. Plays, not being true, were lies, and therefore

* *Precepts in Practice* (1858).

fathered by Satan. Mrs. Walton's attack upon the low-class theatre is based on the same argument.

Theatre of all kinds had long refused to be suppressed. J. M. Dent, whose *Memoirs* covered the 1850's to 1870's, recalled that in Darlington where he was a boy, "The theatre was taboo, and was not allowed in the town, but had to camp . . . in fields. . . . (M)y father and mother looked upon the theatre as the very gate of Hell". Defying their rules, he attended the plays, and found them exciting, romantic, melodramatic—and very, very moral. ". . . right and wrong were very clearly defined . . . in all the plays I saw in this old Barn, I remember none that had the least taint of sensuality in it, and almost every one . . . pointed a moral or called for heroic deeds. . . ."[11] Dickens and Jerrold agreed that this sort of performance was quite innocuous, unlike that of certain West End theatres.[12]

But it was, regrettably, only one side of the picture. An earlier, violent Gothic melodrama lingered on, and much coarse farce was played in "penny gaff" and other low-class theatres. This cheap drama romanticized the criminal; peep-shows dealt lavishly in murder and hangings, and even by the 1840's, "Villainy had, almost imperceptibly, become more intense. Murderers as well as seducers were less inclined to repentance and remorse. . . . Gloating over evil, as distinct from mere ruffianism, was becoming a force in fiction".[13]

Evangelical reformers of the 1840's and 1850's found stage entertainment with its powerful appeal to the emotions a serious obstacle to their work for the elevation of the masses. The evangelical tendency to evaluate all issues in terms of uncompromising good or evil came to the fore, and for twenty or thirty years they made little distinction between one kind of play and another. They could point with some justice to a decline in the quality and moral tone of the pantomime;[14] indeed Dickens called attention to the growth of the unhealthy excitement generated by the danger of acrobatic displays. His observation that "everybody seems afraid that Blondin may fall before they have time to take their seats"[15] attacks the same human callousness that Hesba Stretton deplored twenty years later in *An Acrobat's Girlhood*.

Otherwise Dickens was a persistent champion of stage entertainment. Very much the actor himself, he loved theatre, music-hall, circus and pantomime. Critical chiefly of the flaring footlights that could ignite the gauzy skirts of the ballet, he ignored the moral dangers of a dancer's life. For him, the world of stage and circus was the "type" of fairyland; its inhabitants, ridiculous, feckless or pretentious as he might represent them, were by these very qualities detached from the harsh world of materialism. Like children, they inhabited a world of make-believe. Entertainers in his own work are usually casual and friendly. Mrs. Jarley, absurd but benevolent Queen of the Waxworks, ever travelling with her entourage, offers in royal fashion a pleasant refuge to Little Nell. Mr. Sleary's squalid little circus is the only real home Cissy Jupe has known. Down to its last member, she can count on the support of the troupe; and the warmth and humanity radiating from the tubby person of Mr. Sleary thaw at last the frozen heart of Mr. Gradgrind himself.

This picture of circus life stands up well when tested by the recollections of "Lord" George Sanger,* or by Rupert Croft-Cooke's account of the Rosaires of more recent times.[16] Not even Mrs. Walton could show the whole circus as wholly evil or the smaller shows as morally harmful. On the contrary, the Dwarfs, the Giant, and the Happy Family in *A Peep Behind the Scenes* are kindly and helpful to the sick woman and the footsore child. Her chief target was the cheap low-class theatre offering trivial melodrama, or the low lodging-house where the actors, of necessity, made their temporary home; and her essential concern, completely justified by the facts, was for the health and moral safety of the child actress forced into this life by her unscrupulous father.

The law offered little or no protection to the child performer. Twelve years after the publication of *A Peep Behind the Scenes*, Hesba Stretton was writing *An Acrobat's Girlhood*, an indictment of the nation's failure to protect the child entertainer.

> It was murder, though the law could not punish it . . . they had kept within the law. Somebody told me that in other countries children are not allowed to perform in theatres and shows, and they are obliged to send to England for children when they want them. Children's lives are held more precious there than with us—ay! and children's souls; for they say in those countries that it is not

* Sanger's Circus with its well-known high float carrying the "Britannia" player with her lion at the apex would seem to be the one described by Mrs. Walton in Chapter VII of *A Peep Behind the Scenes.* Sanger's Britannia was of sterner stuff than the girl described by Mrs. Walton in Chapter X.

> good for the morals of innocent little creatures to be brought before the public on the stage. But it is not thought so in England. (Page 66.)

The movement to prevent or at least to regulate the employment of children in theatres and pantomimes had begun in earnest in the 1870's. It attempted to extend the protection of children under the Factory Laws to other children working as entertainers or exploited as little beggars. The National Society for the Prevention of Cruelty to Children arose out of it, Hesba Stretton taking an active part in founding the London branch (1884). In *The Lord's Purse Bearers* (1883), she showed in detail a shocking traffic in half-starved infants rented out by their "keepers" to professional street beggars. Other reformers investigated the treatment of the children who lived on canal-boats, and those who spent the winters with their parents in the workhouses and drifted around the country for the rest of the year, picking hops or fruit, hoeing, haymaking, harvesting.[17]

Pantomime Waifs (1884), by E. M. Barlee corroborates many details of *A Peep Behind the Scenes* published seven years before. It may have suggested parts of *An Acrobat's Girlhood*, five years later. Although her chief concern was with souls, Miss Barlee did not forget bodies. Her book analysed and ranked the various types of theatrical performances according to their use (or abuse) of children. Admitting that high-class drama, opera and oratorio used few children and did little physical harm, she lamented that *all* theatrical training, even on this high level, weakened resistance to moral evil. Children must

> . . . practise the various expressions of the passions . . . until each can be assumed at command. Such an education once acquired unhappily extends beyond the stage . . . the danger . . . lies in the power it imparts of deceiving others and simulating right to cover wrong. (*Pantomime Waifs*, p. 28.)

Ballet, pantomime and music-hall, along with low-class theatres dealing in farce, low comedy and melodrama were, in her opinion, very harmful to children thus employed, who, when they outgrew theatre work, were, at the best, unfitted for less exciting occupations. The work of the Theatrical Mission in London, as outlined in the articles by Anne Beale in *The Girls' Own Paper* (1884) included attempts to train, or find employment for those leaving the stage.

It did much more than give religious instruction to the members of its Scripture Union. Particularly concerned with the welfare of stage children (many as young as four or five), it supplied cheap meals, ran a lending library, kept a register of names and addresses, and traced runaways. It held sewing classes and temperance meetings too; had branches in all large cities, and maintained a home in Paris for young actresses. Anne Beale claimed for it a membership of five thousand from the twenty-one thousand people working in London's forty theatres.

One of the prime concerns of reformers was acrobatics in all its forms. Acrobatics brought in the hazards of a cruel training and dangerous performances; Miss Barlee stresses the ease with which the flimsy existing laws could be evaded by labelling the children of the troupe "apprentices". Even Charlotte Yonge was convinced of the dangers, for she introduced a stolen child (who dies of injuries received) into *Nuttie's Father* (1885), and an "apprenticed" child into *The Long Vacation* (1895). The issue was evidently a live one for some years.

Although both Mrs. Walton and Hesba Stretton were concerned with the degrading effects of the entertainer's life and its great danger to health, there was otherwise no resemblance between their books. Hesba Stretton never obscured her main point—that Trixie was *one of many* such victims of human greed and indifference.

> . . . (T)here are thousands of children employed in theatres and shows, and how many of them grow up to be strong men and women?

The painful facts of the acrobat's training and life were kept before her reader, as was the public responsibility for the situation.

> For it is folks who pay to see such things that are most to the blame . . . she was cruelly done to death in England for the entertainment of the people. They did not know, you say; but they ought to have known it. They have reason and sense; they must know such a life is not fit for a child. (Page 54, 59.)

The tale required the reader to think about the price of his entertainment in human life and health, its emotional possibilities being played down. It was, in effect, a case-history, an example that illustrated Miss Barlee's book or the reports that finally brought about the various acts governing Dangerous Performances and the Prevention of Cruelty to Children.[18]

Mrs. Walton, on the other hand, overwhelmed thought and reason by emotion. Rosalie is a special child, set apart by her superior refinement and beauty, her innocence, her religious faith.

> . . . (S)he had never wandered about the fair, but had kept quietly in the caravan, as her mother had wished her to do so; she knew very little of what was going on in other parts of the ground. (Chapter XIII.)

The tale hinges upon her escape from the life of the fairground and theatre, that nineteenth-century extension of Bunyan's Vanity Fair.

There is much conflicting evidence about the fairs. On the one side stands the drinking, the brawling, the crime. "The love of ugliness . . . exclusively and for itself as the greatest pleasure in life," said R. H. Horne, was exemplified in these fairs,[19] and Kingsley showed one such in *Yeast* (1848). But quite another side is found in William Richmond's recollections of Sevenoaks Fair in the late 1840's,[20] or in Masefield's *Grace Before Ploughing* (1966). In children's books, it finds its happiest expression in *Jackanapes* (1884).

Obviously the conduct of fairs was better regulated by law in the late 1870's and 1880's than it had been earlier; doubtless many children, seeing only what they wanted to see, missed much of the vulgarity and brutality of the cruder shows.

Could Mrs. Walton have realised how enthralling was her description of the sideshows?

> . . . the Fat Boy, whose huge clothes were being paraded outside . . .; the Lady Without Arms, whose powerful feats of knitting, sewing, writing and tea-making were being rehearsed to the crowd; the Entertaining Theatre, outside which was a stuffed performing cat playing on a drum, and two tiny children of about three years old, dressed up in the most extraordinary costumes, and dancing with tambourines in their hands; the Picture Gallery, in which you could see Adam and Eve, Queen Elizabeth and other distinguished persons; all these were on Rosalie's right hand, and on her left was a long succession of stalls on which were sold gingerbread, brandy-snap, nuts, biscuits, cocoa-nuts, boiled peas, hot potatoes, and sweets of all kinds. Here was a man selling cheap walking-sticks, and there another offering the boys a moustache and a pair of spectacles for a penny each. . . .
>
> How glad Rosalie was to get past them all. . . . (Chapter XIII.)

Not so the little reader. At this point, Mrs. Walton retrieved religion and pathos with some skill, and the next page took Rosalie into the Royal Show of Dwarfs, and a fresh recollection of her grief. Then the writer sent her home by a different way, giving us a thoroughly satisfactory peep at the toy stalls and the Happy Family:

> . . . various animals living on the most friendly terms with each other—a little dog in a smart coat, playing with several small white rats, a monkey hugging a little white kitten, a white cat, which had been dyed a brilliant yellow, superintending the sports of a number of mice and dormice; and a duck, a hen and a guinea-pig, which were conversing together in one corner of the cage. (Chapter XIII.)

These engaging descriptions undoubtedly weakened Mrs. Walton's theme of spiritual search and pilgrimage; hoping to show the vanity and tediousness of fairground life, she displayed instead its colour, the charm and gaiety of these little shows, and the genuine kindliness of the show people.

Like *Little Meg's Children*, *A Peep Behind the Scenes* (tract elements and all) dovetails perfectly into the traditional fairy and folk tale. Like Little Heroine of these tales, shabby little Rosalie is other than she seems. Passing through vicissitudes without complaint and without loss of faith and integrity, she attains a rightful security and love. Like Cinderella she has a cruel stepmother, a floor to scrub, unkindness to bear. Mother Manikin, the dwarf, is fairy-like in her oddity and helpfulness, re-appearing in time of need. The villains, however, Rosalie's father and stepmother, are far below fairy-tale standards; creatures rather of squalid melodrama, they fail to convince.

Writing with declared religious purpose, Mrs. Walton had actually produced a most unlikely hybrid: an Evangelical fairy-tale. Hesba Stretton, on the other hand, with avowed social purpose and in the quietest of tones, created an acrobatic troupe that is a floating fragment of hell, with attendant demons in the shape of the Lafosses, tormenting their miserable victims, forcing them into performance at the price of life or health. Running counter to the popular taste for pantomime, this tale made little impression on its own time and is hardly known today, whereas the lurid novels of Amye Reade on the same subject—*Ruby* (1889), and *Slaves of the Sawdust* (1892)—

enjoyed quite a wide circulation, and the pathetic and emotional *Peep Behind the Scenes* was one of the best-known children's tales of the century. It has been in print ever since, and is (1979) listed along with *Christie's Old Organ* in the offerings of the Lutterworth Press. In 1918 it was filmed, Mrs. Walton and officials of the R.T.S. approving the first showing on December 11th of that year by The Studio of Portsmouth Road, Thames Ditton, who had purchased the rights from International Exclusives.

Looking at Mrs. Walton's work as a whole, the modern reader is struck by its sentimentality and its preoccupation with death, particularly in the books for children. Before her time, only the Rev. Legh Richmond had dealt so fulsomely and successfully in deathbed and graveyard scenes; in the same way, Mrs. Walton was attempting to present Christian death in good Evangelical fashion as the crown and triumph of earthly life. But her stories are so lacking in proportion that life does not have a fair chance. The notorious *Little Dot* (1873) illustrates this point; nevertheless the tale was so much to the public taste that the Religious Tract Society ran a magazine entitled *Our Little Dots* (1887–1922) and published a Little Dot Series of stories. *Christie's Old Organ* (1874), Mrs. Walton's "street arab" tale has the reputation of being more cheerful, perhaps because the child lives (although the old man dies—through nine of the fourteen chapters). It is certainly much more restrained in style. *A Peep Behind the Scenes* keeps Rosalie's mother on her death-bed for slightly over half of the book. In fact, had Charlotte Yonge been writing her *Macmillan's* articles in 1889 instead of 1869, she would have had to replace Mrs. Sherwood by Mrs. Walton as "first in the field of pious slaughter". A fair cross-section of Mrs. Sherwood's writing reveals that she much preferred a living child to a dead one; this can hardly be said of Mrs. Walton.

Mrs. Walton's language likewise contributes to the pathetic effect. Situation is heavily underlined by hypnotic repetition of simple emotive words: *little*, *poor*, *old*, *honest*, etc. Mrs. Sherwood had introduced this device with "Little" Lucy, "Little Henry", etc. Miss Charlesworth used it constantly, as she did "the Child" (borrowed perhaps from Dickens' *Old Curiosity Shop*). Mrs. Walton makes great play upon *Old*—Old Treffy, Old Grumpy, Old Solomon, the old organ, etc.—and uses *poor* excessively in *A Peep Behind the Scenes*, particularly about the dying mother. The device was overworked by this time, and no one else seems to have adopted it.

A Peep Behind the Scenes was also Mrs. Walton's contribution to the long Victorian list of pilgrimage books. Equally congenial to her was the theme of storm and wreck, lighthouse and lifeboat. These had greater immediate allegorical relevance in an industrial society than either *Pilgrim's Progress* which demanded awareness of rural life and occupations, or Bishop Wilberforce's *Agathos* which assumed a knowledge of chivalry. Wreck and storm, ship and lighthouse were significant themes in an England that was the world's chief trading nation. Entering children's books with *Robinson Crusoe*, they had been brought up to date throughout the century in the works of Marryat, Ballantyne and Kingston. Both Hesba Stretton and Mrs. Walton seized upon them, utilizing for background the identical circumstances currently inspiring Samuel Plimsoll's campaign for safety at sea, and Mrs. Mary Sewell contributed *Davie Blake the Sailor* (1874 ?) to the tract tale appeals. Hesba Stretton's *The Crew of the Dolphin* (1876) showing the chief cause of wreck to be the greed of shipowner and merchant is a fictional extension of Plimsoll's arguments and of the many articles upon the subject in the periodicals of the day.[21] Mrs. Walton, who had grown up in Hull and was well informed about the lives of fishermen and sailors, made the matter of wreck and rescue the occasion for numerous religious messages. "And are *you* on the rock, my lad?" asks the old visitor to the lighthouse in *Saved at Sea* (1879). The grown-up Christie, who has become a lay-preacher in a Yorkshire fishing village, preaches four sermons, makes two converts, and conducts three hymn-singings in the course of the twelve short chapters of *Christie the King's Servant* (1898). This book was apparently intended for a Service of Song. Both *Little Dot* and *Christie's Old Organ* were used thus.[22] Like A.L.O.E. and "Charlotte Elizabeth", Mrs. Walton seems to have written her own hymns for inclusion in her tales (Fig. 26).

In conclusion, one can only say that Mrs. Walton was a sincere and devout Evangelical born fifty years too late; an excellent clergyman's wife; and a very uneven writer. One at least of her books—the completely morbid *Nobody Loves Me* (1883), in which a destitute, senile old woman, Old Grumpy, adopts a doomed tubercular orphan child of four—would have been better left unwritten. Most modern readers would say the same of *Little Dot*. Her most promising tale, with its splendid wealth of detail about fairground life, and its sadly unexplored possibilities for character development, is swamped in the wave of sentiment and surface refinement marking so much popular literature between 1880 and 1914. Her genuine concern for the spiritual and physical welfare of children was unavoidably sentimentalized by the demands of the times, demands with which the Tract Societies were willing to comply so long as their own basic requirements of a repentance, a conversion, and a Christian death scene were included in each tale. From the modern secular point of view, the best books about orphans at this time were written by the practical and tough-minded Frances Hodgson Burnett. Nevertheless, as an *Evangelical* masterpiece of pathos and religious faith, only *Little Henry and his Bearer* and *Jessica's First Prayer* can be said to equal or surpass *A Peep Behind the Scenes.*

CHAPTER XI

THE BENT TWIG

"JUST as the twig is bent, the tree's inclined"? Not necessarily, judging by the state of the Evangelical orchard in the second and third generation. Certainly many children of Evangelical families inclined devoutly to their parents' beliefs, lived up to them and passed them on. The famous American missionary family, the Scudders, are a notable example. Maria Charlesworth and Mrs. Walton are themselves examples, and A.L.O.E. successfully combined and disseminated eighteenth-century moral principle and strong Evangelical conviction. William Carus Wilson loomed terrifyingly over certain sensitive imaginations committed to his charge, thus attaining literary immortality as Jane Eyre's Mr. Brocklehurst. Popular preacher, copious writer of hell-fire tracts, he was as uncompromisingly Calvinistic as any seventeenth-century Puritan. The general tone of *The Children's Friend* in its early years suggests that Charlotte Brontë's portrait was a fair likeness: yet William Carus Wilson had warm supporters among his former scholars (as Mrs. Gaskell discovered with the publication of her life of Charlotte Brontë). Among them was Emma Jane Worboise, whose novel *Thorneycroft Hall* (1864) depicts a benevolent and well-loved Carus Wilson.

But even as the frail physiques of the Brontë sisters suffered under the hardships of intensive Calvinistic cultivation, their startling talents survived and flowered. In spite of—perhaps because of—emotional deprivation in the House of Desolation, the abilities of the young Rudyard Kipling were stimulated in these painful years. A youthful John Ruskin, guarded, guided, loved and disciplined by his Evangelical parents in a fashion which makes the upbringing of the little Fairchilds look positively neglectful by comparison, grew up to shape much of Victorian thought.

In fact, the bending and pruning of the Evangelical twig, with its consequent diversion of natural impulse and energy, has often *encouraged* talent: it certainly removed distraction, concentrated genius, inculcated application and attention. It is not surprising that many descendents of the early Evangelicals made an indelible mark upon their own times.*

As might be expected, their influence was most immediately apparent in the field of religion, where interesting mutations—Tractarianism, for instance, and Liberal Christianity—occurred in the second or third generations of Evangelical families. Benjamin Jowett was one of the most influential voices of Liberal Christianity, and Charles Kingsley of Christian Socialism. A volcanic upheaval in the Church of England resulted from the actions and writings of John Henry Newman, Henry Edward Manning (son of Wilberforce's close friend), and Wilberforce's own sons, Robert Isaac and Henry. All four became active Tractarians and later Roman Catholics. A second group of Tractarians which included William Sewell, W. E. Gladstone, and Samuel Wilberforce remained within the Church as its vigorous defenders. Henry Sykes Thornton, after a lifetime of strict Evangelical probity, came under the ban of Canon Law by marrying his deceased wife's sister. Marianne, his sister, was a Liberal Christian of broad views. Francis Newman, Annie Besant, and several of the brilliant descendants of James Stephen repudiated their religious faith along with their childhood Evangelicalism to become outspoken freethinkers, agnostics, humanists or atheists. Others in an age of doubt turned with relief to the apparent certainties of science.

The Tractarians in particular had a strong and beneficial influence upon books for the young. Their work, usually of a high literary standard, included fine hymns by John Mason Neale and Mrs. C. F. Alexander as well as Sabine Baring-Gould's "Now the day is over". Bishop Samuel Wilberforce's *Agathos* with its echoes of Spenser was often preferred to *The Pilgrim's Progress* in Anglican households. Moreover, with Charlotte Yonge's *Monthly Packet* (1851–1898) and Mrs. Gatty's *Aunt Judy's Magazine* (1866–1885), the long and depressing monopoly of the Evangelical children's Sunday magazines was broken, and after 1870 the Tract Societies extended the range and interest of their children's periodicals.

The skilfully written novels of Elizabeth Missing Sewell and Charlotte Yonge broke sharply with the conventions of the tract

* As did some descendants of Victorian Evangelicals, e.g. Field Marshal Montgomery, a grandson of the noted Broad Church Evangelical, Dean F. W. Farrar, author of *Eric, or Little by Little* (1858).

tale. Both women were dedicated Anglicans strongly influenced by the Oxford Movement; both had been impressed by Harriett Newman Mozley's ironic analysis of the failure of a narrowly-Evangelical education to develop conscience. In *The Fairy Bower* (1840) and its sequel, *The Lost Brooch* (1841), she had shown a spoilt girl, who both as child and as young woman, displays selfishness, dishonesty and callous disregard for the rights and feelings of others. An excellent training in Evangelical doctrine has left these deplorable traits quite unmodified, the girl simply assuming that those who do not share her beliefs do not matter and acting accordingly.[1]

Elizabeth Sewell had in childhood suffered agonies of guilt from the practice of rigorous religious self-examination demanded at her Evangelical boarding school. To it, she said, she ascribed

> . . . the fatal necessity of using in those early years my common sense as a defence against the workings of a morbid and over-strained conscience. It laid the foundations for a sophistical habit of mind; and some of the actions of my life for which I most condemn myself can be traced to it. (*Autobiography* . . ., p. 27.)

Her own novels, arising out of the doubts and difficulties of her own religious development, were widely read in the 1860's and 1870's. So closely were the works of Charlotte Yonge scanned for religious dogma that she refused to edit a series of children's tales for Macmillan's on the ground that the need to present a variety of religious opinion and belief would prejudice her own position, her names being taken as "a pledge for the strict line of distinctively Anglican orthodoxy . . .".[2] Mrs. Gatty and Mrs. Ewing likewise were on the fringes of the Tractarian group.

All these writers stressed development of character over a period of time and showed the inner life of the individual enriched by participation in the life of a revitalized Anglican church. All stressed a disciplined personal piety, respect for tradition, and the importance of the sacraments. All repudiated the sudden dramatic conversions, religious clichés and simplified doctrine of extreme Evangelicalism. Books such as Elizabeth Sewell's *Margaret Percival* (1847), Charlotte Yonge's *The Daisy Chain* (1856) or *The Young Stepmother* (1861), and Mrs. Ewing's *Six to Sixteen* (1875) deal realistically with family life, and without exaggeration show how religious belief (or the lack of it) governs and influences conduct.

What of the descendants, real or spiritual, of the Evangelical children's writers themselves? The Rev. Legh Richmond in the first generation of them was predeceased by both his disappointing son Nugent, and his promising son, Wilberforce. One of his grandsons was the husband of the late nineteenth-century writer, Emma Marshall. Some of Mrs. Cameron's many children became missionaries; her son, the Rev. George Cameron, was her biographer. Mrs. Sherwood's family moved quietly back into the moderate Established Church. Her only surviving son, the Rev. Henry Martyn Sherwood (the original Henry Fairchild and Henry Milner) took Holy Orders in the 1830's and became Vicar of Aston White Ladies in time for the Coronation celebrations of 1837. There F. J. Harvey Darton found and interviewed him after 1900. He had restored his church; and had held his vicarage longer than any other parish priest in the country. The children's tales written by Mrs. Sherwood's daughter, Sophia (Streeten) Kelly* (often included in reprints of Mrs. Sherwood's works after 1851) are discouragingly tepid, sentimental and class-conscious, much inferior to the work of her famous mother.

Although there is no record that Maria Louisa Charlesworth and A.L.O.E. ever met, members of the Charlesworth and Tucker families came together in the next generation to forward the work of the most conspicuous Evangelical movement of the period: the Salvation Army. In 1869, Miss Charlesworth's brother, the Rev. Samuel Charlesworth, became Rector of Limehouse in the London slums. Samuel Charlesworth and particularly his wife Maria Amelia, a dedicated Evangelical who regularly conducted religious readings for working girls in local factories, gave the Salvation Army workers sympathetic encouragement in the 1870's. Of their three daughters, the two youngest, Florence and Maud, were to make some stir in the world over the next fifty years.

The influence of *Ministering Children* is clearly discernible in the activities of both. Writing in 1889, Maud Charlesworth (then Mrs. Ballington Booth) ascribed her choice of her life's work to the picture of Christianity in action in *Ministering Children*. She had been, she said, vividly impressed by "the kind, helpful sympathy, expressed oftener by deeds than by words, that was sure to follow whenever trouble or sorrow appeared . . .".[3]

* Her work in relation to her mother's is discussed in my *Mrs. Sherwood and her Books for Children* (1974).

Obviously this testimony would have delighted Maria Charlesworth: it was the very effect she had hoped to produce. She would, however, have been horrified had she known that shortly after her death, this particular niece had taken (at the age of sixteen) her "first step in life-long aggressive usefulness" by accompanying; in 1881, the first female Salvation Army contingent to Paris under the leadership of twenty-one-year-old Catherine Booth.[4]

Seriously perturbed, Samuel Charlesworth opposed his daughter's participation in this project on the grounds of her age; of the well-known hostility of the French to these ultra-Protestant activities; and of her health. He feared she was undergoing a spell of religious neurosis. An undignified wrangle in the press followed his protests, for the Booths at all times welcomed publicity of any kind. Very pretty, talented, highly educated, speaking beautiful French, Maud Charlesworth was undeniably an asset to their cause, which, associated from the beginning with the lowest slum elements, was not yet socially acceptable. Having proselytized successfully in Paris cafés at sixteen, she was arrested a year or two later in Switzerland along with other Salvation Army workers. Her path crossed there with that of Josephine Butler, who spoke highly of her. At twenty-one she led a Salvation Army group into Sweden, and at one point addressed the student body of Uppsala University. In the same year, 1886, she married Ballington Booth in a public ceremony at Congress Hall, Clapton, the public (at a charge of 2/6 per head) being admitted to the wedding breakfast. In 1887, the couple sailed for America to take charge of Salvation Army activities there.

For five years, General Booth had been proclaiming loudly that Samuel Charlesworth's opposition to his daughter's Salvation Army career was based largely on social snobbery, and that Maud's rebellion was motivated by her true desire to serve Christ. Inconsistently, he was even louder in his complaints ten years later when this same rebellious Maud and her husband broke away from his own authority. In 1896, the Ballington Booths resigned from the Salvation Army, claiming that the General's insistence upon keeping everything subject to his own control was damaging the work in America (then, politically, very isolationist). Immediately they set afoot their own Volunteers of America, similarly organized, with Ballington Booth as General, and Ballington and Maud as joint Presidents. Described as a "philanthropic, social and Christian movement", it was still strong in the 1920's.[5]

Maud Ballington Booth devoted her work in part to the rehabilitation of prisoners, founding in 1896 a Volunteers Prison League at Sing-Sing. In 1909, she addressed the Chautauqua circuit on the subject, billed as "the Little Mother of the Prisons". By 1913, the League was said to have had ninety thousand members. She was also a founding member of the Parent-Teacher Association, and wrote two or three books for children; but her real contribution to social reform was this pioneer work in the patrol and rehabilitation system. She died in 1948 at the age of eighty-three.

Following the defection of the Ballington Booths, Salvation Army work in New York was not written off as a loss by the tough old General. They were at once replaced by the more tractable Booth-Tuckers—Emma Booth and her husband, Frederick St. George Tucker, nephew and spiritual son of A.L.O.E. Frederick St. George Tucker had been trained for the Indian Civil Service. Disposed towards religion (his Aunt Charlotte's influence?), he had been converted at twenty by the American evangelists, Moody and Sankey. In the eighteenth-century definition of the word, he was an *enthusiast*, emotional, stubborn, one-idea'd. He was also a talented linguist. His Indian career, which lasted only five years, was punctuated by official rebukes, because he insisted on preaching to the natives. Its highlight was his marriage about 1877 to a missionary eighteen years his senior: feeling himself unduly susceptible to female charm, he had sought a wife who would not be too distracting, and was drawn to this one by her strong religious ardour. The only one in his widespread family connection who sympathised with him at this point seems to have been his Aunt Charlotte (then in the second year of her missionary life) who was a witness at his wedding. In 1881, he joined the Salvation Army, having given up the Indian Civil Service. After the death of his first wife, he married Emma Booth in 1888, adding his name to hers, according to the General's rule.

Booth-Tucker worked both in India and in America, writing a number of books about his Salvation Army experiences, and a life of Mrs. Booth. His writing is dismissed by General Booth's biographer, St. John Ervine (by no means faultless in this line) as careless, sentimental and verbose; but the man himself is admitted to have been completely dedicated, abiding by the rule of poverty, ". . . courageous, and honest and selfless . . ."[6] He stayed by General Booth to the end, his loyalty unshaken by the disruption of the family after Mrs. Booth's death.

While personally deploring the tactics of the Salvation Army in India, A.L.O.E. must have felt a certain pride in her nephew. His was the true Evangelical spirit, and she had done much to form it.

Samuel Charlesworth's second daughter, Florence Louisa (1862–1921), four years older than Maud, had great musical talent. While still a child, she helped her mother to conduct religious readings for factory workers, leading the hymn, playing piano or violin. So fine was her contralto voice that her father had promised her professional vocal training. She decided instead, at nineteen, to marry his curate, the Rev. Charles Barclay. Florence Barclay was an exemplary clergyman's wife, working with village organisations, playing the organ, conducting the choir, raising several children. Then, in her forties, convalescing from a serious illness, she began to write. In 1909 she became the most popular novelist of the decade as *The Rosary* reached a sale of 150,000 copies in its first year before climbing to over a million by 1921.

The nature of the link between *Ministering Children* and *The Rosary* is immediately apparent. Maria Charlesworth had written "to show as in a picture what ministering children are"; Florence Barclay wanted her characters to be an object lesson in living. According to her daughter's account, she deliberately depicted an ideal world—bright, refined and beautiful, "the people charming, amusing, brave and true". She hoped to make her reader forget for a time the dreary realities of her own life, her disappointing acquaintances. Miss Charlesworth's books had avoided the ugliest and most degrading aspects of poverty, and kept evil at a distance. Mrs. Barclay's avowed intent was to avoid all "taint of sin or shadow of shame" and never to represent a character who might "lower the ideals" of her readers.[7]

Both women advocated kindness, sympathy and charity in human relations; both sincerely practised what they preached, Maria Charlesworth giving generously to missions and charities and supporting a London Ragged School, her niece helping to keep up an orphanage and donating generously to hospitals.

Many of Mrs. Barclay's characters, the Hon. Jane Champion, for instance, are ministering children of a larger growth. They follow the path of duty without complaint or deviation, tending the sick, smoothing the way for others. Like Little Jane, Little Rose and others, they move across an ideal background, violence, malice and stupidity being no more evident in their elegant surroundings than in Miss Charlesworth's picturesque village. Both writers were praised by their contemporaries for their effective use of sentiment directed to religious teaching.

There was, however, this essential difference: whereas Miss Charlesworth devised her ideal picture as an example to its reader, Mrs. Barclay produced hers for an escape. Maud Ballington Booth had grasped the spirit of the Evangelical lesson in *Ministering Children*, but her sister successfully cultivated its sentiment. True to the taste of her times, Mrs. Barclay was vague about religion. Nevertheless she was fully convinced that her work carried a spiritual message, and was puzzled and hurt when rebuked for writing a "religiously sensuous" story in which, complained the reviewer, the hero's conduct and reasoning "illustrates the ingenuity with which the scriptures may be twisted when the wish is father to the thought".[8] Such criticism did not diminish her popularity: by 1910, two or three generations of readers had learned in childhood to equate sentiment with religion. Mrs. Barclay's books supplied romantic "escape" literature for those whose ordered world was crashing down after 1914. A century of industrial growth with its attendant problems, over fifty years of scientific questioning and religious doubt separated the post-war generation of 1920 from that which had turned to Evangelicalism after the Napoleonic Wars. Readers who had grown up with *Ministering Children*, *A Peep Behind the Scenes*, and other tract tales enthusiastically accepted Mrs. Barclay's novels, which had a tremendous popularity for about thirty years. They are little known today. Neither their sentimental romance nor their diluted religion could endure the harsh realities of the depression and the second World War.

So much for a few of the children and grandchildren of conspicuous early Evangelicals. What of all the rest? What of the descendants of farm labourers, of Ragged School pupils, of mine and factory workers, of slum dwellers? Those, in short, for whom or on whose behalf so much of the Tract literature was written? It is impossible to be sure: they left so little record. Evangelical discipline and organisation had some unexpected results. The links between Methodism and early trade unionism are well attested.

> ". . . (T)he Methodist and Evangelist training were what the early socialists were made of. There were a lot of them—Christians turned politicians,"

said a former miner in 1969.[9] But to judge from tract tales dealing with workmen and masters, the matter was only superficially touched on in these books at any time; they probably had little influence. Occasionally in books written in the present century we find a glimpse of the effect of Evangelical penetration into sad and difficult lives. Some of Dr. Barnardo's orphans for instance have written of their childhood in the Cottage Homes.[10] A very few others, mostly from homes of above-average literacy for the place and time, have told of their sincere enjoyment of the tract tales: Flora Thompson, George Sturt, Edgar Wallace are among them.

In many such homes the tract tales, accumulated book by book as school and Sunday School prizes, formed the children's only library. Cherished and re-read, such family libraries often accompanied their owners across the sea. Thus a copy of *The History of Susan Gray*, one of the earliest tract fiction books, was presented in a Baptist Sunday School "for good conduct and attendance", in 1884. In 1913, the same book is given "To Muriel . . . for her birthday from Mother"; in 1974 it turns up in a thrift shop in British Columbia. And so with many others, their once-gay covers of scarlet or buff or blue or green soiled, their gilt tarnished, their pages finger-marked, scrawled, spotted with oil or candle-grease. Most bear the original inscriptions, some have the names of three or four owners with different dates. They have been read.

During the settlement of the dominions, remote districts often lacked church services or Sunday Schools, children receiving what religious instruction they got from their parents and their family libraries, if any. The Religious Tract Society and the S.P.C.K. continued to supply books very cheaply, sometimes free, to schools, Sunday Schools and libraries in new lands. Since for two generations or more the hardships of pioneer life allowed neither time nor opportunity for writing, little fiction for the young came out of Canada, New Zealand, Australia or South Africa for many years. In 1930, children of the commonwealth were still reading Ballantyne, Kingston and Henty; contemporary children's literature of the lands of their birth hardly existed. The always-available, cheap and copious supply from Paternoster Row explains in part the long failure of commonwealth countries to produce their own children's literature.

When around 1900 commonwealth writers did make a start, their work was often highly derivative—Marshall Saunders'

Beautiful Joe (1894), for instance; or the works of the popular and internationally-known "Ralph Connor" (the Rev. C. W. Gordon). His *Glengarry Schooldays* (1902), in spite of much lively episode and vivid and authentic pictures of Ontario pioneer life, was little more than a colourful tract tale, almost as heavily laden with sentiment and overt religious teaching as *The Wide Wide World* or *The Robbers' Cave*.

A wide variety of circumstances contributed to the decline of tract literature in the first quarter of this century. After 1870, the influence of the churches and the Tract Societies upon education was gradually undermined by the demands of an industrial society in which technical skill and knowledge of science were increasingly valued. Of the two great original purposes of the tract printings, *literacy* came by about 1880 to be taken for granted, perhaps with undue optimism. *Religious training*, except within the home, dwindled into the brief Scripture lesson at school and an hour or two at Sunday School once a week.

Between 1870 and 1900 too, a whole new group of talented writers for children appeared, whose work set new and exacting standards. Lewis Carroll, George MacDonald and Kipling showed in their different ways lively originality, vivid imagination and remarkable artistic perception. Mrs. Ewing brought a ready sympathy and kindly humour to her graceful tales; Mrs. Molesworth and Frances Hodgson Burnett displayed great psychological insight in their presentation of child characters who were a realistic mixture of good traits and bad. (This type of 'mixed' character had always been frowned on by the Tract Societies, a fact which accounts for the flatness of characterization in the majority of tract tales, a flatness and predictability which no amount of sentiment or action could disguise.) With the tales of Ernest Thompson Seton, Charles G. D. Roberts and Kipling, even the animal story broke away from the well-worn moral or sentimental patterns of the past to show nature realistically in a purely secular light. There was too an enthusiastic revival of folk and fairy tale.[11]

Almost imperceptibly during these years the tract tale was merging with that very large group of books for girls that has recently been described and analysed in *You're a Brick, Angela* by Mary Cadogan and Patricia Craig (1976). Piousness became sportsmanship (boys' school stories being a strong influence here); most of the action took place in schools, but the fondness for type characters and "conversion" of the unbelieving and unconforming indicates the relationship.

Sunday reading, however, lingered on. It took the destructive effects of the first World War to alter the whole climate of belief in which from the time of Mrs. Trimmer it had developed. The inevitable sense of loss, deep and widespread emotional exhaustion, the cynicism and doubt which followed upon two wars within fifteen years, all fostered agnosticism and religious indifference. Economic depression proved that honesty and industry did not necessarily bring their just reward. Everywhere old values were shaken. The discipline of respectability was challenged within the very classes that had upheld it most loudly; close-knit and intense family relationships were regarded askance by a generation with a smattering of Freudian psychology and a passionate admiration for *Sons and Lovers* (1913). In a strong reaction against complacency in religion, the optimism and sentiment so often associated with it in the later tract fiction sounded a hollow note. In the 1920's, the noted American tract tale writer "Pansy" (Isabella Alden) summed up the prevailing attitude. "In these days," she observed sadly, "Christ is not popular."[12]

By the end of the first World War, religious tract fiction with a few notable exceptions had indeed largely sunk out of sight as popular reading. The tales of Mrs. Walton, Hesba Stretton, Silas Hocking, "Pansy" and others were still quite well known to Sunday Schools, and were, apparently, plentiful until around 1930. The remaining English stocks and much information about them and their writers disappeared in the destruction of Paternoster Row by firebombs at the end of 1940. Thousands more of the books vanished into paper salvage during the war years. Today, surviving copies often command respectable prices in the catalogues of the second-hand or rare book dealers, especially those with Kronheim plates, or engravings signed by notable Victorian artists, William Dickes, Alfred Bayes, the Dalziels, and Harrison Weir among them. The work of good contemporary illustrators had been an admirable feature of much R.T.S. and S.P.C.K. publishing of the 1860's and 1870's, although illustration, like content, was much sentimentalized after 1880. It would be interesting to investigate the influence of Tract Society publications upon the illustration of children's books from 1870 into the present century.

CONCLUSION

THIS survey has covered much of the field of English Tract publishing for children in the last century. Stemming from the late eighteenth-century concern over illiteracy, the output of the Tract Societies over the next hundred years illustrates the attempt to reconcile traditional moral and religious training with the increasing demands of industrialisation and the current theories of the inevitability of progress. It was an ambitious and in many ways a successful project, leaving its impress on both education and literature at home and abroad, and implanting Evangelical secular ideals of honesty, industry, cleanliness and respectability in three or four generations of those exposed to Evangelical training.

Tract fiction, which was known to more children than was any other class of story during this period, was peculiar to the nineteenth century. A part of the sociology of literature and education as well as of contemporary religion, it proves to be firmly embedded in its historical background. Rooted in *The Pilgrim's Progress*, the Puritan sermon and the writings of Dr. Watts, it drew its theories of education from those of the Wesleys, Mrs. Trimmer and Hannah More, and its calculated appeal to the emotions from Richardson and the novel of sentiment. Its subject matter (apart from the religious message) sprang from major preoccupations, hopes and anxieties of the century, registering, for example, the shock waves emanating from the French Revolution, the Evangelical outcry for the establishment of Indian missions, the great temperance movement, and the growth of the social conscience.

Whenever possible and practical, original sources have been consulted in an attempt to estimate both the influence of individual writers and the significance of the whole body of tract fiction, hitherto somewhat neglected in the study of children's books. Although the isolated tract tale may be dismissed as trivial and the individual writer ignored, the whole massive output of tract fiction for the young demands more serious consideration. It had a formidable effect upon nineteenth century writing for children, and its influence extended well into the present century, not only in Britain, but in America, in the dominions, and in Europe where the works of many English Evangelical tract tale writers were well known in translation.

From the narrative tracts of 1795–1800, written to convert and train the spiritually ignorant and preserve them from radical influence, there developed in the course of the century several groups of tract tales: the "historical", designed to promote the Protestant view of history; the missionary; and that very large group which called attention to pressing social evils. Perhaps the chief interest of the latter today is that they open a window upon the Victorian scene, giving a startlingly different view from that seen through *Alice in Wonderland*, *The Crofton Boys*, or the stories of Mrs. Molesworth and Mrs. Ewing. Models of literary grace, emotional restraint and pleasant humour, these last display in miniature the best of the Victorian world: its pleasant villages, busy schoolrooms, and tranquil homes. Its children are loved and valued; its events work together for good. But in cold fact, for all its nostalgic charm, this comfortable world was occupied by a mere fraction of the Victorian population. Around and below it lay the dark territories of the tract tale, inhabited by tens of thousands of "the masses" who lived in slum tenements or on the streets of London, Manchester or Liverpool (all favourite cities of tract fiction). Such tales are the equivalents in juvenile fiction of *Mary Barton*, *Alton Locke*, or *Hard Times*—social realism for the young.

Although its content merely brushed the surface of that low life described in depth by Mayhew, Dickens and Charles Booth, this type of tract tale is, within its narrow limits, generally truthful, laying before its readers a wider range of realism than would be approved today. It treats, for instance, quite fully of death. Those who reject this as morbid might, in justice, remember two things: that death in a Christian context loses its terror; and that the sinister morbidity of violence thrust upon today's young viewers of film and television was not a part of Victorian tract fiction. Most of its realism lay in the vivid details of the precarious existence of the very poor. Tract tales show too the pathos and the waste implicit in the making of young criminals, proving that neither the concept of the city as a dehumanizing environment nor that of the "alienation of the individual" of which we hear so much today is new. They are, moreover, worth examining for their evidence on the changes in the status of women during the period.

In the vast field of social reform, however, the contribution of tract literature is easy to overrate. Examined in its contemporary context, it cannot be credited with the earliest exposure of the evils it attacks, or with the first agitation for reform. The anti-slavery movement was over a century old when *Uncle Tom's Cabin* appeared; reformers had argued the cause of the chimney sweep for at least eighty years before *The Water-Babies* was written; and the need for children's hospitals was widely recognised long before the publication of *Alone in London* or "Brenda's" tale of *Froggie's Little Brother*. Like the novel of social purpose; tract fiction underlined an already-existing concern and publicized a contemporary issue. It was, at the most, effective propaganda, dramatizing the matter and keeping it before the public eye. It could hardly do more; the complex reality underlying the pitiful situations depicted was beyond the child's capacity to grasp or the child's ability to mend. Many of the evils displayed in the tract tales are still with us. That they have to date defeated Royal Commissions, scientific investigation, mass education and technical progress, and the efforts of the welfare state would not have surprised those early Evangelicals who ascribed them to the workings of original sin.

These tales do illustrate clearly the development of the new attitude to children throughout the century. Whereas the spiritual deprivation of the young and of the poor is the theme of most of its early nineteenth-century writers, the physical and economic welfare of both groups becomes a prime concern around 1870. At the beginning of the century the child receives religious instruction from adult mentors; by the end, he is the bearer of the spiritual message to the less worthy adult. Is this the beginning of that youth cult of recent years in which childhood (now extended almost to the age of majority) is held to generate spontaneously all its own virtues while deriving its faults and follies from its elders?

Bound by Tract Society regulations, the tract tale appears to have allowed for little development in religious teaching. Assuming the reader's ignorance or immaturity, the earliest writers presented the religious lesson on the primary level, so easily discernible as to leave little to be discovered in the next reading or even in the next book. Some writers showed great skill in diversifying settings and problems and in arousing emotion; throughout the century the range of subject matter widened. The essential theme of repentance followed by conversion and faith was augmented around 1815 by missionary work (i.e., conversion in exotic settings); the 1840's brought in the reclamation of the slums.

All this had lent itself to the religious approach of the tract tale. But by 1860, secularisation was advancing rapidly, and tract tale writers accommodated their religious themes to the demands of the times, demands guided by the vast interest in travel, discovery, colonization, and the growth of scientific and industrial knowledge. As the proportion of religious instruction dwindled its tone became less urgent, less insistent upon the recognition of sin (the "wicked heart" of Mrs. Sherwood's tales). The wicked heart and the conviction of sin came to be obscured by the idea of a wicked slum and the conviction of a faulty society. It became easy to think of the central characters of children's tract tales as innocent victims of circumstances instead of as sinful creatures possessing free will who could, if they would, be restored to the status of children of God. By the time of Freud and the war of 1914–1918, the repudiation of Evangelical belief was well under way.

As literature, tract fiction has in this century been considered dull, morbid, and intrinsically worthless. Some of the weaker tales are indeed so; others are skilfully written in excellent English and far from dull. As *tract* fiction, originally devised as part of a serious scheme of education, they deliberately subordinated imagination and literary grace to the simplest of religious teaching and moral training, thus enabling their writers to break down early Evangelical and Nonconformist prejudices against fiction, and establish its respectability and its value as a vehicle of moral teaching. At the time, the tract tale itself was locked into the conventions, clichés and stereotypes which eventually led to its being discarded altogether.

Throughout the century, the tract tale and the related habit of Sunday reading worked to standardise popular reading matter and condition taste and response. Mistress and maid alike became avid readers of sentimental fiction; since both could have grown up on the Sunday School books of Mrs. Sherwood, "Old Humphrey", and the Rev. Legh Richmond, some community of taste was only natural. The sympathetic and sentimental outlook fostered in youth by such juvenile reading favoured social action on behalf of the unfortunate, creating readers for the novel of social purpose as well as for the novel of sentiment. It furthered the clichés and discouraged the critical faculty; as a democratising influence it flattened literary standards. It may help to explain the vast popularity of Mrs. Henry Wood, Hall Caine, Marie Corelli, Augusta J. Evans

Wilson, Mary J. Holmes, Florence L. Barclay, and other writers of high-powered romance in which sentiment, well disinfected by religious platitude, governed the actions of wholly predictable idealised characters. Religious implications in their works which might have aroused serious thought, soul-searching or self-questioning usually vanished in a fog of emotion or were pushed aside in sensational action. The extraordinary resentment aroused by Hardy's *Tess* (1891) and *Jude the Obscure* (1895) indicates the extent of his deviation from the accustomed literary paths.

Offensively didactic to modern taste, the tract tales preach, exhort, persuade and passionately seek to inform. Tone, style and message found for a hundred years a ready response from groups of people who were contemporaries of Napoleon and Wilberforce, of Darwin, Livingstone and Carlyle, of J. H. Newman and Charles Dickens, those makers of history, pioneers of science, great thinkers and writers of the age. If we can rid ourselves of our modern prejudices, and lay aside for a moment the habits of dissection, analysis and apportioning blame to the past, it is possible to recover from the tract tales something of the nineteenth-century background, and to hear in the words of their authors some smaller but no less authentic voices of the times.

GENERAL BIBLIOGRAPHY AND NOTES

Bibliography

Place of publication is London unless otherwise stated.

ALTICK, R. D. *The English Common Reader . . . 1800–1900*, Chicago, 1957.

ANDREAE, Gesiena, *The Dawn of Juvenile Literature in England*, Amsterdam, 1925.

BARCLAY, F. L. *The Life of Florence L. Barclay by One of her Daughters*, New York & London, 1921.

BARRY, Florence, *A Century of Children's Books*, 1922.

BATHO, Edith C. & Bonamy Dobree, *The Victorians and after . . .*, 1938.

BEAMES, Thomas, *The Rookeries of London*, 1852, reprinted 1970.

BEST, G. "Evangelicalism and the Victorians" in *The Victorian Crisis of Faith*, Ed. A. Symondson, 1970.

BOOTH, Maud B. *Beneath Two Flags*, New York & London, 1889.

BRIGGS, Asa, *Victorian People*, 1954.

BROWN, F. K. *Fathers of the Victorians*, 1961.

BUTLER, Josephine, *The Salvation Army in Switzerland*, 1883.

CASSERLEY, J. V. *The Retreat from Christianity in the Modern World*, 1952.

CAZAMIAN, Louis, *The Social Novel in England 1830–1850*, Paris, 1904; trans. 1973.

CHADWICK, Owen, Ed. *The Mind of the Oxford Movement*, 1960.

——— *The Victorian Church Vol. I*, 1966; *Vol. II*, 1970.

CHAPMAN, Raymond, *The Victorian Debate: English Literature and Society 1832–1901*, New York, 1968.

CLARK, G. Kitson, *An Expanding Society: Britain 1830–1900*, Melbourne, London & New York, 1967.

——— *The Making of Victorian England*, 1962.

COLLIER, R. *The General Next to God*, 1965.

CROFT-COOKE, Rupert, Ed. *The Circus Book*, 1948.

CROUCH, Marcus, *Treasure Seekers and Borrowers*, 1962.

CRUSE, Amy, *After the Victorians*, 1938.

——— *The Victorians and their Books*, 1935.

CUTT, M. N. *Mrs. Sherwood and her Books for Children*, 1974.
DALZIEL, Margaret, *Popular Fiction 100 Years ago*, 1957.
DARTON, F. J. H. *Children's Books in England*, 2nd edition, 1958.
——— *The Life and Times of Mrs. Sherwood*, 1910.
DAWSON, E. C. *Missionary Heroines in India*, 1908.
DENT, J. M. *Memoirs of J. M. Dent 1849–1926*, 1928.
DICTIONARY OF NATIONAL BIOGRAPHY (D.N.B.)
DISHER, Maurice Willson, *Blood and Thunder*, 1949.
——— *The Greatest Show on Earth*, 1937.
DORÉ, Gustave, & Blanchard Jerrold, *London: a Pilgrimage*, 1872.
EDEN, Emily, *Letters from India* (2 vols.), 1872.
——— *Up the Country* (2 vols.), 1866.
EGOFF, Sheila, *Children's Periodicals of the Nineteenth Century*, 1951.
ERVINE, St. John, *God's Soldier: General William Booth* (2 vols.), 1934.
FOSTER, Warren D. Ed. *Heroines of Modern Religion*, New York, 1913.
FRIED, Albert, & Richard Elman, Eds. *Charles Booth's London*, 1971.
"G.C.", "A.L.O.E." in *Sunday at Home* parts 1 & 2, 1894.
GASKELL, Peter, *Artisans and Machinery*, 1836.
——— *The Manufacturing Population of England: Its Moral, Social and Physical Condition . . .*, 1833.
GIBERNE, Agnes, *A Lady of England: The Life and Letters of Charlotte Maria Tucker*, 1895.
GIBBS, M. E. *The Anglican Church in India 1600–1970*, New Delhi, 1972.
GREENWOOD, James, *Unsentimental Journeys or Byways of the Modern Babylon*, 1867.
——— *The Wilds of London*, 1876.
GREGG, Pauline, *A Social and Economic History of Britain 1760–1950*, 1950
HARRISON, Brian, *Drink and the Victorians*, 1971.
HOUGHTON, Walter, *The Victorian Frame of Mind*, New Haven, 1957.
HOWSE, E. M. *Saints in Politics*, Toronto, 1952.
JAEGER, Muriel, *Before Victoria*, 1956.
JAMES, Louis, *Fiction for the Working Man 1830–1850*, 1963.
KITTERINGHAM, Jenny, "Country Work Girls in Nineteenth-century England" in *Village Life and Labour*, Ed. Raphael Samuel, London & Boston, 1975.
KNIGHT, Charles, *Passages of a Working Life* (3 vols.), 1864–65.
LAIRD, M. A. *Missionaries and Education in Bengal 1793–1837*, 1972.

LE ROUX, H., & Jules Garnier, *Acrobats and Mountebanks*, Trans. A. P. Morton, 1890.

LONGMATE, Norman, *The Workhouse*, 1974.

MACKENZIE, Helen D. *Six Years in India: Delhi: The City of the Great Mogul . . .*, 1857.

MARSHALL, Emma, "A.L.O.E." in *Women Novelists of Queen Victoria's Reign*, Ed. Mrs. Oliphant, 1897.

MAYHEW, Henry, *London Labour and the London Poor* (4 vols.), 1861.

MEARNS, Andrew, *The Bitter Cry of Outcast London etc.*, 1883; reprinted Leicester, 1970.

MOZLEY, Dorothea, Ed. *The Newman Family Letters*, 1962.

NEUBURG, Victor E. *The Penny Histories*, 1968.

PAFFORD, J. H. P. "Introduction" to *Isaac Watts: Divine Songs*, 1972.

PARLIAMENTARY PAPERS 1814–15; 1816; 1831–32; 1833; 1843.

PIKE, E. Royston, *Human Documents of the Industrial Revolution*, 1966.

——— *Human Documents of the Victorian Golden Age*, 1967.

PINCHBECK, Ivy & Margaret Hewitt, *Children in English Society Vol. II*, 1973.

PLUMB, J. H. *England in the Eighteenth Century*, 1950.

PUSEY, E. B. *Parochial Sermons Vol. III*, 1878.

——— *Sermons . . . from Advent to Whitsuntide*, 1848.

RAYMOND, E. T. *Portraits of the Nineties*, 1921.

REFORMATORY AND REFUGE UNION, *Jubilee Report: Fifty Years Record of Child Saving 1856–1906*, 1906.

RELIGIOUS TRACT SOCIETY, *Catalogues.*

——— Minute Books of the Copyright Committee.

ROBSON, Isabel S. *The Story Weavers*, 1900.

RODGERS, Betsy, *The Cloak of Charity*, 1949.

ST. JOHN, Judith *et al.* Eds. *The Osborne Collection of Early Children's Books 1566–1910*, Toronto, 1958, revised Toronto, 1966.

——— *The Osborne Collection . . . 1476–1910, Vol. II,* Toronto, 1975.

SANGER, Lord George, *Seventy Years a Showman*, 1926.

SANGSTER, Paul, *Pity my Simplicity*, 1963.

SEELEY, R. B. *Memoir of the Life and Writings of Michael Thomas Sadler*, 1842.

SEWELL, Eleanor L. Ed. *The Autobiography of Elizabeth Missing Sewell*, 1907.

SMITH, Sarah, *Log Books 1859–1871* (ms.).

SOCIETY FOR THE PROPAGATION OF CHRISTIAN KNOWLEDGE, *Catalogues.*

TILLOTSON, K. *Novels of the Eighteen-forties*, 1954.

TONNA, Charlotte Elizabeth, *Helen Fleetwood*, 1831.

TROLLOPE, Frances, *Michael Armstrong*, 1840.

TURNER, E. S. *Roads to Ruin*, 1950.

WARREN, Max, "The Church Militant Abroad: Victorian Missionaries" from *The Victorian Crisis of Faith*, Ed. A. Symondson, 1970.

WEBB, R. S. *Notes Regarding the Life of Hesba Stretton . . .*, (ms.).

WIGGINS, Archibald R. *The History of the Salvation Army Vol. IV*, 1964.

WINGFIELD-STRATFORD, E. *The Squire and his Relations*, 1956.

YONGE, Charlotte, "Children's Literature of the Last Century" in *Macmillan's Magazine*, July 1869.

YOUNG, G. M. *Victorian England: Portrait of an Age*, 1936.

YOUNG, Kenneth, *Chapel: The Joyous Days and Prayerful Nights of the Nonconformists . . . 1850–1950*, 1972.

Notes

CHAPTER I

1. Dickens, C.: "Frauds on the Fairies" in *Household Words* (1853), p. 97–100.
2. From *Bella and Monsterina* (Wellington, c. 1809), p. 44 and *How to be Happy, or Fairy Gifts* (1828), p. 210.
3. Kilner, Dorothy: *Jemima Placid* (c. 1785). It was reprinted in Charlotte Yonge's compilation *A Storehouse of Stories* (1870) and appeared in shortened form in E. V. Lucas' collection *Forgotten Stories* (1906).
4. Trimmer, Sarah: *Easy Lessons for Young Children* (1787), Lesson VIII. Reprinted in L. de Vries' *Flowers of Delight* (Toronto, 1965), p. 159.
5. D'Épinay, Mme.: *The Conversations of Emily*. Abridged from the French (1815), p. 259–61. The original (1774) was awarded the prize for utility by the Académie Française, in competition with Mme. de Genlis, who had submitted *Adèle et Théodore*.
6. Darwin, Erasmus: *A Plan for the Conduct of Female Education in Boarding Schools* (Derby, 1797), XVI–XXII, p. 45–55.
7. Pinnock, William: *Catechism of Morality* (4th edition, 1827), Ch. 1, in which the Reasons for the Practice of Personal and Relative Duties are given. One of Pinnock's many standard catechisms.

8. Vol. II, 1802 edition.
9. "On Presence of Mind" from the Fourteenth Evening of *Evenings at Home* (1792–96), Vol. III, p. 97–111.
10. Mrs. Trimmer considered *Original Poems* a moral rather than a religious work: "If *moral improvement* be the object . . . the end may be as effectually answered by such poetry as is here offered to the public, as by composition in the highest style, for very great attention has been paid to principle from beginning to end . . ." (*Guardian of Education*, Vol. IV, 1805, p. 77).

    The verses were, of course, adopted by Evangelicals, many in the succeeding book, *Hymns for Infant Minds* (1808) being strictly Evangelical in tone, e.g. XXVII; XXVIII; L; LI; LXXII.
11. Examples include Mrs. Sherwood: *Ermina* . . . (1831); Miss Sandham: *Friendship* (1820); Mrs. Hofland: *Matilda or the Barbadoes Girl* (3rd edition, 1816); and the anonymous *The West Indian* . . . (1827).

    See also Keir, David: *The House of Collins* (1952), p. 21 & 22, on the tobacco merchants of Glasgow.
12. Trimmer, Sarah: *Instructive Tales* (1831 edition), Ch. XIV, p. 113–27.
13. Sherwood, M. M.: *Stories Explanatory of the Church Catechism* (1817), Ch. XXII, p. 153. This was written around 1810 and is said to have been printed in Calcutta around 1814.

Chapter II

1. Altick, p. 37.
2. *A Brief View of the Plan and Operation of the Religious Tract Society* (1828), p. 11 & 12.

    See also Green, S. G.: *The Story of the Religious Tract Society for 100 Years* (1899), p. 6 & 7.
3. James, p. 116–17.
    Sangster, p. 52–59.
4. Bamford, S.: *Passages in the Life of a Radical* (1893). Vol. I, Ch. IV, VIII & IX; p. 86–87.
5. Altick, p. 66–77.
    Gregg, p. 267–75.
6. Plumb, p. 214.
7. See, for example, discussions in Brown, Howse, Jaeger, Plumb, Sangster and G. M. Young.
8. *Gentleman's Magazine* (June, 1796), i, 505.
9. Capt. Sherwood's account of this experience is found in Darton (1910).

10. Tonna, Charlotte Elizabeth: *Personal Recollections* . . . (1847), p. 50.
11. Brown, Ch. VI.
    Hopkins, Mary Alden: *Hannah More and her Circle* (New York & Toronto, 1947), Ch. XX.
    Jones, M. G.: *Hannah More* (1952).
    Clarke, W. K. L. "Good Mrs. Trimmer" in *Eighteenth Century Piety* (1944), p. 118–25.
    Yarde, D. L. *The Life and Works of Sarah Trimmer, a Lady of Brentford* (Hounslow & District Historical Society, 1972).
12. Vol. I (1802), p. 267–68 & 392–93. Both books are praised, *Susan Gray* for "interesting and affecting narrative" and its use of "all the arguments which Reason and Religion can furnish" to check vanity and the love of dress; *Margaret Whyte* for its presentation of death, "full of reasonable hopes of a happy immortality . . . without those gloomy fears or enthusiastic raptures . . ." The review concludes with the hope that these writers will produce some tales "in which merit meets with a reward in this world."
13. In Mrs. Sherwood's textbooks such as *Introduction to Astronomy* (1817), *Introduction to Geography* (1818), each item of information is tagged with an appropriate Biblical quotation. Her Millenarian theory is found in the last three parts of *The History of Henry Milner* (1826, 1831, 1837), and in *The Millenium* (1829).
14. *Guardian of Education* V (1806), p. 94.
15. Day, Thomas: *The History of Sandford and Merton* (1837 edition), p. 12–13.
16. *The History of Margaret Whyte* (Bath, 1818), p. 54–55.
17. Assortments of these tracts may be found in any of the numerous tract magazines listed in Egoff. Notable examples are: *The Children's Friend* (1826–60); *Youth's Instructor & Guardian* (1817–55); and the *Sunday Scholar's Magazine* (1821).
18. *The Correspondence of William Wilberforce* . . . (1840), Vol. I, p. 250.
19. *Harry Beaufoy* . . ., p. 168.
20. Sandham, Elizabeth: *The Twin Sisters* (1810), Ch. XII.

Chapter III

1. *Anna Ross* (1825 edition), p. 47–48.
2. Best, p. 42–43.
3. Brown, Ch. IX.
   Methodist Magazine XLII contains a report of the May 1819 meeting of the British and Foreign Bible Society.
4. M. G. Lewis to William Wilberforce, October 16, 1817.

5. Brown, Ch. VI.
Hopkins, Mary Alden: *Hannah More and her Circle* (New York & Toronto, 1947), Ch. XVII, XVIII & XIX.

6. Robbins, William: *The Newman Brothers: An Essay in Comparative Intellectual Biography* (1966), p. 44–47.
Westminster Review Vol. X (1856), p. 46–47.

7. See Egoff.
Juvenile Missionary Magazine (1844–45). The building, upkeep and journeys of the L.M.S. vessel *John Williams* are described. [John Williams was the missionary sent to the South Seas in 1817 by the L.M.S. In 1839, he was slain by cannibals who had been angered by the conduct of crews of whaling vessels.]

8. Knight, Vol. I, p. 223.
Altick, p. 206–10.

9. Altick, Ch. V & VII.
Clark, Ch. VI.
Knight, Vol. I, p. 241.
Jones, William: *The Jubilee Memorial of the Religious Tract Society 1799–1849* (1850).

10. James, p. 2–3.
Silver, P. & H.: *The Education of the Poor: The History of a National School 1824–1974* (London & Boston, 1974).

11. *A Brief View of the Plan and Operation of the Religious Tract Society* (1828), p. 4–9.

12. Trollope, II. p. 294–95.

13. Seeley, and Parliamentary Papers (1816), III.

14. Tonna, p. 369–70.

15. Burt, Thomas: *Pitman and Privy Councillor . . .* (1924), p. 49 ff.

16. *The Rioters* (1827), p. 122.

17. Gaskell (1836), p. 139. See also Ch. II & VI.

18. Tonna, p. 249.

19. Longmate, Norman: *The Waterdrinkers* (1968), p. 121–33.
Young, K. p. 118–20.

CHAPTER IV

1. Sewell, p. 80.

2. Keddie, Henrietta ("Sarah Tytler"): *Three Generations: The Story of a Middle Class Scottish Family* (1911), p. 226.

3. Stirling, A. M. W.: *Life's Mosaic* (1934), p. 130.

4. Darton (1958), p. 179.

5. Yonge, C.: "Didactic Fiction" in *Macmillan's Magazine*, August 1869.
6. *The Poor Man's Guardian*, 9 July 1831; 8 December, 1832; December 1835. See also *The Penny Satirist*, *The People's Hue and Cry*, *The Penny Times* and *The Radical* during these periods.
7. Only after 1850 were the old Evangelical tracts gradually discarded. Those written to counter infidelity, political agitation, Popery and Sabbath breaking were numerous during the 1830's and 1840's. As late as 1851, "Henry Briggs the Socialist" appeared in the S.P.C.K. catalogue along with "A Few Words on the Sin of Lying", "A Kind Caution to Profane Swearers" and warnings against Mormonism, the Church of Rome, fortune-telling and drunkenness. By 1860, when the whole range of the publications had widened and secularised, there was a good choice of sensible school textbooks, and "Henry Briggs" had vanished.
8. Tonna, p. 398.
9. Clark, G. Kitson: "The Romantic Element 1830–1850" in *Studies in Social History* . . . Ed. J. H. Plumb (1955), Ch. VII, p. 236.
10. The findings of Dalziel do not seem to take into account enough of "the garbage" complained of by the disillusioned Knight (Vol. II, p. 328). This material is analysed in some depth in James, Ch. IX. Knight felt that an improvement in the moral tone of printed matter took place in the 1830's. Undoubtedly, by 1840 a much wider range of respectable domestic magazines was beginning to cater to newly literate working people. The real test of improvement would of course be the extent to which the respectable reading matter had displaced "the garbage" among its habitual readers. Of this, there is little evidence, and no way to find out.
11. Knight, Vol. III, p. 228.
12. *Past and Present*, Bk. III (1843), p. 334.
13. Wilberforce, William: *The Correspondence of William Wilberforce Edited by his Sons* . . . Vol. II (1840), p. 450–51 & 478–79.
14. Ponsonby, A.: *More English Diaries* (1927), p. 197–98.

    Shaftesbury's intense self-criticism is admirably explained by Georgina Battiscombe in *Shaftesbury: A Biography of the Seventh Earl* (1974).
15. "Self-Examination" from *The Book of Children's Hymns and Rhymes* Collected by the Daughter of a Clergyman [1859], p. 147.
16. "Public Instruction" in the *Quarterly Journal of Education*, Vol. VII, (1834), No. XIII, p. 70.
17. These figures were arrived at by a count of magazines noted in Egoff, but the list is by no means comprehensive.

Chapter V

1. Charlesworth, Samuel: *In Memoriam: A Brief Memoir of Maria Louisa Charlesworth* (Saffron Walden, c. 1881). Written for limited circulation by her brother.
   "In Memoriam" in *Women's Work in the Great Harvest Field* (1881).
2. *In Memoriam: A Brief Memoir* . . . (see note 1 above).
3. The lives of Mrs. Ewing and her sisters supply examples, as do the books of Charlotte Yonge.
4. *The Cottage and its Visitor*, p. 4–5.
5. Barclay, p. 49–54.
6. Jeffries, R. *Hodge and his Masters* (1879).
7. Kitteringham, p. 98–112. See also the Sixth Report of Children's Employment Commission on Agricultural Labour Gangs (Parliamentary Papers, V, 16, 1867). Excerpts are quoted in Pike (1967) and it is reviewed in *Leisure Hour* (1 June, 1867), p. 413–15.
8. Tyrwhitt, R. St. John: "Thoughts on Christian Art" in *Contemporary Review* III (September, 1866), p. 188.
9. *All the Year Round* (8 September, 1860), p. 517–20.
10. Sidgwick, F. Ed.: *The Complete Marjory Fleming* . . . (1934), p. 107.
11. Mayhew, Vol. III, p. 380–99.
12. Printed by J. Harkness, Preston, 1842.
    "Barbarous Murder of a Child by a Schoolmistress". H. Disley, Printer . . . St. Giles. (n.d.).
13. Dalziel, Ch. V.
14. Knight, Vol. II, p. 328–30.
15. Leavis, Q. D.: *Fiction and the Reading Public* (1932), p. 63.
16. Wilberforce, Samuel: "Preface" to *Agathos and Other Sunday Stories* (1840).
17. Thompson, Flora: *Lark Rise to Candleford* (1965 edition), p. 396 & 427.
    Nesbit, E.: *The Would-be-goods* (1901), Ch. II.
18. Pusey (1848), p. 57–58.
19. "The Spring Morning" from *The Book of Children's Hymns and Rhymes* Collected by the Daughter of a Clergyman [1859], p. 136. The unacknowledged author may have been Lady Flora Hastings.
20. Pusey (1848), p. 57 ff.; Pusey (1878), p. 260.
21. Hill, Octavia: Homes of the London Poor (1875), p. 111.

Chapter VI

1. Houghton, p. 79–81 & 85–86.

2. "Sage of Chelsea". A review of *The Letters of Thomas Carlyle to his Brother Alexander*, Ed. E. Marrs, in the *Times Literary Supplement*, 24 April, 1969, p. 435.
3. Mayhew, Macaulay and *Punch*: See excerpts quoted in Pike (1967), p. 26–33.
4. *The Family Times* (19 December, 1849).
5. Maxwell, Christabel: *Mrs. Gatty and Mrs. Ewing* (1949), p. 114 & 125–26.
6. All the domestic journals around 1850—*The Family Friend, The Family Economist, Howitt's, Eliza Cook's, Household Words*, among them—display this faith in science and the certainty of progress. Science is thought of as the skill of practical accomplishment: in Macaulay's phrase, "everything that promotes the convenience of life". ("Sir James Macintosh", *Critical Essays*, 1835.)
7. *D.N.B.*
8. Giberne, p. 161, 164.
9. Carlyle, Thomas: *Past and Present* (1843), p. 264.
10. Eliza Cook (1812–1889), journalist, popular poetess and editor of *Eliza Cook's Journal* (1849–54). See Hudson, Derek: *The Forgotten King and Other Essays* (1960), and *Good Words* (1876) for information about her.

    For Samuel Smiles see Briggs; and also Smiles, Aileen: *Samuel Smiles and his Surroundings* (1956).
11. *The Crown of Wild Olive* (1865), Lecture I.
12. *Times*, 7 November 1850.
13. Sala, G.: *Life and Adventures of George Augustus Sala* (New York, 1895), Vol. I, p. 214–15.
14. Maxwell, Christabel: *Mrs. Gatty and Mrs. Ewing* (1949), p. 89.
15. *Narrative of a Mission of Inquiry to the Jews from the Church of Scotland* (Philadelphia, 1842), v.
16. Giberne, p. 123–24. The allusion is doubtless to the Operative Jewish Converts' Institution, which did printing.
17. Scott rehabilitated the Jew in fiction with the attractive figure of Rebecca in *Ivanhoe* (1819), which followed soon after Maria Edgeworth's *Harrington* (1817). George Eliot's *Daniel Deronda* (1874–76) was an important novel; minor works on similar themes included those of Grace Aguilar, Mary Bennett, and the Rev. J. H. Ingraham (*A Prince of the House of David* etc.), and Wallace's *Ben Hur*. There were plays with Old Testament themes; and the French Jewish actress, Rachel, was a noted stage personality.
18. *Sunday at Home* (1894), p. 453–56 & 466–69.

19. Eden (1866), Vol. II, p. 89–90, 175, 216–17.
    Eden (1872), Vol. I, p. 153–54; Vol. II, p. 155–57, 165–66, 226
    Mackenzie, p. v., 4–13, etc.
    Helen Mackenzie was a strict Evangelical and a tireless visitor of missions and schools of all denominations except Roman Catholic.
20. Laird, Ch. I & II.
21. *Ibid*, p. 235 & 259–60.
22. A.L.O.E.: *Little Bullets from Batala* (1875–76), p. 65–79. See also Giberne, p. 333.
23. A.L.O.E.: "The Pugree with a Border of Gold" and "The Broken Fence" from *A Wreath of Indian Stories* [1876].
24. Sherring, M. A.: *The History of Protestant Missions in India from . . . 1706 to 1881* (1884 revised edition), p. 438.
25. Mill, J. S.: *Autobiography and Other Writings*, Ed. J. Stillinger (Boston, 1969), p. 66.
    Young, G. M.: "Macaulay" in *Victorian Essays*, Ed. W. D. Hancock (1962), p. 45.

Chapter VII

1. Thomas Arnold to J. C. Platt, January 20, 1839. *The Life and Correspondence of Thomas Arnold*, Ed. Arthur P. Stanley (1858), p. 126–27.
2. Pike, (1967), p. 255–56.
3. Bruton, J.: "The Pauper's Consolation" from *Innes's Budget of Merry Songs* (c. 1845). Sung to the tune "Chapter of Accidents".
4. See note 1 above—*Life and Correspondence . . .*
5. "The Girl from the Workhouse" in *All the Year Round* (October 18, 1862), p. 132 ff.
   Thackeray, Anne: "Little Paupers" in *Cornhill* XXII, (September 1870), "Pauper Girls" in *Westminster Review*, Vol. 93 (1870), article VI.
6. Gregg, p. 489.
7. Bamford, Samuel: *Passages in the Life of a Radical*, and *Early Days* (2 vols.), (1893), Vol. I, Ch. VII & VIII.
8. "A.C.S.": "An East End Transcript" in *Sunday at Home* (1898), p. 634–37.
9. Mayhew, Vol. II, p. 74–79.
10. House, Humphrey: The Dickens World (1941), Ch. II, III & IV.
    Gilbert, William: "The Abuse of Charity in London" in *Contemporary Review* XXXI, March 1878.
    Mayhew, Vol. IV, p. 448.
11. Dalziel, p. 15.
12. Introduction to *The Parent's Assistant* (1897 edition), p. x.

13. Shaen, M. J. Ed.: *Memorials of Two Sisters, Susannah and Catherine Winkworth* (1908), p. 100.
14. Cruse (1935), p. 157 & 301.
15. Doyle, John A. Ed.: *Memoir of Susan Ferrier* (1898), p. 302.
16. Mary Sewell was the mother of Anna Sewell, and the author of numerous pathetic works in verse, including "Mother's Last Words", *The Children of Summerbrook*, "Our Father's Care", *Homely Ballads* etc., and a number of tracts. Her life was written by A. E. Bayley ("Edna Lyell") in 1889. Susan Chitty: *The Woman Who Wrote Black Beauty* (1971) is a biography of Mary Sewell as well as her daughter.
17. Osborne, Edgar: Introduction to *The Osborne Collection* . . . Vol. I, see St. John (1958).

Chapter VIII

1. *Jessica's First Prayer* is said to have been translated into every European language as well as into many Asiatic and African tongues.
2. *Woman*, November 19, 1966. Letter column.
3. Friedrichs, Hulda: "Hesba Stretton at Home" in *The Young Woman* No. 22, (July 1894), p. 327–33. Includes photographs.
4. "Hesba Stretton"—I. Memoir specially written for *The Sunday at Home*; II. A personal note by Mrs. Hesba D. Webb (a niece of Hesba Stretton) in *The Sunday at Home* (1911), p. 121–25.
5. Hesba Stretton to Mrs. Pattison, April 16, 1886?. University of London Library A.L. 225.
6. Webb.
7. Friedrichs, p. 333, see note 3 above.
8. For a detailed account of this firm see Cutt. See also Brown, P. A.: "Houlston of Wellington . . ." in *Shropshire Magazine* (Shrewsbury, April 1959), p. 15–16.
9. Many Evangelical and Methodist families were surprisingly tolerant in the matter of novel reading. See for instance Altick p. 117–23. The Benjamin Gregory he cites was friendly with relatives of Hesba Stretton in Shropshire.
10. No. 14, New Street, Wellington has disappeared, although the buildings at either side (intact in 1968) give an idea of what it was like. The site is now occupied by three small shops.
11. "A Provincial Post Office" in *All the Year Round* (February 28, 1863).
12. Post Office Tales in *All the Year Round* include: "The Postmaster's Daughter" (November 5, 1859); "Felicia Crompton" (January 10,

1863); "The Travelling Post Office". *Mugby Junction* (Christmas Number, 1866).

The bookshop and bindery appear in the novel *Hester Morley's Promise* (1873), and the short story, "The Real Murderer" (*All the Year Round*, January 2, 1864).

13. See for example, "The Postmaster's Daughter" (*All the Year Round*, November 5, 1859); "Winnifred's Troubles" (*The Welcome Guest*, Nos. 96 & 97, 1861); and "Lord Westbourne's Heir" (*All the Year Round*, August 10 & 17, 1872).
14. Tales and payments are listed in a separate account book.
15. Smith, August 1865 to May 1866. Their efforts to establish a closer degree of intimacy never quite succeeded.
16. From *Christ's Musts . . .* (1894). This sermon is reprinted in *The Best of Alexander Maclaren*. Edited by Gaius Glenn Atkins (New York, 1949).
17. *Ibid.*
18. Smith, April 2, 1866.
19. Wood, C. W.: *Memorials of Mrs. Henry Wood* (1894), p. 325.
20. Letter in possession of M. N. Cutt. Details about Ben's daughter as supplied by her granddaughter, Mrs. Howard R. Walker of Blue Mound, Kansas, to the Osborne Collection.
21. *Sunday at Home* (1911).
22. Webb.
23. *Ibid.*

Chapter IX

1. E. Nesbit to Ada Breakell. Moore, D. L.: *E. Nesbit: A Biography* (1967), p. 107.
2. Lee, Amice: *Laurels and Rosemary: The Life of William and Mary Howitt* (1955), p. 322.

   Reports of the Epping Forest Commission (1872 and later).

   Papers of the Arbitration Proceedings (1879–81).

   LeFevre, G. J. S.: *English Commons and Forests* (1894).

   Townley, H.: *English Woodlands and their Story* (1910).

   Squatters' rights depended upon twenty years' occupation of the site, certified in legally acceptable fashion. Since villagers' rights to common had been given in many cases two or more generations earlier, their documentary proof was not usually to be found when those intent upon getting the land for mining, construction or railways demanded it. Those forced out of their living quarters and into the local workhouse could then be hired out locally and their wages claimed by the parish in lieu of workhouse keep.

3. "The Black Country" in *Edinburgh Review* (1863).
4. Longmate, Norman: *The Waterdrinkers* (1968), p. 125.
5. Page, H. A.: "The National Refuges for Homeless Children" in *The Sunday Magazine* (1874), p. 126–30. Details of the training ship *Chichester*, which accommodated 220 boys and was supported by voluntary contributions.

   Wynter, A.: "The London Gamin" in *Good Words* (March 1, 1867), p. 160–67.
6. Young, G. M.: "The Age of Tennyson" in *Victorian Essays* . . . Ed, W. D. Hancock (1962), p. 57–58.
7. Maria Rye was a member of the committee of 1856 which petitioned for a Married Women's Property Bill. She later devised and partially financed a project of the 1860's and 1870's to salvage destitute children and have them adopted abroad, mostly in Canada. Others engaged in child salvage were Annie Macpherson, William Quarrier of Glasgow and Dr. Barnardo. There was also the Church of England Children's Society. Contemporary articles on these ventures are found in *Good Words* (1871, 1882); *Sunday at Home* (1898). Fuller accounts include: Pike, G. H.: *Children Reclaimed for Life* (1875), with an introduction by Hesba Stretton; Birt, Lillian: *The Children's Homefinder* . . . (1913); Rudolph, E.: *The First Forty Years* (1922); and the centenary books on the Barnardo homes (1966). A wide coverage is found in Pinchbeck & Hewitt. These authors are hostile towards Maria Rye and her efforts, though John Stroud, *Thirteen Penny Stamps* (1971) takes a kinder view, as did her contemporaries.
8. Smith, March & April 1868.

   March 10: Startled Mr. Stevens by saying I intended to ask Mr. Wills' advice about "Little Meg".

   March 13: . . . displeased with the Tract Society.

   March 28: . . . saw Mr. Stevens, C. W. Wood, Mr. Seeley, Houlston & Wright; resolved upon asking so much a thousand for "Little Meg".

   April 23: Went to see Nisbets' about "Little Meg". The Tract Society offers only £50 for it and are quite aggrieved that I do not accept it gratefully. Told Mr. Stevens to send the ms. to Nisbets.

   April 24: . . . Dr. Davis offering £25 for the first 1000 of "Little Meg" & £10 per 1000 afterwards; we were utterly amazed . . .

   April 25: Dr. Davis repeated his offer . . .

   April 28: A letter from Dr. Davis saying his offer was a mistake and the Society could not give it.

   April 29: . . . Sam Manning offering £5 per 1000 only . . . excessively indignant.

April 30: Mr. Wright offered 4 guineas per 1000 without seeing the ms. . . . Mr. Stevens brought a note from Dr. Davis offering £6. 5 per 1000. I suppose we must take it . . .

May 4: . . . agreed about Meg at last.

See also Minute Book of Payments in R.T.S. Archives, 1868.

9. Bell, E. Moberley: *Octavia Hill* (1942).
   Hill, Octavia: *Homes of the London Poor* (1875).
10. Read, Herbert: *The Innocent Eye* (New York, 1947), p. 46–47.
11. Thackeray, Anne: "Betsinda and her Bun" in *Cornhill* XXXVI (September, 1877), p. 325–32.
12. Pike (1967), p. 287.
13. Grollman, Earl A. Ed.: *Explaining Death to Children* (Boston, 1967), p. 27 ff.; 36–47.
    Also Butler, Francelia: "Death in Children's Literature" in *Children's Literature* Vol. I (Storrs, Connecticut, 1972), p. 104–24.
14. *The Clives of Burcot* is probably the worst of her early efforts. There is not much to be said for *Paul's Courtship* (1867), or for the short stories "The Ghost in the Clock Room" (*All the Year Round*, December 13, 1859) and "The Withered Daisy" (*All the Year Round*, November 23, 1861).
15. *The Monthly Reporter*, March 1869. The monthly organ of the R.T.S.; the quotation comes from the leading article.
16. Bell, E. M.: *Josephine Butler* (1963).
    Collins, Philip: *Dickens and Crime* (1965 edition), Ch. IV.
    Deacon, R.: *The Private Life of Mr. Gladstone* (1965).
    Harrison, Brian: "Underneath the Victorians" from *Victorian Studies* Vol. X (1966–67), p. 239–62.
17. "Between the Cradle and the Grave" in *All the Year Round* (February 1, 1862), p. 454–56.
    See also *Good Words* (1868), p. 360–68; (1871), p. 790–94; and (1874), p. 659–64.
18. Thackeray, Anne: "Chirping Crickets" in *Cornhill* XIX, (1869), p. 235–42.
19. "Aunt Judy's Correspondence" from *Aunt Judy's Magazine* (1871), p. 127.
    Maxwell, Christabel: *Mrs. Gatty and Mrs. Ewing* (1949), p. 148.
20. Forster, E. M.: *Marianne Thornton* . . . (1956), p. 210.
21. Among these articles are:
    "The British Pompeii" in *Chambers's Journal* (1859).
    "Manchester Free Libraries" in *Chambers's Journal* (1860).
    "Aboard an Emigrant Ship" in *All the Year Round* (1862).

"A Provincial Post Office" in *All the Year Round* (1863).
"The Blackburn Sewing Schools" in *Temple Bar* (1863).
"A Summer Day in the Wrekin" in *Leisure Hour* (1864).
"Gypsy Glimpses" in *All the Year Round* (1869).

22. Keddie, Henrietta: *Three Generations* . . . (1911), p. 341–42.
23. Pike, (1967), p. 156 (taken from Census figures of 1851).
24. "Modern Domestic Service" in *The Edinburgh Review* (April, 1862), p. 426.
25. *Cornhill* XXX (September 1874), p. 281–96. Reprinted in Vol. VII of the *Collected Works of Miss Thackeray* (1875–76).

CHAPTER X

1. *Ministering Children* until 1924. *A Peep Behind the Scenes*, 1962. This and other of Mrs. Walton's books are kept in print by the Moody Institute in Chicago.
2. Lewis, Mary A.: "Cheap Literature for Village Children" in *Macmillan's Magazine* (July, 1878), p. 210–22. Reprinted in Littell's *Living Age* (1878).
3. Salmon, E.: *Juvenile Literature as It Is* (1888), p. 176–77. See also summary of Charles Welsh's survey of reading habits, p. 13 ff.
4. Details of the career of the Rev. O. F. Walton come largely from the *Clergy List* . . . (1917). The Jerusalem Bishopric was governed jointly by the Churches of England and Prussia, and from its founding in 1841 to its dissolution in 1886 to be reconstituted under Anglican auspices alone, it was a fruitful source of discord. One reason was that enthusiastic Evangelicals in the Holy Land insisted upon proselytizing among Christians of the Orthodox Church as though they were pagans or Roman Catholics. The Rev. O. F. Walton may have been caught in these disagreements. The details about Cally are found in J. H. Maxwell's *Tourist Guide to the Stewartry of Kirkcudbright* (1873), and the *Third Statistical Account of Scotland . . . The Stewartry of Kirkcudbright* (1965), p. 160–61. Details of York and Wolverhampton are found in local directories of the 1880's and 1890's.
5. For this recollection I am indebted to the kindness of the Deputy Librarian of the Tonbridge Branch of the Kent County Library, and Mrs. Pankhurst, Leigh, Tonbridge.
6. *The Correspondence of William Wilberforce* (1840), Vol. I, p. 49–53.
7. Corner, Julia: *Little Plays for Little People*, Series the First, (1853), p. viii–ix of the 1870 edition.

8. Garstin, Crosbie, Ed.: *Samuel Kelly, an Eighteenth-century Seaman . . .* (New York, 1925), p. 162.
9. Day, Thomas: *Sandford and Merton* (1837 edition), p. 193–94.
10. Doré & Jerrold, p. 164–5 & 170–71.
    See also: Mayhew, Vol. I, p. 42–44.
11. Dent, p. 5 & 17.
12. *All the Year Round*, (July 21, 1860), p. 352–54; (September 29, 1860), p. 597–600.
13. Disher (1949), p. 138.
14. Horne, R. H.: "The Burlesque and the Beautiful" in *Contemporary Review* (October, 1871), p. 391–406.
    See also: *Saturday Review* (January 5, 1884), p. 18–19.
15. *All the Year Round* (June 29, 1861), p. 324–27.
16. Croft-Cooke; Disher (1937); Sanger. Also see Mayhew, Vol. III, p. 98–112 & 149–61.
17. Smith, G. *Our Canal, Gypsy, Van and other Travelling Children*, A Lecture. (January 7, 1886. Privately printed.)
    See also: Reformatory and Refuge Union *Jubilee Report*.
18. Acts are listed and commented upon in Reformatory and Refuge Union *Jubilee Report*. Relevant articles are found in: *The Sunday Magazine* (1874), p. 150–51; and *The Saturday Review* (May 17, 1884), p. 642–43.
19. Horne, see note 14 above.
20. Stirling, A. M. W.: *The Richmond Papers* (1926), p. 108–09.
21. *Cornhill* XIV, p. 37 ff.
    All the Year Round (1860), p. 321–26; & 342 ff.
    And many others. See also Turner, Ch. VII.
22. According to K. Young, Ch. 3, the Service of Song consisted of the reading of "an edifying though not necessarily religious" story, with breaks for the singing of hymns, solo or anthems. It was often held on a Sunday afternoon. Among stories used in Services of Song were: *Jessica's First Prayer*; *Little Dot*; *Christie's Old Organ*; *Dick's Fairy* (by Silas Hocking); and *Teddy's Button* (by Amy Le Feuvre).

Chapter XI

1. Published by Burns. See Tillotson, K. and "Newman's Sister Harriet and *The Fairy Bower*" a talk on the B.B.C. Third Programme, July 17, 1952.
   See also: Tillotson, K. & G.: *Mid-Victorian Studies* (1965).
2. Nowell-Smith, Simon, Ed.: *Letters to Macmillan* (1967), p. 87–90.

3. Booth, p. 260.
4. Ervine, Vol. I, p. 523–27 & 585–601; Vol. II, p. 659–67 & 759–66.
5. Foster, Ch. X.
   Wiggins, Vol. IV, p. 355–60.
6. Ervine, Vol. I, p. 539–43.
7. Barclay, p. 215 & 240–41.
8. *The Bookman* (American), November 1911. *The Nation* (November 16, 1911) described this book as "a slough of sentimentality".
9. Bullock, J.: "A Miner's Story". *The Listener* (February 13, 1969), p. 200.
10. See: Hitchman, Janet: *The King of the Barbareens* (1960); Holmes, G. V.: *The Likes of Us* (1948); Norman, Frank: *Banana Boy* (1969) for some accounts of Barnardo upbringing in this century.
11. Crouch, Ch. I–III.
12. Alden, Isabella M.: *Memories of Yesterdays*, edited by Grace Livingstone Hill (1931), p. 280.

Author Booklists

Short title lists of the works of Maria Charlesworth, Hesba Stretton, Charlotte Tucker (A.L.O.E.) and Mrs Walton

The following lists are arranged in chronological order of first book publication. Where it has proved impossible to confirm the date of first publication the British Library receipt date is shown in square brackets. Place of publication is London unless otherwise stated.

Maria Louisa Charlesworth (1819–1881)

Maria Charlesworth's books were all first published by either Seeley, Burnside and Seeley, or Seeley, Jackson and Halliday.

1846 *The Female Visitor to the Poor*. Published in a revised edition as *The Cottage and its Visitor* in 1856.

1848 *A Book for the Cottage, or the History of Mary and her Family*.

1849 *Letters to a Friend under Affliction*.

1849–55 *Letters to a Child*.

1850 *The Light of Life*.

1853 *Sunday Afternoons in the Nursery*. Selections from this volume were subsequently issued as packets of 6 reward books (1s, or 2d each) in 1862.

1854 *Ministering Children*. A number of excerpts from both this volume and its sequel, see below, were published as reward books, for example: *The Blind Man's Child* (1872); *Little Jane and Tales* (1872); *Ruth and Patience* (1873); and *Rose, the Ministering Child* (1873).

1856 *Africa's Mountain Valley*.

1856 *The Sabbath Given; The Sabbath Lost*.

1858? *The Life of a Baby*.

1858 *The Ministry of Life*

1860 *England's Yeomen*.

1860 *India and the East: a Voice from the Zenana*.

1862 *The Sailor's Choice or Lennie's Friends on Shore*.

1867 *Ministering Children: a Sequel*. Also found as *The Basket Maker's Shop* (1926). See *Ministering Children* (1854) above.

1869 *The Last Command* (A booklet explaining the Communion Service.)

1871 *Where Dwellest Thou, or The Inner Home.*

1872 *Eden and Heaven.*

1876 *Oliver of the Mill.*

1878 *The Old Looking Glass, or Mrs. Dorothy Cope's Recollections of Service.*

1879 *The Broken Looking Glass.*

1882 *Heavenly Council in Daily Portions* (notes from M.C.'s Bible Classes, Edited by Maria Barclay).

* * *

The *Song of the Ministering Children* exists, but no copy has been traced.

Hesba Stretton (Sarah Smith), (1832–1911)

Hesba Stretton's books were issued by a number of publishers, but especially by the Religious Tract Society and H. S. King.

1864 *Fern's Hollow.*

1865 *The Children of Cloverley.*

1865 *Enoch Roden's Training.*

1866 *The Fishers of Derby Haven.*

1867 *The Clives of Burcot.* Reprinted as *The Price of a Secret, or the Clives of Burcot* in 1909.

1867 *Jessica's First Prayer.* (First appeared in *Sunday at Home*, 1866).

1867 *Paul's Courtship.*

1867 *Pilgrim Street.*

1868 *Little Meg's Children.*

1869 *Alone in London.* (Also appeared in *Sunday at Home*).

1869 *David Lloyd's Last Will.* (First appeared in *Leisure Hour*, 1868).

1870 *Nellie's Dark Days.*

[1871] *Max Krömer.* (First appeared in *Leisure Hour*, 1871.)

1872 *Bede's Charity.* (Also appeared in *Sunday at Home*).

1872 *The Doctor's Dilemma.*

1873 *Hester Morley's Promise.*

1873 *The King's Servants.* (First appeared in *The Day of Rest*). *Old Transome* and *Faithful in Much* are parts of this book which sometimes appeared separately.

1873 *Lost Gip.* (First appeared in *The Day of Rest*).

1874 *Cassy.*

1875 *Brought Home.*

1875 *No Work No Bread.*

1875 *The Wonderful Life.*

1876 *The Crew of the Dolphin.*

1876 *Friends Till Death and Other Stories.*

1876 *Left Alone and Michael Lorio's Cross. Left Alone* was subsequently published separately in 1888.

1876 *Michael Lorio's Cross and Other Stories.*

1876 *A Night and a Day.* (Winner of the American Tract Society's Gold Medal.)

1876 *The Storm of Life.* (Also appeared in *Good Words*, 1876).

1876 *Two Christmas Stories.*

1876 *The Worth of a Baby and How Apple Tree Court was Won.*

[1878] *Mrs. Burton's Best Bedroom and Other Stories.*

1878 *A Man of his Word.*

1878 *Through a Needle's Eye.*

1879 *A Thorny Path.* (First appeared in *Sunday at Home*).

1880 "*Facts on a Thread of Fiction*" *: In Prison and Out.* (First appeared in *Sunday Magazine*, 1878.)

1881 *Cobwebs and Cables.*

1881 *No Place Like Home.*

1882 *Two Secrets and A Man of his Word.*

1882 *Under the Old Roof.*

1883 *The Lord's Purse Bearers.*

1884 *Carola.*

[1884] *The Sweet Story of Old.* (Unrelated to Mrs. M. A. Hallock's book of the same title published by the R.T.S. in 1860.)

1887 *A Green Bay Tree.*

1887 *Her Only Son.*

1887 *The Ray of Sunlight; or Jack Stafford's Resolve:* a collection of stories by H.S. and other popular writers.

1888 *The Christmas Child.*

1888 *A Miserable Christmas and a Happy New Year.*

[1888] *Only a Dog.*

1888 *Papers on the Parables.*

1888 *Sam Franklin's Saving Bank.*

1889 *An Acrobat's Girlhood.*

1891 *Half Brothers.*

1894 *The Highway of Sorrow* at the close of the nineteenth century.

1894 *Paul Rodents* (with Sergius Stepniak).

1897 *In the Hollow of His Hand.*

1898 *The Soul of Honour.*

1903 *Good Words from the Apocrypha*: selected and arranged by H.S. *et al.*

1903 *Parables of Our Lord.*

[1904] *Jessica's Mother*. (First appeared in *Sunday at Home*, 1866. It seems probable that an earlier edition was issued, but it has not been traced).

1906 *Thoughts on Old Age.*

1908 *The Christmas Child and Other Stories* (including *Only a Dog*, *Sam Franklyn's Saving Bank* and *The Worth of a Baby*, all previously published separately).

n.d. *On and Off Duty.*

n.d. *Poison in the Packet.*

n.d. *A Sin and a Shame*. All three of these stories are mentioned in the Minutes of the R.T.S. Copyright Committee, but no editions have been traced.

Charlotte Maria Tucker (A.L.O.E.), (1821–1893)

A.L.O.E.'s principal publishers were Gall and Inglis, and Thomas Nelson, both firms printing in London and Edinburgh. Many of her short tales were first printed in periodicals: *The Family Treasury of Sunday Reading*; *The Children's Paper*; or *The Christian Juvenile Instructor* (which she edited for a time). She also contributed two religious novels: *Daybreak in Britain* and *Mahala* to the R.T.S. magazine *Sunday at Home*.

Many of the short tales were collected and reprinted by Nelson in the "Giving Light" series or the "Favourite Stories for the Young" series, some appearing in more than one volume. A "Pearls of Wisdom" series of 24 short tales, published by Morgan and Scott, London, appeared in the 1880's and 1890's. There were also Picture Reward Cards with verses by A.L.O.E. and a set of four Picture Story Books from Nelson in the 1870's.

1852 *The Claremont Tales; or Illustrations of the Beatitudes.*

1853–56? *The Adopted Son* [1877].

1853–56? *Angus Tarlton* [1877].

1853–56? *Life of Luther*, taken chiefly from D'Aubigne's *History of the Reformation* [1873].

1853–56? *True Heroism.*

[1854] *Glimpses of the Unseen.*

1855 *Wings and Stings: A Tale for the Young.*

1856 *The Giant-Killer; or the Battle which All Must Fight.*

1856 *New Year's Address for 1857: As Ye Sow So Shall Ye Reap.*

1856 *Upwards and Downwards; the Sluggard and the Diligent.* Subsequently reappeared as *Upwards and Downwards and Other Stories* in 1874.

1857 *Rambles of a Rat.*

1857 *The Robey Family; or Battling with the World.* (A sequel to *The Giant-Killer*, see 1856 above).

1857 *The Young Pilgrim: A Tale Illustrative of "The Pilgrim's Progress".*

1858 *Flora; or Self-deception.* Appeared abridged as *The Ruler's Dream* in the "African Home Library" series, 1947).

1858 *Futteypoor; or the City of Victory.*

1858 *Harry Dangerfield, the Poacher.*

1858 *The Mine; or Darkness and Light.*

1858 *Ned Manton; or the Cottage by the Stream.*

1858 *Old Friends with New Faces.*

1858 *Precepts in Practice; or Stories Illustrating the Proverbs.*

1858 *The Story of a Needle.* Also found as *The History of a Needle.*

1859 *The Christian's Mirror; or Words in Season.*

1859 *Idols in the Heart.*

1859 *New Year's Wishes.*

1859 *Whispering Unseen; or "Be Ye Doers of the Word . . .".*

1860 *Gain and Loss.*

[1860] *Invited Guests: a Religious Tract for Children.*

1860 *The Lost Jewel.*

1860 *Pride and his Prisoners.*

186? *The Convict's Child; or the Helmet of Hope; Friend and Foe; or the Breastplate of Righteousness; A Hasty Blow; or the Sandals of Peace; Proved in Peril; or the Shield of Faith; The Sailor's Home; or the Girdle of Truth; Son of Israel; or the Sword of the Spirit.* Six tract tales which appeared bound together in one volume as *The Christian's Panoply* in 1870, but were issued earlier as a packet of books. They also appeared, ostensibly as a single story in six parts, in [1865], as *Ned Franks, or the Christian's Panoply.*

1861 *Illustrations of Parables.*

1861 *My Neighbour's Shoes; or Feeling for Others.*

1861 *Parliament in the Playroom.*

1862 *Christian Conquests.*

1862 *Christian Love and Loyalty.*

1862 *The Light in the Robber's Cave.* Later appeared as *The Robbers' Cave: A Story of Italy.*

1862 *The Shepherd of Bethlehem, King of Israel.*

1862 *War and Peace: A Tale of the Retreat from Cabul.*

1863 *The Crown of Success; or Four Heads to Furnish.*

1863 *New Stories.*

[1863] *Picture Reward Cards Illustrating the Life of Christ*: two series.

1863 *Poetry by A.L.O.E.*

1863 *Pretty Presents for Pets.*

1863 *The Silver Casket; or Love not the World.* Also subtitled *The World and its Wiles.*

1863 *Sketch of the History of the Jews.*

1863 *Stories from Jewish History, from the Babylonish Captivity to the Destruction . . . .*

1864 *Exiles in Babylon; or the Children of Light.*

1864 *Miracles of Heavenly Love in Daily Life.*

[1864] *Stories for the Young* (six numbers).

[1864] *Tit, Tiny and Tittens, the Three White Kittens: Rhymes. . . .*

1865 *Our Sympathizing High Priest: Meditations on the Daily Sorrows of the Saviour.*

1866 *Fairy Know-a-bit; or a Nutshell of Knowledge.*

1866 *Rescued from Egypt.*

1866 *The Straight Road is Shortest and Surest.*

1866 *The Wanderer in Africa: a Tale Illustrating the Thirty-second Psalm.*

1867 *The Children's Treasury.* Later became *The Children's Tabernacle: Handwork and Heartwork* [1871].

1867 *The Holiday Chaplet of Stories.*

1867 *The Lake of the Woods: A Tale Illustrative of the Twelfth Chapter of Romans.* Later subtitled *A Story of the Backwoods.*

1867 *Poems and Hymns.*

1867 *Sheer off; or the Two Schoolmasters of Colne.*

1867 *The Sunday Chaplet of Stories.*

[1867] *Thoughtful Alice and Other Stories.*

1867 *Triumph over Midian.*

1867 *Zaida's Nursery Note-book for the Use of Mothers.*

1868 *Castle of Carlsmont: a Tragedy in Five Acts in Verse.*

1868 *House Beautiful; or the Bible Museum.*

1868 *Hymns and Poems.*

1868 *Living Jewels; or Diversities of Christian Character Suggested by Precious Stones with Biographical Examples.*

1868 *On the Way; or Places Passed by Pilgrims.*

1869 *A Braid of Cords.*

1869 *Claudia.*

1869 *The Golden Fleece.*

1869 *Hebrew Heroes: a Tale Founded on Jewish History.*

1869 *Places Passed by Pilgrims: 12 Tales Illustrating "The Pilgrim's Progress".*

1870 *Be on your Guard; or a New Year's Address to Sunday Scholars.*

1870? *The Cord of Love.*

1870 *Cyril Ashley.*

1870 *Daybreak in Britain.* (First appeared in *Sunday at Home*).

1870 *A Gift Book for the New Year.*

[1870] *New Year's Hymns* (six hymns).

1870 *Picture Story Book.*

1871 *Dora's Mistake; or The Children's Tabernacle.*

1871 *Freedom: a Tale of the Early Christians.*

1871 *The Hymn my Mother Taught Me and Other Stories.*

1870 *Is There Heart in It? A New Year's Address for 1871.*

1871 *The Lady of Provence; or Humbled and Healed.*

[1871] *New Year's Hymns* (six hymns).

1871 *Sunday Picture Book Illustrating the Life . . . of Christ.*

1871 *A Wreath of Smoke and Other Stories.* (First published in *The Leisure Hour*).

1872 *Edith and her Ayah and Other Stories.*

[1872] *New Year's Story for 1873: Trusty and Truthful.*

1872 *The Olive Branch and Other Stories.*

1872 *The Silver Keys.*

1872 *Try Again and Other Stories.*

1873 *The City of Nocross and its Famous Physician.* (This appeared in in *The Family Treasury* as "The Great Imposter or Popular, Pleasant, Pernicious".

1873 *A Friend in Need and Other Stories.*

1873 *Good for Evil and Other Stories.*

1874 *An Eden in England.*

1874 *Fairy Frisket; or Peeps at Insect Life.*

1874 *The Father's Letter: A New Year Story.*

1874 *The Little Maid.*

[1874] *Norah's Trial.*

1875 *The Backward Swing.*

1875 *The Brother's Return and Other Stories.*

1875 *The Children's Garland; a Picture Story Book.*

1875 *The Children's Posy: a Picture Story Book.*

1875 *Every Cloud has a Silver Lining and Five Other Little Books.*

1875–76 *Little Bullets from Batala.*

1875 *The Message of Hope and Other Stories.*

1875 *Only a Little and Other Stories.*

1875 *The Spanish Cavalier; a Story of Seville.*

1875 *The Truant Kitten and Other Stories.*

1875 *The Victory and Other Stories.*

1876 *Haunted Rooms.*

1876 Nelson's Packet Stories—packet 1, 2, 15, 18, 39 & 40.

1876 *The Tiny Red Night-cap and Other Stories.*

[1876] *A Wreath of Indian Stories.*

[1877] *Blind Alice and her Benefactress.*

1878 *Christ and the Soul: Texts Selected and Spiritual Song.*

1878 *Pomegranates from the Punjab: Indian Stories.*

1880 *The Zenana Reader.*

[1881] *Hours with Orientals.*

[1882] *Seven Perils Passed.*

[1883] *Life in the Eagle's Nest: A Tale of Afghanistan.* Also appeared as *The Eagle's Nest.*

[1883] *Mahala, The Jewish Slave: a Story of Early Christianity.* (First appeared in *Sunday at Home*).

1884 *Life in the White Bear's Den.* Later appeared as *The White Bear's Den: a Tale of Labrador.*

1884–93 *Pearls of Wisdom from the Parables of Christ.* 24 tales similar to the Nelson Packet Stories (see 1876 above), issued by Morgan & Scott.

1885 *Harold Hartley; or Pictures Drawn in an English Home.*

[1885] *Pictures of St. Paul Drawn in an English Home.*

1886 *Pictures of St. Peter in an English Home.*

1887 *The Fairy in the Spider's Web.*

1887? *In the Spider's Web: a Story of the Indian Mutiny.*

1887 *Percival's Picture Gallery.*

[1888] *The Battle of Life; or What is a Christian?*

1888 *Driven into Exile: a Story of the Huguenots.* (*Rich toward God* by Barbara Hallihan, 1974, is based on this book).

1888 *The Hartley Brothers; or the Knights of St. John.*

1889 *Beyond the Black Waters.*

1889 *Harold's Bride.*

1890? *Ben Stone.*

1890 *The Blacksmith of Boniface Lane.*

1890? *Sophie Claymore.*

1890? *The Teacher Taught.*

1890? *The Whirlpool.*

1890? *The Wondrous Sickle and Other Stories.*

[1891] *Black Yarn and Blue and Other Tales.*

[1891] *The Little Brother.*

[1891] *The Rope Cable Cut and Other Stories.*

[1891] *The Two Crutches and Other Stories.*

[1891] *The Two Dinners and Other Stories.*

1892 *The Iron Chain and the Golden.*

1893 *The Forlorn Hope.*

[c. 1895] *Tales Illustrative of the Parables.*

1896 *Story of Dr. Duff.*

1901 *The Two Pilgrims of Kashi and Other Stories.*

[1932] *Grannie's Love Proof; or Words without Deeds or Little Husks without Seeds.*

Mrs. O. F. Walton (Catherine Augusta Walton), (1849–1939)

All Mrs. Walton's books were published initially by the Religious Tract Society.

[1872] *My Little Corner: a Book for Cottage Homes.*

1873 *Little Dot.* Also became A Service of Song in the 1880's.

1873 *My Mates and I.*

1874 *Christie's Old Organ*, (Wheeler, J. B. *Our Home in Heaven or Echoes from "Christie's Old Organ"* [1881]).

1877 *Angel's Christmas.*

1877 *A Peep Behind the Scenes.*

1879 *Saved at Sea: a Lighthouse Story.*

1879 *Was I Right?*

1880 *Little Faith: the Child of the Toy Stall.* (First published in *Sunday at Home*, 1879).

1881 *Olive's Story; or Life at Ravenscliffe.*

1883 *Nobody Loves Me.*

[1884] *The Four Little Preachers: a New Year's Address to Sunday Scholars.*

1884 *Shadows, or Scenes in the Life of an Old Armchair.* (This was filmed as "The Old Armchair" by Screen Plays in 1920, and released in London, May, 1921. [From Minutes of R.T.S. Copyright Committee.])

[1885] *Taken or Left.*

1886 *Golden Threads for Life's Weaving.*

1886 *Launch the Lifeboat.*

1886 *Our Gracious Queen.*

1886 *Poppy's Presents.*

1889 *Winter's Folly.*

1890 *The King's Cup-Bearer: The Story of Nehemiah.*

1890 *The Mysterious House.* (First appeared in the *Child's Companion and Juvenile Instructor* for 1889).

1893 *Nemo, or the Wonderful Door.* (Appeared as *The Wonderful Door*, 1903).

1897 *Audrey, or the Children of Light.*

1897 *Elisha, the Man of Abel-Meholah.*

1898 *Christie the King's Servant.* Also appeared as *A Service of Song, Founded upon . . .* c. 1900.

1901 *Pictures and Stories from Queen Victoria's Life.*

1906 *Dr. Forrester.*

1906 *Unbeaten Paths in Sacred History.*

1907 *The Lost Clue.*

1919 *Strange Diana.*

INDEX